RECOGNITION

The Key to Identity

Catherine Monnet, Ph.D.

THE KEY TO IDENTITY

iUniverse books may be ordered through booksellers or by contacting:

iUniverse
1663 Liberty Drive
Bloomington, IN 47403
www.iuniverse.com
1-800-Authors (1-800-288-4677)

Because of the dynamic nature of the Internet, any web addresses or links contained in this book may have changed since publication and may no longer be valid. The views expressed in this work are solely those of the author and do not necessarily reflect the views of the publisher, and the publisher hereby disclaims any responsibility for them.

Any people depicted in stock imagery provided by Thinkstock are models, and such images are being used for illustrative purposes only. Certain stock imagery © Thinkstock.

ISBN: 978-1-4917-6613-2 (sc)
ISBN: 978-1-4917-6612-5 (e)

Library of Congress Control Number: 2015906227

Print information available on the last page.

iUniverse rev. date: 05/26/2015

CONTENTS

Introduction xi

PART I: WAYS AND MEANS TO
   RECOGNITION.......................................1

Chapter I: The Material Self 3

My Body, My Self: Looks Matter...3
Age and Gender: Absolutes? Not Really 10
Speech and Language: You Say What You Are,
   You Are What You Say 18
Clothing: From Bikinis to Burkas, Making a
   Statement 20
Material Possessions: "Look What I've Got!" 24

Chapter II: The Social Self...............................32

Work Dethroned: Are You What You Do?.........................32
Significant Others: Finding Your Mirror 46
Groups: Show Me the Company You Keep 62
Media: Spreading the Word, It's All about Me...................72
Animals: Recognition from our Fellow
   Earthlings...79

Chapter III: The Spiritual Self...............................84

The Soul: Eternal Recognition 84
A Soulless Spiritual Self...95
Death: Recognition beyond the Grave..............................101
Non-Recognition: Getting Away from It All 107

PART II: ORIGINS 113

Chapter IV: Back to the Beginning...................... 115

Consciousness: the Understated Problem 116
Recognition: Binding, Attention, Memory 119
Conscious Recognition: Moving Forward....................... 121
Animal Consciousness and Recognition 123
First Humans and Conscious Recognition....................... 125
Self-Recognition: Language and Thought....................... 129

Chapter V: From Infancy to Self.......................... 138

The Selfless Infant 139
The Mirror Stage: Recognizing a Self 141
Shame: The *Look* of the Other... 148
Theory of Mind: Discovering How Others Think 151
Developing a Narrative Self: Learning to
    Tell a Story 153
Summary... 160

**PART III: THE *SUBJECT* OF SELF
RECOGNTION** 161**

Chapter VI: The Self: Seeking a Definition........ 163

The Self: A Brief Historical Background........................... 163
The Me: The Empirical, Social Self................................... 168
A Narrative Self: The Story of Your Life 172
Fictive or Real: Is Anybody in There? 176
Identity: Who Am I?... 181
Creating an Image: Minds and Mirrors............................. 187

**Chapter VII: Cultural Differences: We Mustn't
Generalize**... 195

Chapter VIII: The Evaluative Self, How do I Rate? .202

Self-Esteem: An Overrated Goal...................................... 204
The Social-interest / Self-interest Divide:
    Altruism vs. Egoism 214

Altruism: Good for Goodness' Sake 216
Egoism & Narcissism: The Modern Epidemic...................217
Authenticity: The Paradox of a True Self......................... 221

PART IV: MORAL IMPLICATIONS.............. 231

Chapter IX: Mutual Recognition:
Recognition as Respect 233

Kant, Hegel and Sartre…... to Make my Case................... 234

Chapter X: Non-Recognition II,
Denying the Other as Other 249

Chapter XI: A Psychological Approach to Moral
Recognition....................................... 257

Empathetic Recognition, Feeling vs. Rationale 262

Chapter XII: The Ambiguity of Mutual Recognition:
The Never Ending Dilemma.................267

Conclusion 269

Endnotes 273
Selected Bibliography... 299
Index.. 309

A special thanks to Mary Bartlett for her generous editorial assistance.

INTRODUCTION

Esse est percipi (To be is to be perceived)
George Berkeley

Just what is recognition? It is a term we use every day in many different contexts. Recognition is identifying something previously seen, heard, or known; perceiving something as true, or acknowledging something as valid. But as related to human behavior, recognition involves the notion of acknowledging a person's achievements, services or merits, and might include expressing approval or appreciation. Recognition involves the right to be heard or given attention, and when extended beyond the individual, it may be an official act, as when one nation acknowledges the existence of another nation or government.

My interest in the subject of recognition was inspired by a remark made by my French sister-in-law. She had worked hard all her life assisting her husband in their upholstery business, raising a family, giving everything she had to give in terms of time, effort, care and affection to everyone she knew. Late one evening in a melancholic mood she said, "Catherine, all I ever wanted is a little recognition." I immediately understood what she was talking about. She didn't want money, she didn't want gifts, she didn't want praise; she just wanted "a little recognition." It didn't seem like a lot to ask for, but apparently, it was something she felt she wasn't getting. Thinking about her remark, it struck me that this is precisely what most of us want. Our need for recognition is expressed by what we say and do, through our work and affiliations, in the partner we choose, even in the clothes we wear.

My interest in consciousness, self-knowledge, theory of mind, and intersubjectivity, prompted me to learn more about this very basic and essential concept. But curiously, as I began doing research, I discovered that there has been relatively little written on the subject of recognition *per se.* I'm not sure if this is because the importance of recognition is too obvious or because as a theme, it's too vast and amorphous to even begin writing about. On the other hand, there has been an enormous amount of research and literature on the subject of self, including self-knowledge, self-esteem, self-confidence, the spiritual self and every other self-oriented subject. The whole field of psychology is necessarily concerned with the self, and psychotherapy presupposes that what we call our *self* is both something we can come to know and something amenable to change.

The objective of most popular psychology books written on the above subjects is to help people understand and perhaps modify their selves. Most of us believe we have a better chance of changing our self than we have of changing the world we live in. Those who choose the latter, courageous as they may be, must necessarily work with others to do so, and ultimately working with others begins with an understanding of how they think and function as individual selves. I believe that the need for recognition is a very important element in this understanding.

How we seek recognition in our everyday life and the psychological, sociological and philosophical foundation for this search, is the subject of this book. My main thesis is that without recognition we neither have a consciousness of self nor can we have meaningful relationships with others. Meaning is relational, each mind is a community of minds and the construction of self and others is only achieved through a *shared* reality.

Before introducing this book's organization, I would like to preempt a couple of obvious objections to my thesis, the first being that we don't all need or desire recognition.

When I discussed this subject with friends, some said, "I could care less about recognition," or "What others think is unimportant." If recognition is perceived simply as a form of admiration for personal traits, behaviors and actions, then many of us probably don't see it as essential but I would argue that everyone wants a minimum of recognition. No one wants to be taken for a mere object, leaned on like a lamppost, kicked aside like a broken bottle, ignored when seated in a restaurant. One reason common courtesy is so important is that it is a sign of recognition. In civilized society, we even recognize unconscious beings, (comatose patients), or those with a potential for consciousness (fetuses), and even the irretrievably unconscious (the dead). As William James wrote in 1890, "No more fiendish punishment could be devised, were such a thing physically possible, than that one should be turned loose in society and remain absolutely unnoticed by all the members thereof."[1] Humane treatment implies recognition and I believe everyone wants to be recognized as a free, sensitive human being.

Though the importance of recognition seems self-evident, like many subjects related to self, a preoccupation with such a need can be interpreted as egotism. Accordingly, I'll be pointing out that a search for recognition, especially in the modern occidental world where individualism, independence and autonomy are highly valued, may easily turn into an obsession. However, the concept of recognition is very different from very popular notions of self-esteem, feeling good about ourselves and appreciated or approved of by others for who we are and what we do.

My thesis is that recognition is *existentially* important, essential to constructing a self, to interpreting reality and creating a meaningful life. As I say this, I'm aware that I slide back and forth between a sort of Sartrean existentialism and a Darwinian determinism, a balancing act between defending both our free will in constructing ourselves and the constraints of our biological and social situation in determining our choice.

Finally, claiming that recognition is important for meaning and morality is not intended to be a reductionist thesis. In studying any phenomena, definitions open up one way of considering something, but close off others. Every subjective mental state, including motivations for our behavior, can be seen from different angles. I believe that the need for recognition is a very interesting part of our mental life, but not the only important part. In exploring the way in which recognition functions in our lives, I found the subject both enriching and unifying, due to its interdisciplinary nature. It involves neuroscience, anthropology, psychology, sociology, as well as philosophy which is why I've organized my book into four complimentary parts, each considering recognition in a different way.

PART I

The first section deals with our practical daily lives by looking at how individuals commonly seek recognition. I have used William James's discussion of the Material, Social and Spiritual self in organizing this section.[2] I'll be pointing out the various ways we are recognized and recognize others, such as our physical self, material possessions, our social interactions, work, activities, significant others and group affiliations, as well as our spiritual beliefs and approach to death. These views are based on my own experience, observation and reflection, plus some researched historical background.

PART II

Since one of the best and most often used methods of understanding any phenomena is to explore how, when and where it began, the next section considers "Origins." The appearance and development of recognition basically coincides with that of consciousness itself, so a discussion of consciousness is unavoidable. In this section, I'll venture into evolutionary anthropology and developmental psychology, using documented research to support my case. In scientific terms, it involves both the *phylogeny*, (how human groups evolve, from australopithecines to hominids, to modern man), and the *ontogeny*, (how individuals develop, from their infancy to adulthood) in considering recognition.

PART III

The subject of recognition is compelling because it is so basic to explaining who we are. Through recognition from others, we are essentially constructing recognition of our self, as a unified, coherent, meaning-bestowing person. There has been an enormous amount of literature about the self, from genuinely scientific, to popular theories for self-improvement. My discussion of selfhood is based upon previous studies, well-developed theories and personal reflection. To examine recognition, I found it necessary to discuss different aspects of selfhood, including philosophical definitions of the self, modern notions of the social or narrative self, sociological theories concerning images and identity, and very importantly, cultural differences in relation to these theories. The section ends with a discussion of evaluative considerations of self, the popular notions of self-esteem, egoism and narcissism, empathy and altruism, and finally the concept of an authentic self.

PART IV

The last section, "Moral Implications", is a consideration of recognition in its philosophical and existential sense. I'll be discussing why recognition is so important for us as human beings, including recognition as a normative concept, that is to say, why we should or ought to recognize others and in what way recognition, especially *mutual* recognition, is important for notions of respect, merit, justice, equality, dignity, authenticity, and a meaningful existence. Mutual recognition and all that it implies, is important not only for the rights of individuals, but the rights of nations, governments and ideologies, and for the harmonious and peaceful future of humanity. Pointing out the necessity for mutual recognition, cannot be overstated, since morality would not be a concern in a world of one.

Another admission is that I'm mostly basing my observations on modern Western culture. I was born and educated in the United States, have lived most of my adult life in France, and spent the last five years working and living in China which has increased my sensitivity to cultural differences. Though most of the psychological research and literature that I've read concerns Western and especially North American cultures, I'm aware of the danger of cultural reductionism, describing a 'universal self' in terms of one culture (Western) and even less objectively, one subculture (white, educated, middle-aged persons). To avoid a too limited perspective I'll point out some observable difference between Western/individualistic and Eastern/collectivist cultural values and behavior.

One last point: I would also like to state what this book is *not* intended to be. Though I am advocating a need for recognition for oneself as well as others, this is not a "How To" book. I hope that what I've said about recognition will be informative, thought provoking and hence useful. Also, this is not a comprehensive research book. Though I've tried to support my views with authoritative sources and well known theories, I've conducted no personal experiments, surveys or clinical tests. There are aspects of the subject I've overlooked, others I've emphasized too much, and certainly much more to be explored concerning such a rich subject.

PART I

WAYS AND MEANS TO RECOGNITION

Observing myself and others, I realized just how much of what we do and say is motivated by a need and desire for recognition. How the other sees us often guides, directs, explains, and regulates our behavior, teaching us what is acceptable or inacceptable, encouraging us to conform or be unique, belong or reject. Each of us creates an identity by means of a continual exchange of recognition between our self and others. This chapter will point out some of the more observable ways in which we are recognized. I'll be developing some subjects more than others, not based on their importance but rather on their familiarity and relevance.

In order to present the most basic ways in which we seek or bestow recognition, I have followed the categorizations of William James, who discussed consciousness of self in his famous work, *The Principles of Psychology.* What James called the "me" or "empirical self" continues to be an insightful and pertinent explanation of selfhood and seems a logical way of analyzing how recognition influences our self-construction. James' classifications were:

1) the Material Self
2) the Social Self
3) the Spiritual Self
4) the Pure Ego.

In this section, I will follow James' order by discussing the first three selves; material, social and spiritual, saving a discussion of the pure ego for the third section of this book. It will become evident that the material, social and spiritual selves are inextricably interrelated. Even James seems to mix them up at times. For example, he includes a person's family as part of the material self as well as social, or a person's working role as related to his material possessions, as well as his social honor. Consequently, my categorizations are also a little arbitrary since these different forms of recognition are not distinct, but rather combine to create a sort of gestalt sense of self.

Chapter I

The Material Self

My Body, My Self: Looks Matter

People appear to us incarnate, or embodied, at least initially. When we communicate with others we don't have to physically see their body to know they exist *as* a body. We recognize their voice or imagine it when we read their words, and in whatever way we interact with someone we never doubt they exist physically. Our body is the basis of intersubjectivity, that is, how we reveal ourselves to each other as human beings and intentional subjects. The body is a public and objective means of recognizing not only who a person is, but what a person feels or thinks. Before we had symbolic speech, the body, through gestures, growls, and smiles, was the way we expressed feelings or intentions.

Our body often reveals our true thoughts. Body language, our non-verbal communication using postures, movements, and facial expressions, reflects mood and internal feelings. Often, it seems our body has a mind of its own. We sweat or shake (and stink) when afraid, turn red when embarrassed, hang our head when sad or ashamed, raise our brows when surprised, grate or bare our teeth when angered. We use our body to dissimulate what we're really thinking, something actors, prostitutes, and politicians do quite well. Mind and body are inseparable, regardless of what Descartes claimed, and recognition reflects our mental-corporal functioning.

Long ago, recognizing other physically beings was essential for our very survival. Just like any other animals, (although animals do a lot more sniffing than people), spotting kin, friends and foes, was essential for humans in order to recognize predators and prey or members of their own group. Sight is one of our most basic means of recognition. Sound, smell, and touch, play a strong role, but sight predominates, which is one reason our physical appearance is so important. Before DNA testing, we counted on physical resemblance for recognizing paternity: strong paternal resemblance encouraged strong attachment from the father (the mother's DNA used to be beyond a doubt). Recognizing members of one's family, clan or country based on physical features such as skin, eye, or hair color, insured a sense of identity as being "one of us" or "one of them."

Physically, our bodies in size, shape and form, expose more than our health and well-being; they also express our inner self. Early in human history, qualities such as facial symmetry indicated freedom from disease and suitability for mating. Paleontologists conjecture that if we look at how the human face and body evolved, certain features predominated over others; for example, a shorter distance between the upper lip and the brow in men, exaggerating the size of the jaw, or a particular waist and hip ratio in women. Evolutionary psychologists have come up with various hypotheses as to why such traits were preferred, most of which had to do with maximizing reproduction and survival, health and well-being. Attractiveness, in its literal sense, has its roots in the quest for reproduction potential and fertility.

How prehistoric people perceived their corporal self, how they presented themselves to others, and whether body image was of value in creating a sense of self is a matter of speculation. We know from paintings, artifacts and jewelry that people in primitive societies used adornment and were conscious of their bodies, but were they conscious of being attractive, desired, or admired? Did they have physical predilections; make comparisons like we do today or worry about their bodies fitting within a norm?

From the time we've had written records, we know that humans had a concept of beauty based on what was perceived as 'attractive'. This perception has evolved over time and continues to do so with a great deal of debate and variation. But it is hard to discount the importance of attraction and attractiveness since even animals attract with their physique, from peacock feathers to deer antlers. Today, body image continues to be important in determining how we are recognized as well as how we view ourselves. As always, the criteria, whether we fit in or stand out, are found attractive or repugnant, accepted or rejected, are culturally and socially defined.

Our early ancestors needed recognition for survival. Today, physical recognition has evolved to become an intentional and symbolic form of how we want rather than need to be recognized by others. When we meet someone for the first time, we are immediately aware of and react to their body. To know a person's mind takes time, a very different process. Our physical self has importance because it is apparent, public, substantial and real. Those who are in the public-eye are recognized immediately by their physical image, and their fame is directly related to how frequently they're seen on television, in magazines, or on the Internet.

Recognition is when something or someone looks alike or unlike what has already been experienced. The more familiar a person is, the more we can discern an anomaly in the way he or she usually appears. Those who are less familiar or less like us, tend to be less distinguishable. People of different ethnicities tend to objectify others. For example, Asiatic people, whether they are Korean, Japanese, Chinese, Vietnamese, may 'all look alike', to someone who is Western whereas for an Asiatic person, the opposite is true. One of my Chinese friends identified another houseguest as looking Korean, whereas I was unaware of any distinguishing traits. By the same token, my Chinese friend was hard pressed to identify one of my Western friends as Italian, based only on physique. These are examples of how easy it is to objectify those who do not share our looks. During war or ethnic conflicts we often attribute physical stereotypes to the enemy, turning individuals into an undifferentiated mass.

Personal attitudes towards physical appearance range from indifferent to obsessive. Some people don't seem to care about their physical appearance. Perhaps they are less conscious of their looks, are indifferent, or reject an emphasis on physical appearance as superficial. For people who downplay their physical self, other characteristic or qualities are more important or preoccupying and more representative of their personhood. However, a person's initial physical appearance and how he or she is recognized by others can have a huge influence on whether or not physical appearance becomes important in later life. For example, who can resist a pretty baby? Being physically pleasing is reinforced by the reactions of others. The cute child will be showered with smiles and positive feedback. How does this influence people as they age? When people are extraordinarily attractive, within their social context, they often become more conscious of their looks which can easily become a dominant force in constructing their sense of self. Certain social roles or professions, such as models, actors, or dancers, require a continual consciousness of physique.

A dear friend of mine, an ex-model, turned heads everywhere she went. Consequently, she would never go out of the house without being what she considered presentable. She spent most of her time exercising, primping, collecting flattering clothing, and spending afternoons in beauty spas. Her reputation as a beauty limited her life to a particular field of activities. As she aged, in spite of some recourse to aesthetic surgery, she experienced an existential crisis. She was no longer recognized for her youthful beauty.

The importance of our physical self is contingent upon the culture we live in. Beauty has always been a subjective value (the irony of beauty contests) and what is considered a beautiful body has varied throughout history from voluptuous fleshy Rubens women to emaciated run-way models. Being overweight, once a sign of wealth is now sometimes identified as a sign of a poor diet and low income level. White skin was once associated with aristocracy; peasants were tanned. Centuries later, until the dangers of skin cancer were revealed, tanning was in vogue among the wealthy, evidence of the fact they could afford a beach vacation in winter. Variations in what qualities have aesthetic value are countless, but they are all reflections of societal and cultural norms. In any case, how we are seen by others, whether we are regarded in a positive or negative way, influences our self-concept and self-esteem.

Being thought of as attractive and accepted rather than rejected is a hard notion to dispute. However, our physical appearance has turned into a modern obsession. The 'youth and beauty' mantra is used constantly to advertise and sell just about any product on the market, from toothpaste to cars. It's no surprise that the physical self has become such a preoccupation. We believe our appearance is important for everything from finding a partner to getting a good job, and we have more and more choices to achieve the desired result by altering the way we appear. Resources such as cosmetics, aesthetic surgery, Draconian diets, muscle building, and fashion are all aimed at modifying and improving our physical appearance, so that we are seen as we want others to see us and as we want to see ourselves. If we can manage to modify the way we look, the result is a feeling of control, rather than helplessness. (Incidentally, one explanation for anorexia is "If I can control my body, I can control my life").

One other point; what about the blind? Obviously, visual recognition is not the only way to gain recognition or be recognized. Those who can't see at all construct a sense of others and of themselves based on sound, touch, and smell. The notion that the blind may *see* others for who they really are has been a recurring theme in books and movies, proving that physical appearance is sometimes a misleading and superficial way to recognize other people. And for those who have their sight, it is also true that the way we see another person, once we know them personally, is influenced by their character or personality. Someone who is kind, thoughtful, and generous, seems more physically attractive whereas negative character traits can transform a beauty into a beast.

The way our body is perceived, in terms of age, body size, skin color, and anomalies, is unfortunately not only a source of positive, but often negative recognition. Being outside the norm, such as in height or weight, can have an influence on how we are perceived by others. The effect this has on our self-concept and life choices varies from one person to another. Those who are physically handicapped or disfigured often suffer not only from their inability to function as most people do, but also from being treated as different or odd. People often mock what they fear and being other than physically normal is an unconscious threat to those who make fun of abnormality. Fortunately, humanity has evolved and we no longer display freaks (physical malformations, dwarfism, even obesity) to be gawked at and humiliated, as they once were in carnivals and circuses. But disfigurement is still used as a method of punishment in some cultures, so that a traitor, thief, or adulteress is easily recognized and constantly displayed to a condemning public.

Regardless of how familiar or different a person looks, he or she is nonetheless recognizable. Identity photos serve this very purpose. And though some people may not be concerned by the appearance of their body, it still somewhat influences the way they are seen and how they see themselves. We are categorized and put into groups despite our desire to be identified as such. Age and gender are two very good examples of this categorization.

Age and Gender: Absolutes? Not Really

Age and gender are two seemingly incontestable ways we are physically recognized. These two basic physical facts of our existence play an enormous role in our behavior, how we relate to others, and our self-concept.

Aging affects us all, slowly but surely, depending upon our genes and life style. Gender has always mistakenly believed to be purely genetic. However today, we are increasingly finding technical methods of altering our bodies. With aesthetic surgery, special diets, health programs, and for some, relatively stress-free living, we have managed to somewhat control the aging process, at least from a physical point of view. For some, gender has also become a matter of medical choice. With genetic engineering, it seems almost anything will be possible in the not too distant future.

___*Age.*___ Gerontology is a science which studies old age and the process of aging. When we talk about aging, we immediately think of the elderly, but of course, we start aging as soon as we are born. We are commonly recognized and categorized according to our age group. Each stage from infancy, toddlerhood, childhood, adolescence, and on throughout adulthood is distinguished by certain social and cultural norms in terms of emotional and intellectual maturity as well as physical ability. Concurrently, each group has particular privileges (it's accepted that babies cry and the elderly kvetch). Your age group determines certain legal rights; (18 year olds can marry and vote), and certain expectations; (capable adults should be self-sufficient), and each age group has its own inherent needs and desires for recognition.

We don't all age at exactly the same rate. Some young people seem advanced for their age, and some elderly young for their age, always according to cultural and social standards. Ironically, the young often want to be recognized as older and the old as younger, perhaps because in most modern societies, it is the young to middle-aged adults who apparently set the standards, and fulfill roles of productivity, authority, and power. There are certain prejudices in modern societies, more or less justified, that certain individuals are too young or too old to hold a job, raise a family, or assume certain responsibilities.

It is generally acknowledged that there are times in our aging process when we experience an identity crisis, one during adolescence and the other in later life, passing from adulthood to old age. From personal speculation, both these passages represent a radical transition in recognition coming from others and a simultaneous change in recognizing oneself. The adolescent becomes conscious of an independent self, responsible for his or her decisions and acts. The elderly person may lose this sense of independence and consequently personal responsibility.

Attitudes towards the elderly differ from one culture to another, and thus, the transition from adulthood to old-age can vary tremendously. The elderly might be rejected and forgotten or respected and revered, depending upon the individual, the family, and the cultural context. Aging is not only physiological; it is also social and takes place within a relational context. Aging research has shown that, "The aging organism does not operate in a vacuum, but is engaged in a reciprocal interaction with a particular environment, and is itself the product of life-course experiences during a given slice of history. Physiological aging is only one of many factors that determine the condition and statuses of old people." [1]

Ideally, if not debilitated by dementia, or loss of memory, the elderly command special respect, and privileged recognition. Eric Erikson saw old age, the last or eighth stage of life, as associated with wisdom. Old age can be an affirmative experience, what Erikson labels "Integrity," when a person has a sense of life's wholeness and coherence, and it can also be negative, which he calls "Despair," when a person has a sense of life's meaninglessness or stagnation. Both these attitudes can produce a synthesis of "Wisdom" which is an informed and detached attitude toward life when confronting death. [2] Some elderly people slide gracefully into this state of wisdom, and others fight or resist it almost as fervently as death. For some, part of the effort to remain looking young is to be recognized as such, reinforcing one's belief that aging and dying is still a long way off. Of course, as an aging person, I've discovered that just looking young is not the only goal. Staying healthy, energetic and capable both mentally and physically for as long as possible is important for profiting from life to its fullest, as well as maintaining a sense of recognition.

Gender. From infancy, gender identification and sexual orientation are probably the most basic factors in forming our human relationships, influencing our role in society, and creating our sense of self. Stereotypical assumptions about what kind of behavior is appropriate for which sex and what constitutes being masculine or feminine, still exist in many societies and cultures. Men are sons, brothers and fathers, they may be expected to do manly things; be protectors, providers, fight in wars, like sports, and other testosterone oriented activities. Women are daughters, sisters, mothers, expected to do womanly things; raise children, be homemakers, and be generally nurturing and caring. These clichés of gender roles are only relatively universal, but they do persist, even in today's Western culture. Walk into any modern toy store to see how gender stereotyping is still in effect.

The concept of masculinity or femininity and its relative importance has changed throughout the ages and differs from one society to another. The idea of what is acceptable or optimal behavior for men and women is still evolving. However, quite commonly, men need or want to be recognized for their masculinity and women for their femininity, whatever that may entail, in order to emphasize or confirm their sexual identity, and in many cases to perhaps attract another person of the opposite or same sex. There is often societal pressure to fit into one gender type or another. The occurrence of a certain event such as an accident or illness in which a recognizable sexual attribute is changed or modified (examples: prostate cancer, impotence, a hysterectomy, the ablation of a breast), a man or woman may feel their sexual identity jeopardized. Feeling sexually insecure in reaction to social standards can have an effect on how a person recognizes him or herself as representative of their particular gender.

Optimally, a man who manifests feminine qualities or a woman who appears masculine is comfortable with his or her outward image. The importance for a confidence in self-concept is rooted in the alignment of how we are seen and how we see ourselves. Preconceptions, ignorance, lack of empathy, prejudice, and fear have created much misunderstanding concerning deviance from standard male/female gender identity and sexual attraction. Unfortunately, even from a very young age, some boys are identified as "girly" some girls as "boyish" because they behave in socially defined ways that correspond to the opposite sex. Their behavior may contradict expectations, but the recognition they receive from others will eventually tend to either stifle their inner nature and outward behavior or re-affirm it. We are becoming more scientifically sensitive to the difference between nurture and nature, and the fact that small differences at birth can widen into a gender gap largely due to upbringing and culture.

One current example of an attempt to limit the gender gap and encourage greater equality is taking place in Sweden. In a few experimental preschools, there is a program designed to discourage male and female stereotypes. Pronouns like him and her are replaced by the neuter word, *hen*. The children are not referred to as *he* or *she*, but as *friend*. Teachers are trained to treat all toddlers in the same way. Some Swedes see this program as admirable and progressive while others criticize it as artificial 'gender madness.' [3]

It is important to acknowledge that despite common beliefs, gender is not only a genetic, black and white, male and female issue. Our gender is determined by a combination of nature and nurture. Our sexual development is an interaction of different physical systems, including the brain and hormones released by the glands, as well as culture. The nuclei of the brain mediating our sexual self-consciousness are influenced by hormones and experience during infancy. Most of us are born with two X chromosomes, or an X and a Y, that effect our brain development, which is in turn determined by the production of estrogens or androgens, and the presence of female or male gonads. Neuroscientists Gillian Einstein and Owen Flanagan write, "At about the sixth week of gestation, the primordial gonads have formed from a gonad that is undifferentiated between female and male. Developing simultaneously is an undifferentiated structure called the urogenital groove, the progenitor of the external genitalia. So, we begin undifferentiated." [4]

According to gender research, both sexes have a feminine and masculine component, and it is the gonadal steroids that influence the sexual dimorphism of the frontolimbic structure and the resulting feminized or masculinized circuitry of the brain. [5] Apparently, our genotype sets in motion the sexual self, but multiple components, genotypic (our genes), and phenotypic (the outward expression of our genes) determine our gender identification and sexual orientation. "When they are aligned, genotype, phenotype, and brain biology all work together to reinforce one's story as one sex or the other, one sexual orientation or the other." [6]

Scientific findings concerning our gender identity and perhaps our sexual preferences confirm that the most important part of our self-narrative is not purely biological since recognition from our first caregivers during infancy have a great deal to do with our sexual orientation. Recent scientific research has seemed to prove that our gender identification and sexual orientation is decided very early in our development. "Psychological gender is known to be firmly and irreversibly established within the first 18 to 24 months of human life," [7] and this is due to both biological-genetic and social-cultural factors, that is, both neural sex differences and the rearing environment.

Our gender, which is commonly believed to be an incontestable part of our social identity, is greatly influenced, if not determined by the way we are recognized from the time we are born. Our sexual identity and orientation goes beyond the body and the brain, it is more than merely physiological, and a full explanation needs to take into consideration the total social-cultural environment. Our self-concept, as female, male, or both, and our sexual orientation, bisexual, lesbian, homosexual, transsexual, is a conceptual construction with a biological basis, influenced by genetics, early upbringing and cultural environment. The only problem is that the social-cultural environment often takes for granted that those who do not demonstrate expected gender behavior might be ostracized, criticized, or gravely misunderstood. As Einstein and Flanagan said, "Since the subjective perception of one's sex, gender identification, is reinforced by biology and culture and that perception satisfies the standard norm, things seem "normal." When genotypic and phenotypic sex are not aligned as expected, a complex array of types of sexual self-consciousness and stories can emerge. In such cases, what one believes oneself to be and how one is treated by others can clash. One comes into conflict with expectations—cultural and religious—and sometimes with oneself." [8]

In any case, there is no "deviation" in wavering from the norm of male-female-heterosexual attraction, since the non-alignment of physical and psychic gender, as well as same sex attraction has perhaps always been present among Homo sapiens. It has taken a long time for science to prove what has always been apparent in human culture, the sometimes "natural" ambiguity of our gender. Today, the lesbian, gay, bisexual and transgender community has made great progress in being socially accepted in some parts of the world and hopefully, in the near future, they will receive the same basic human rights and non-judgmental recognition as any other social group of people.

Speech and Language: You Say What You Are, You Are What You Say

To continue my discussion of recognition on a corporal or physical level, after sight comes sound, that is, voice, speech and language. We usually recognize people by their speech as easily as by their looks. When you receive a phone call from a family member or friend, their voice is immediately familiar, even a short "hello," indicates who is speaking. Have you ever had a friend try to trick you on the phone by disguising his or her voice? It's usually a failure since the voices of those we know are so recognizable. However, some people are so clever in this rare ability that they turn it into a career. The comedian's art of impersonation is an incredible talent, literally adopting another's persona by imitating the way someone speaks including rhythm, intonations, and pitch.

Speech is also the most revelatory indicator of a person's state of mind. Timbre is one of the best ways of not only recognizing whose speaking but how they're feeling. We know whether people are angry, depressed, confused, or in a good mood, not only by what they say but by the tone of their voice. In terms of how we want to be recognized, we can modify our voice in order to convey a message; we reproach or admonish in a stern voice, or we speak slowly and softly in order to seduce. Very often, what is said, is less significant than how it is said, (or how it is heard), which is why oral speech plays such an important part in how we interpret meaning. Some people are very good at manipulating others in this way. Charismatic leaders, such as preachers or politicians, usually have a very convincing and impressive vocal delivery. The resonating tone and volume of their words can be mesmerizing. Another fascinating use of voice control is in the practice of hypnotism.

Passing from the sound of speech to actual language, human communication, which involves the understanding of other's thoughts, feelings, intentions, beliefs and values depends upon symbolic language. The relationship between language and thought is a fascinating subject in philosophy. One of the main debates is about whether language is a window to the mind or whether language actually constructs thought. In either case, it is certain that the better people can express themselves, the better we know what they're thinking and the better we can understand and empathize with them. There is nothing more frustrating when travelling to foreign countries than not being able to communicate. On a personal note, my marriage got off to a rocky start because of my poor French and my husband's poor English. There were some silly arguments based on simple misunderstandings, as well as an incapacity to be subtle or nuanced enough to palliate our differences. Of course when all else fails we rely on body language. A smile or tears, a fearful scream or cry for help, is understood in all languages, but the more we wish to express, the more we need language.

We definitely rely on symbolic language as a basic means of recognizing ethnicity or culture. We immediately recognize whether someone is American, German, or Chinese, by the language they speak, just as we know when a foreigner is speaking our language according to their accent. Of course there are exceptions, people who are bi-lingual or multi-lingual, and a privileged few who have an exceptional ability to speak other languages without an accent. Such a talent is quite useful for *not* being recognized as in cases of espionage.

Not only does the language or languages you speak say something about your origins, but the way you speak your language, its grammar, expressions, idioms, and vocabulary, says a great deal about your cultural background, education and general attitude. The manner in which one's language is spoken is extremely revelatory. George Bernard Shaw's *Pygmalion*, beautifully demonstrates the importance of speech in creating a personal image. It's the story of a phonetics professor, Henry Higgins, who transforms a Cockney flower girl, Eliza Doolittle, into an aristocrat by changing the way she speaks. Of course he also dressed her in fine clothing, but without proper speech, she never would have fooled the English gentry. Here is the perfect example of how recognition from the other can alter someone's self-concept. Being seen differently, Eliza suffered an existential crisis, finding herself estranged from the riff raff of her former street life, but having a hard time finding her place among the British upper class. If the way someone appears to us visually does not coincide with their way of speaking, we have the impression that something is out of sync, because we are accustomed to a certain style of language conforming to a certain visual image.

Clothing: From Bikinis to Burkas, Making a Statement

What is one of the principal ways we are recognized physically? By our clothing and more specifically, how we adorn ourselves. From the beginning of social existence, people have been decorating their bodies with jewelry, clothing, hairstyles, body paint, tattoos, and even ceremonial scarring among other customs. Clothing, first used for protection and comfort, evolved as a source of recognition, indicating social status, rank, group affiliation, and religious beliefs, as well as personal expression. Body covering is an almost universal practice. Total nudity exists in only a very few societies and in those cases there is often some minimal covering of the female or male sex organs. The exception in modern society is naturalist camps where nudity has a specific purpose and philosophy which is to be comfortable and unashamed to expose one's body and be naked with other like-minded people. (From my experience of naturist life styles, children and adults are comfortable with nudism whereas adolescents usually cover themselves).

In today's world, our clothing is often a matter of choice, and what we wear is an expression of our self, bohemian or conventional, casual or formal, consciously fashionable or outmoded. One's dress can make a declaration. "I am tough, feminine, gay, rich, sexy etc." Kenneth Gergen discusses postmodern consciousness and what he calls the "pastiche personality," with a need to continually change personality by changing style. Women particularly, he claims, since high fashion could not survive if they "did not insist on new vocabularies of clothing in the same way they require fresh insights, new experiences, and informed opinions to properly construct themselves." [9]

However, whereas Gergen sees the individual demand for change as influencing the market, Anthony Cohen sees the individual "managed and manipulated" by the market, in which our freedoms of choice are relentlessly determined by the economics of fashion.[10] He says that mass marketing, "In order to entice me to consume *their* products as an expression of *my* identity, they try to create an entire persona for me." [11] Whether individuals influence the market or the contrary, and it is probably a bit of each, the multi-billion dollar fashion industry employing millions of people around the world, would not be so lucrative if it didn't rely on people's need for social recognition.

Clothing can be used to acquire status or to be identified as belonging to a particular ideological or cultural group. Gang members and neighborhood delinquents are just as conscious of dress as the bourgeoisie. Tattoos and droopy torn jeans are a source of recognition in the same way as designer dresses and a Louis Vuitton bag, as each adornment symbolizes adherence to a distinct cultural group. Regardless of social status, fitting in stylistically is just as much an indication of one's attitude towards self, as standing out. Adolescents are particularly sensitive to conformism and wouldn't be 'caught dead' wearing certain articles of clothing. We all tend to try to amorphously fit in with others, by adhering to an unstated fashion code, wearing bikinis on the beach or evening gowns at the opera. There is conventionally appropriate clothing for different social situations.

But fitting in is becoming increasingly globalized, transcending particular cultural situations. Casual dress is the dominate trend. With mass communication, television and Internet, we can see that we are going towards more and more homogeneity. Western dress has been adopted by almost every culture on earth, having replaced or being worn in addition to customary clothing styles. Our clothing, like commercial shopping centers, is starting to look alike around the world, such as the now well familiar unisex look of jeans and a tee-shirt, or the ubiquitous somber business attire worn by men and women in every part of the world.

Does this conformity reflect a part of our passive willingness to fit-in to modern Western standards? It would seem that our increasingly conformist style of dress reflects our common desire to be recognized as part-of, rather than distinct-from others around the world. Total uniqueness in terms of style is nearly impossible and quite ironically, even non-conformism - from artistic flare to shocking clothing and adornment - can reflect a socially acceptable or anti-socially rejected statement of being recognizably 'different.'

Some famous celebrities rely on fashion to project their overall image and make a point of being recognized via a particular way of dressing. As we well know, celebrities are paid millions to advertise certain brand names. The psychological ploy is that if a famous person wears X and I wear X, I will be recognized as being like the celebrity wearing what I wear. (For more on clothing and appearance as a statement of self, see the social psychologist R.A.R. Gurung who specializes on the subject).

But, clothing is not always a choice. Uniform codes of dress are imposed for many professions, such as certain factory workers, salespersons, airline personnel, the military, prisoners and prison guards. These mandatory dress codes serve many purposes, which include the ability to identify people in particular roles, such as policemen and medical personnel. Some uniforms create anonymity: individuals do not stand out and avoid inciting narcissism or jealousy. Priests' vestments, or nuns' habits, and school uniforms are examples. These imposed dress codes can serve as a way to identify someone as belonging to a group, but they can also serve as a way of limiting someone's access to recognition as a unique, self-expressive person. In cases of total body covering, such as the burqa, it is a way of limiting a person from any externally social recognition whatsoever.

Material Possessions: "Look What I've Got!"

Continuing with a discussion of the "material self," I'd like to discuss material possessions. In the same way that our clothing and adornment are sources of recognition and express our inner self, so is a good part of what we possess. Beyond the bare necessities, our material possessions reveal something about our identity. And consequently, our identity is reaffirmed by other's recognition of what we possess.

This is the existential conclusion argued by Sartre in *Being and Nothingness*. In his discussion of "doing and having," he contends that appropriation is in effect an act of self-creation. "The pen and pipe, the clothing, the desk, the house – are myself. The totality of my possessions reflects the totality of by being. I *am* what I have." [12] Obviously, you don't need to be an existentialist philosopher to come to this conclusion. On television, I recently heard a similar comment by a contemporary Chinese fashion designer. "What you buy is what you are, so it depends upon how you define yourself." [13]

When a person is located on the bottom rang of Maslow's pyramid of human needs in which mere survival is an achievement, he or she has little hope of possessing anything more than what is essential for survival. But once a person has the chance to acquire material possessions, such as a house, car, or any other material object, they become indications of social status and life style. Once we have attained a modicum of what is necessary for our health and comfort, our acquisitions reflect what we value and are expressions of our self.

There are those who reject or discredit materialism of any kind, perhaps on grounds of religious belief or simply because they have chosen to lead a more intellectual or spiritual life. Ascetics do exist, those refusing to indulge in materialistic pleasures and casting off any recognition of the empirical self, which I might add, earns them another form of recognition. But most individuals today take advantage of earthly comforts if they can, and despite their religious or spiritual beliefs, they would probably agree with the familiar expression, "You can't take it with you." On the other hand, according to certain religions even today, some people's belief in an afterlife does include a 'reborn' empirical self and a selection of accompanying material rewards.

In modern society, we sometimes falsely presume that if people don't have the same material comforts as others in their socioeconomic group, it is because they can't afford them. It is rare to see people living below their means, despite occasional tales of frugal millionaires rejecting comfort and popular commodities. More often, the rich take advantage of their wealth, and buy what they can afford. This doesn't mean that some wealthy people are not very magnanimous, contributing to charitable enterprises, but they almost always assure themselves and their immediate family with a minimum of comfort before giving anything away. We are much more accustomed to reading about how rich people flaunt their wealth in outrageous ways, expensive homes, yachts, jewelry, clothes, *les signes extérieures de richesse* as they say in French, than about contributing to society. This is not new; as history has taught us, pharaohs, emperors, aristocrats, were infamous for lavish egocentrism. But this phenomenon also points out the irony of recognition. Such ostentatious displays of wealth gain the admiration and envy of some, but the disgust or resentment of others.

Excessive material success epitomizes contradictory recognition. On the one hand, it's the motivating force according to capitalistic principles and a Protestant work ethic and on the other hand, it's seen as despotic egocentrism. Christianity valorized the meek and the poor. Quotes attributed to Jesus notwithstanding (*It is easier for a camel to go through the eye of a needle, than for a rich man to enter the kingdom of heaven,* and *Blessed are the meek, for they will inherit the earth),* doesn't keep Christians from seeking material success. Even the non-wealthy sometimes aspire to material comfort and outward signs of wealth to such an extent that they live way above their means. A nineteenth century, economist Thorstein Veblen labeled this 'conspicuous consumption.' [14] The social psychologist William Swann writes, "In recent years, the widespread availability of consumer credit has not only fanned the flames of conspicuous consumption but altered its character. Now that people can buy on credit items that they cannot truly afford, they can, at least for a time, take on the appearance of being far more wealthy than they actually are. Propelled by a desire to impress their fellows and, perhaps, themselves, many people have struggled to bolster their self-esteem by consuming themselves into poverty." [15] In existential terms, this demonstrates that for many people, *having* more represents *being* more, or in other terms, a richer life is a fuller life.

There are historic reasons for our consumerism. In the mid-nineteenth century in America, the idea that material wealth was a sign of greed or waste was replaced by a new secularized version of the Protestant work ethic. Industrialization brought on mass production and political economists began urging immediate consumption to replace "saving for a rainy day." Asceticism came to be seen as paralyzing the economy, whereas buying boosted it, and America, like many other industrialized nations, became a consumer society. Even back in the 1920s, the implication was that consumption was a way to show our patriotism, as was expressed in this local Indiana newspaper, "The American citizen's first importance to his country is no longer that of citizen but that of consumer."[16] Closer in our memory, threatened by a recession in 2007, President G.W. Bush encouraged the American people "to go shopping more," to boost and demonstrate their faith in the American economy.

In a consumer society, the simple psychological observation that our self-identity is related to what we possess has been the major strategy for advertising. To sell their products, anything from houses to perfume, publicity consultants know that you have to appeal to a social image. If you want to be recognized as a successful person you should drive a certain car, as a real man you should drink a brand-name beer, or to be an attractive woman you should use a particular shampoo. This is also why advertising agencies pay millions of dollars for well-known actors to advertise their products. If someone you know and admire uses a certain product, you might believe it is worth more than competing products. Since you recognize the actor, you therefore use the same product and recognize yourself as being equally important.

There is some intrinsic pleasure derived from the material objects we possess regardless of the recognition they brings us; the speed of a Ferrari, the comfort of a private jet, the beauty of a diamond ring, the pleasure of looking at a Renoir painting every day in our living room. But ultimately, the value of material objects or status symbols is only relative to a social context, the meaning bestowed upon them by others in a particular time and place. If they are recognized as rare or expensive, and only accessible to wealthy elites, the pleasure is derivative rather than inherent. A real diamond is shiny and sparkly and can be considered intrinsically beautiful, but a quality fake diamond, worth a financial fraction, can be just as beautiful.

Not all material property is bought in the consumer market. We also have inherited property, land, a home, or other memorable objects that we "just can't throw away," even if no longer useful. We surround ourselves with things that have sentimental meaning, that remind us of our past, that bring us psychological comfort. We collect things, or know people who do, such as stamps, dolls, jazz records, and lace underwear. Collections, casual or obsessive, are quite revelatory of our personality. They might indicate some hidden frustration or unconscious desire, an inherent passion or satisfying pastime. Sometimes our possessions are shared with others, displayed on shelves, even entered in contests while others are stashed away in attics, or hidden in drawers. Very often, we surround ourselves with things that reflect our identity, our interests and passions, items from our past, diplomas, medals, trophies, photos, signs of accomplishment as well as memorable souvenirs, not necessarily for external recognition, for others to see, as much as for our sense of self-conservation, perpetuating self-recognition. Whether such memoires cover every wall or are discreetly guarded in boxes, they are reminders of who we are; they are tangible objects preserving intangible recognition.

The notion of recognition coming from material possession, or property, has it's antecedents in philosophy. Hegel, like John Locke before him, [17] saw our property as coming from labor, as he discussed in the Jena Lectures. "All that I have, I have through work and exchange, i.e., in being recognized"….. "At the same time I externalize this existence of mine, making it something alien to myself, and preserve myself therein. In the very same thing I see my being-recognized, being as knowing. In the former I see my immediate Self, in the latter my being-for-myself, my personhood. I therefore see my being-recognized as [my] existence, and my will is this counting-for-something (*diss Gelten*)." [18]

Hegel's rather obtuse terminology makes the simple point that through labor, one externalizes oneself and preserves one's self in what is produced. We make a material object that becomes a possession, but this possessed object takes on a spiritual meaning because it is recognized by others as being *mine*.

Sartre also considered that an activity, especially our creative work, is transitional between doing and having; our actions are ways 'to be' or 'to have.' According to Sartre, "One does (= makes) an object in order to enter into a certain relation with it. This new relation can be immediately reducible to *having*." [19] But Sartre did not limit possession simply to material objects. He includes knowledge, such as scientific research, as being an effort to appropriate. The contents of knowledge, that is, immaterial thoughts, are maintained in existence by me, by my thinking about them.[20] In the same spirit as Hegel, Sartre claims that what is possessed, one's property, is at once external and independent, and something which is mine and therefore a "subjective emanation" of ourselves. "There is within the same syncretism a self becoming not-self and a not-self becoming self." …. "The possessor is the raison d'être of the possessed object." [21] This is true for created objects, but also objects that we purchase. Money represents power, not as a possession in itself, but as a means for possessing, "…to buy an object is a symbolic act which amounts to creating the object," says Sartre. [22]

This relation between activity and possession exemplifies the link between our material self and our social self and introduces the next category I'd like to discuss. As I mentioned earlier, the different sorts of selves interconnect since in reality we are only one self.

Chapter II

The Social Self

How we are perceived by others and how we perceive ourselves is accomplished through both *having*, and *doing*, but being recognized socially constitutes who we are. We might say *I have blue eyes*, or *I have a beautiful home*, in much the same way as, *I have a steady job*, or *I have a husband*. Our social self, as we will see, begins with our physical and material self, but it extends to our active and relational self, which is why the following discussion concentrates on work and various forms of interrelationships.

Work Dethroned: Are You What You Do?

Work is one of the most important and time consuming activities in our lives; our job, the services we render, the products we make, our professional activities, constitute some of our greatest sources of social recognition.

When children are asked *What do you want to be when you grow up?*, they will tell you what kind of job they would like to do; the assumption being that your job or career is equivalent to what you will *be*. Often one of the first things people ask each other when they have just met is *What kind of work do you do?* This is a question we need to ask in order to situate or categorize someone, quite apart from physical characteristics like gender, age, and ethnicity. At a recent dinner in Paris, an American tourist asked me, "What is your daytime activity?" I found this a curious formulation. Was this a politically correct way to determine if I was gainfully employed? And speaking of politically correct, the formulation of euphemisms for jobs considered modest is a good example. A trash collector is a 'waste management and disposal technician' a fork lift driver is a 'vertical transport engineer,' or a telephone salesperson is a 'communications executive.'

There is a direct connection between the kind of work you do, and your social and economic status. Like a name and an address, a job is something every able adult is supposed to have. Most applications ask for your occupation. If you are unable to specify a job, you're stuck putting unemployed, retired or other, none of which are necessarily an accurate description. Some retired people suffer an identity crisis when they stop working. My own father died of a heart attack three months after he was asked to retire at age 73. I still believe it was triggered by depression because he no longer felt useful and had lost an important part of his identity. In 1913, the social theorist Max Weber wrote that in our American society, our major sense of value was centered on our work, and personal worth was organized around work to such an extent that many individuals couldn't find meaning in any other way. Consequently, this created a problem of leisure time, especially for those who retired.

Some fortunate people find their work inherently valuable, an end in itself rather than a means to an end. They work with passion and are committed and engaged. Money or public recognition has little relevance. Certain professions come to mind, such as sports, creative arts, research, teaching, the medical arts, and humanitarian and benevolent aid work. Then again, a person can feel committed and engaged in any line of work. There are happy plumbers, farmers, doormen and dog walkers. It is fulfilling to be accomplished in something, to be an expert, experienced, and authoritative, taking pride in what you do, or feeling that you contribute to society or a common good, without considering monetary reward or public success. But even if recognition is not the goal for some it is still usually appreciated and reassuring.

Some professional activities are more dependent upon public recognition than others, competition sports for example. Being the best, seeking first place, setting a world record, or bringing home a gold medal, is a major motivation. Performing artists, singers, dancers, actors, thrive upon recognition. Their professional careers depend upon it. As a former dancer, I can speak from experience. There is a fair amount of narcissism necessary as far as your body is concerned since it is essential for technique, grace, control, and ability to interpret the choreography. You spend hours looking at yourself in the mirror, correcting and perfecting. However, the mirror is not a reflection of yourself, it represents your public, and what you need in order to be a successful dancer is to perfect your image. The art of cooking is another clear example. Food is necessary for survival, but in almost every corner of the world, we have elevated it to an art form, inspiring thousands of new cookbooks, cooking shows and world famous restaurants where people spend a fortune for a single meal. Whether cooking for friends or clients, a talented chef seeks appreciation of what is prepared. Some professions simply wouldn't exist without public recognition.

Creative artists may or may not be looking for personal recognition, preferring recognition for their creation rather than themselves. And though there is the rare creative artist who hides all her paintings in the attic, most dream that their art will be discovered and appreciated by the public. It is difficult to work in a vacuum, spending hours, days, months and sometimes years on a creative project with no acknowledgement for your work. Writers, artists, composers, as well as scientists, often create without any assurance that their work will ever be appreciated or even considered critically, yet there remains a glimmer of hope that someone someday will recognize their work. It takes dedication, and a certain 'madness,' to persist. And the irony for a recognized artist is that she might still ask herself, is it really good?

The success or public value of artistic creation can be ephemeral, a passing fashion. Recognition might come immediately or it may take years, it may last months or it may last centuries. How many popular artists have come and gone? What makes a work of art a classic? Graffiti for example, originally produced as a means of recognition, marking territory, or making a statement, was once considered vandalism. Now it is a respected art form. We could say the same thing about rap music.

Some creative artists have been declared ahead of their time, like Stravinsky or Van Gogh, which is another way of saying that their contemporary public didn't recognize their work. Magritte waited until the end of his career for his paintings to become popular. When the New York public began paying a fortune for them he claimed that success came too late. Perhaps his disappointment was partly the realization that his talent as an artist had to become fashionable. It is indeed a pity when the value of a painting depends upon the price it earns at an auction, as if to say that public recognition corresponds with a price tag.

Fame and success in certain sectors are nothing but extensive public recognition, being in the public eye, acknowledged by the masses. People are said to identify with famous people, that is, they project part of their own self onto the person they admire. They recognize themselves in them, boosting self-esteem. Every culture develops its own hero system, and cultural heroes serve as idealized role models. The general public creates heroes and stars, political and ideological and religious leaders. We inflate their deeds, turn their narration into myth, and pass on their reputation from generation to generation. Some idolized characters are not even real, cartoon creatures, action heroes, legendary lovers, all created in books or the cinema. They become universal references, immortalized in print and film, and kept alive in the minds of individuals and whole societies. Now, with the help of media, especially the Internet, some people become famous or infamous, idolized as well as criticized practically overnight. Immortality is accessible to everyone.

Work is seen not only as a means to an end, in the form of survival or comfort, but as a virtue in itself. This is partly due to the historic evolution of the work ethic in Western societies and partly due to our relatively comfortable level of subsistence, a view introduced in social theory over a century ago. Thorstein Veblen in *The Theory of the Leisure Class* (1899) speaking of conspicuous-consumption claimed that once a society rises above a certain level of economic security; work is not motivated by comfort but the prestige of doing well. Max Weber in *The Protestant Work Ethic and the Spirit of Capitalism* (1905) reconciled monetary profit and religion, showing that work in itself was essentially virtuous. [23]

To understand how and why we have come to have such an almost universal attitude towards work as essential for our sense of self-worth, I'd like to briefly discuss how this concept of work has evolved.

Today, only a few groups of people continue to elude the modern work culture. There are still some hunter-gathering societies, African or Australian aboriginal communities, who spend only a few hours a day working. The rest of the time is spent in leisure, telling stories, and philosophizing. [24] These groups are a window to pre-historic societies, and it might surprise us that they don't work endlessly merely to survive. It's fun to speculate, as anthropological psychologists or ethnographers often do, as to how work roles developed. It was probably natural that the testosterone equipped men hunted while the childbearing women gathered. Activities were carried out based on group needs, acquiring food, tending the fire, constructing shelter, making clothes, fighting off predators, healing wounds, with someone, a chief or leader, to coordinate. Tasks were probably chosen or assigned by those who were most capable or best suited to carry them out. Then, through mimicry and later through deliberate instruction, tasks were passed on. More societal needs required more tasks, and more work roles were established within the community.

From the very beginning, there was some inequality in terms of physical and mental capability, some members of the community were weaker, some stronger, some quicker, some more nurturing, some more aggressive. The larger the social community, the more complicated things became, and with the confrontation of different rival communities and mixed cultures, a whole new set of inequalities must have appeared. Consequently, hierarchies developed in the expanding social structure.

If we jump historically to early civilization in the Western world, we know that work was not always an optimal means to an end, nor an end in itself. In Greek and Roman times, the word for work, *ponos,* meant "pain" or "sorrow," and manual labor, reserved for slaves, was held in low regard. Later, for Hebrews and Christians in the Middle Ages, work was still considered unpleasant, seen as God's punishment for man's original sin. With the Protestant movement of Martin Luther, though social status was related to what sort of work a man did, there was still the constraint of non-mobility since a person should not try to alter the profession to which he was born as it would be to go against God's laws. However, with the advent of John Calvin, God's 'Elect,' who would inherit eternal life, were those who were hard-working and active. Helping the less fortunate was disdained since it would rob them of their chance to prove themselves.

It was Max Weber, the German economic sociologist mentioned earlier, who came up with the term "Protestant ethic," which emphasized the importance of hard work, discipline, and postponed gratification. A few social elements during the 16th century that helped the Protestant ethic take hold were a rapid increase in population, inflation and high unemployment. (Sound like the 21st century?) With the Protestant Reformation, all kinds of work, even the most menial, were ordained with divine dignity, and one had the moral right to choose one's work. This philosophy coincided conveniently with rising capitalism. [25]

From World War II onwards, women significantly began joining the work force and they have increasingly assumed more jobs with greater responsibility, prestige, and higher wages. But there are still stigma and obstacles in many parts of the world for women. Even in Western societies, there is a gap between gender, work and salary. Women often start careers later in life, are more likely to change or interrupt careers to raise a family, and many give their children or husband's work priority "The net result is that the support for the experience of self that women find in work is often less than their male counterparts. Commonly, women experience conflict between the support of the self, found in work and their other goals in living." [26] It seems that women more often face a conflict of roles than men do, in which case a woman's recognition for professional success and her ability to think and work independently, must be balanced with recognition for her role as mother, or her capacity for nurturing and being emotionally responsive to family members or the larger community.

It is obvious, in light of the history of work ethics in Western culture that the current emphasis on personal, individual success, particularly in the U.S. has its Protestant antecedents. For a great majority of working people who are not passionately engaged in the work they do, the result is a feeling of non-recognition or alienation. Since the advent of the industrial age, factory work and routine manual labor has reduced workers to automatons, with little control, alienated from the product of their labor. This alienation was presciently observed by Hegel, who wrote in 1805, in the Jena Lectures that labor is a means of self-recognition, consciousness making itself into a thing, "*das sich zum machen des Bewußtseyns.*" [27] In other words, by 'objectifying oneself,' putting the self into an object, selfhood is put in jeopardy of dehumanization. A person no longer works for himself but for the industrial enterprise or for society in general. He becomes part of a human machine, a fragmented part of the labor force, which is depersonalizing, and effaces any sense of recognition.

Hegel's theory of alienation, dating from the Jena lectures but only first published in 1931, undoubtedly impressed Marx, since it was echoed in his early writings. "What constitutes the alienation of labor? First, that the work is external to the worker, that it is not part of his nature; and that, consequently, he does not fulfill himself in his work but denies himself, has a feeling of misery rather than well-being, does not develop freely his mental and physical energies but is physically and mentally debased. . . . His work is not voluntary but imposed, forced labor. It is not the satisfaction of a need, but only the means of satisfying other needs. . . . Finally, the external character of work for the worker is shown by the fact that it is not his own work but work for someone else, that in work he does not belong to himself but to another person." [28]

The writings of Marx and socialism in general, raise fears, especially in the U.S. Some Americans are afraid that his socialist ideology will destroy liberty, free enterprise and human progress. However, I find the psychology of his discourse quite perceptive. Even the respected humanist psychologist, Abraham Maslow, who believed that it was a strong desire of every person to reach his full potential, thought that it was important that a person's work be consistent with his personal program. Like Hegel and Marx, Maslow attributed dissatisfaction with work to a feeling of alienation, when people see no purpose in their work other than earning money. [29]

Alienation was an inevitable consequence given some of the deplorable working conditions during the industrial revolution, but in the beginning of the 20th century, formerly oppressive factory conditions improved. They coincided with the emergence of "scientific management," which improved productivity. But scientific management also exacerbated the problem, "work could be broken down by management into components so simple that even the most ignorant and unmotivated worker couldn't help but master them."....but "it downplays the importance of workers' feelings about themselves, their work, and the tasks they were required to perform." [30] After WWII however, with the development of new psychological theories such as behaviorism, it became evident that the worker needed to be self-motivated. Human relations departments developed in order to help workers feel useful and important, by instituting awards, social events, and company newsletters. To further improve employer and employee relationships, job enrichment programs were put into place. The historian Roger B. Hill wrote, "Factors such as achievement, recognition, responsibility, advancement, and personal growth which, when provided as an intrinsic component of a job, tended to motivate workers to perform better." [31]

We are now immersed in the information age, which presents some advantages for work satisfaction. There is more emphasis on skill, challenge, and autonomy, and workers have more control over their work. Nonetheless, not everyone has the opportunity to work in an enriching environment. Education and training are prerequisites for working in high responsibility positions, white collar or service jobs. These positions are reserved for people who have proved themselves according to specific standards, through specialized education, or professional training. It seems that our present education system, especially higher education, is oriented towards acquiring a good job rather than overall knowledge or general culture. Business management and computer sciences have become more practical and lucrative than the humanities, and the changes in university curriculums reflect this trend.

Today, as throughout history, the work you do, the job you have, is evaluated in a hierarchical way; in most cases directly related to how much money you make. Certain fields of work are immediately associated with high incomes, such as CEO's, surgeons, Wall Street traders, lawyers, and leading politicians, whereas a lack of education and training, is assumed to lead only to low paying jobs. Unfortunately, some of the most laudable and important roles for the well-being of individuals and the future of humanity, mothers (no wages), teachers or nurses (low wages), or prostitutes, (yes, they fill an important role), as well as hundreds of other dirty, smelly, noisy, or dangerous necessary jobs, receive little social recognition. Why are the masses of people who work in low-status jobs that are less desirable and less satisfying not given the recognition they merit? This rhetorical question is easily answered in a world of superficial values in which success is equated to financial gain.

A couple of additional observations; there are some working age people who can't work, or have very limited possibilities for working, such as the physically or mentally ill. Not everyone can find recognition through labor. Secondly, it should also be noted that not all work is legitimate. There are also the corrupt and dishonest; thieves, drug dealers, mercenaries, whose activities may earn millions. Their 'professions' have no positive value, and only lead to self-serving, negative and destructive consequences. Can this be considered work? It's an activity with a payoff. Ironically, drug lords, sensational criminals, à la Bonnie and Clyde, heads of crime gangs, and even some well-known corrupt leaders, are more publically recognized than hard working little-people. They are admired heroes in their immediate entourage and detested by society at large. Making a living, and occupying a role, negative as it may be, can earn someone recognition even though it is in contradiction to universal values.

Lastly, on the other end of the spectrum, there are the privileged few, the aristocracy or the very wealthy, who don't need to work. Some flaunt and waste their riches, but many make their contribution to society by financing charities, research, foundations, hospitals, schools, museums, or any other project that is beneficial to humanity. Philanthropists are duly recognized for their generosity. But obviously, monetary wealth is not necessary for benevolent action. Self-sacrifice, forgoing personal comfort and pleasure in order to serve others, is highly respected and rare. Some individuals become inspirational heroes recognized throughout the world, while thousands of others may only receive recognition within their immediate communities. Although, I believe that in cases of true altruism and generosity, recognition is not a motivation but a consequence of one's work. (I will have more to say about altruism in Section 3)

I would like to recapitulate my thoughts about work and recognition. Not everyone chooses the work they do. For many it is a matter of survival, from gathering wood to weaving carpets, and in some oppressive societies, and even in some liberal societies, there is little opportunity for mobility. The identity of these individuals is nonetheless related to the work they do, but given their lack of choice, the recognition they may hopefully gain from others and that they can have for themselves is limited. In a sense, it renders their efforts to survive as decent human beings all the more honorable.

For those who have a choice, (and I weigh my words since *choice* is so equivocal), some consider their work an end in itself, and some consider their work a means to an end. Some find their work inherently valuable. They take pleasure in what they do regardless of the financial gain and immediate public recognition. Their own self-recognition is measured in terms of an accomplishment, relative to a personal goal, which is indirectly defined and becomes meaningful within a socio-cultural context.

If there is no inherent pleasure in the work one does and public recognition or financial gain becomes the main objective, the result may be disappointing. Adaptation theory, advanced by the psychologist Harry Helson, explains this sense of disappointment. "Those who set their sights on high salaries, luxurious houses, or fancy cars, for example, may be chagrined to learn that the "glow" produced by the fruits of their labors is surprisingly short-lived." [32] We judge our current experiences relative to earlier ones and our current prosperity to what we've become accustomed to. As soon as we adapt to a certain level of comfort or affluence, (home appliances, a car, big house, new clothes) we no longer appreciate what we have but crave more.

The current problem in many wealthy Western nations is that economic growth has slowed down and the majority of people, the massive middle class, can no longer acquire new things at the same rate. The same conditions that were present in the 16th century appear today, a rise in population, a lack of employment and an economic imbalance between "the haves and the have nots." Many people who have work feel exploited, alienated and dissatisfied with their lives. If they are unhappy with their work role to begin with, the level of comfort, material goods, and social status do not compensate for an insatiable need for more. The social psychology professor William Swann writes, "Even if the struggle to improve our financial status by increasing our work hours does not leave us feeling controlled, the positive feelings accompanying the new material possessions acquired with our increased income will vanish rapidly. The pursuit of more becomes a Sisyphean task that is unsatisfying at best and alienating and deflating at worst." [33]

People work for many reasons, and when I claim that work is either a means to an end or an end in itself, I am generalizing. An individual has many conscious and unconscious reasons and motives regarding work, that are difficult to identify or classify. But regardless of the motive, regardless of the work we do or don't do, it remains a major source of recognition in society today.

Significant Others: Finding Your Mirror

When Freud was once asked in an interview to define psychological health, his answer was "lieben und arbeiten," love and work.[34] Contemporary psychologists, like Maslow, Rogers and Erikson, have also stressed the importance of both competence and devotion to loved-ones as fundamental to our sense of self-worth. [35] Like work, our personal relationships, especially significant others in our lives are very important for recognition.

The analysis of interpersonal relationships with people who mean the most to us, our family, friends and colleagues, is an enormous interdisciplinary subject.

Psychologists, psychotherapists, and sociologists, spend their entire professional lives investigating and developing theories about how we relate to others. Many therapists, counselors, and social workers are abandoning the individual-centered approach, proposing that an individual's problems are inherently the byproducts of troubled relations with others, within the family, the workplace and school. Thus, rather than just exploring the individual's unconscious or modifying his or her behavior, increasing numbers of therapists help individuals explore their relationships.[36] There is also a flourishing market for psychological literature available to help us deal with our personal relationships. I would like to point out a few observations and theories about significant others and our sense of recognition.

William James said that a person whom one loves reflects the "most particular social self." He adds that for most people, "to his own consciousness he is not, so long as this particular social self fails to get recognition, and when it is recognized his contentment passes all bounds." [37] Our feelings of accomplishment in important domains such as work, can be crushed to insignificance or elevated to ecstasy, depending upon the reaction of the ones we love. Think a child's joy when proudly showing his mother an excellent grade at school, a husband sharing his happiness and relief with a job promotion, or a young couple presenting their aging parents with a long awaited grandchild. On the contrary, think of the disheartened feeling and disappointment when efforts or accomplishments are not acknowledged by someone you hold dear. On a personal note, I was very sorry that my father died before I earned my doctorate, one of his long awaited wishes for my future.

When we refer to significant others, who are they? First of all, some of our significant relationships are given, others are acquired. Generally speaking, our parents, children, and immediate family, are givens, whereas our eventual partners, friends, and some close colleagues, are chosen. (Again, the word choice is somewhat equivocal).

Our earliest caregivers, usually our mother and father, are the first and most important people from whom we seek recognition. When we are growing up, the family, especially the mother, has the most influence on our future self.

As concerns our choice of partner or friends, the consensus among psychologists is that our close relationships tend to reaffirm the person we believe ourselves to be. Close relationships can be fleeting, or lasting. What we seek in a temporary or romantic encounter, -- often during a period of courtship and seduction -- can be very different from what we need in long-term relationships or enduring partnerships such as marriage.

There is nothing more emotionally intense that falling in love, but we know from common experience, and as confirmed by studies in neurochemistry, that intense passion can't and doesn't last. The levels of dopamine and adrenalin in the brain are similar to the high of cocaine and this chemical balance cannot be sustained. Sooner or later, serotonin kicks in and the madness of passionate love wanes. [38]

It is doubtful that anything like romance today existed in the first known societies or early civilizations.

Our concepts of romantic relationships in pre-historic times or early civilizations are often influenced by sentimental novels and Hollywood films, projecting our own romantic experiences on historic characters, rather than learned from actual recorded history. Though we don't know how important intimate relationships were to a meaningful existence long ago, there is no doubt of their importance today.

We do know something about the beginnings of courtly love, a concept brought by the Arabs when they conquered Spain in the middle of the 11th century; French noblemen were charmed by the idea, and helped its spread through the rest of Europe. But romantic love and marriage seldom coexisted. Marriage was still a feudal business transaction, arranged in the interest of family and territory. Love was reserved for the ideal lover, an often clandestine, adulterous affair. Courtly love flourished but underwent dramatic changes in the following centuries and it became fashionable for men to fall in love with eligible maidens. The idea that love was an important factor for marriage developed progressively, while adulterous liaisons were considered immoral and loveless affairs superficial. Thus, love, sex and marriage became conceptually united, until marriage became a matter of mutual free choice.[39]

Today, it seems common for people who fall in love to envisage a future marriage or at least to develop a long lasting relationship. The original unconscious attraction might be as Freud said a recall of the first object of heterosexual love, the "opposite-sex parent." [40] Recent studies seem to confirm Freud and his idea since a majority of people either deliberately seek a mate who resembles the opposite sex parent or a partner who is as unlike the opposite sex parent as possible.[41] In any case, falling in love or infatuation, the sudden, intense longing for the loved one, seems nearly universal.[42]

I'm not going to venture into the mysterious mechanisms of passionate love, that is, who we fall in love with and why, as fascinating as that might be, [43] but I would like to briefly discuss what individuals usually seek from their partner when they are in love. The romantic idealization of the loved one can cause a person to do everything possible to win his or her romantic partner. Since there is often intensified sexual arousal when people become infatuated, they will tend to concentrate on the guises of seduction and to look for recognition based on mostly superficial qualities, such as looking one's best, wining-and-dining, lavish gifts, or romantic get-a-ways. The lover who wants to conquer or win the beloved may consciously or unconsciously present a self that is not entirely sincere, adopting whatever identity necessary to win the loved one's heart. Usually the self that the lover projects will be seen by the beloved as improving his or her self-worth, the more attractive the lover, the more one is worthy as well as fortunate to be solicited by someone so recognizably desirable.

Consequently, because the beloved's self-esteem has been so highly elevated in these circumstances, the lover must be kept and protected like an object. The potential problem in this idealized romantic situation is its fragility and lack of permanence. The beloved must persistently elicit the same reactions from the lover whose feelings are often conditional, "I'll love you as long as ..." The possibility of losing your lover at the height of a romantic affair can be emotionally devastating, and sometimes catastrophic. Winning and keeping a loved one, or recuperating from the loss of a loved one has always been the theme of poems, songs, novellas, and the fodder of countless popular magazines. Obviously, recognition from a person we love is one of the most motivating, driving, sustaining forces known by modern humans.

From an existentialist point of view, it's interesting to recall what Sartre said about the impossibility of the lover's dyad. For Sartre, "in Love, the Lover wants to be 'the whole World' for the beloved." [44] For example, a woman in love wants to know if her lover would "change his life for her," "steal for her," "kill for her." The lover thus becomes the foundation for all values. Most importantly for Sartre, the lover does not want to possess the beloved only as an object, an automaton, or as a result of psychological determinism. "The lover will then feel that both his love and his being are cheapened." [45] This situation has been dramatized throughout the ages in myths like Tristan and Isolde, or Shakespeare's *Midsummer Night's Dream,* or countless fairytales, in which a princess or other character has taken a magic love potion and falls in love with the first person he or she lays eyes on. This infatuation is ultimately unsatisfying for the beloved because he or she has not been consciously and freely chosen by the lover. According to Sartre, every lover wants to be the sole and unique choice of the beloved. He wants to possess "a freedom as freedom," [46] a contradiction that renders the situation doomed to frustration. "Thus it seems that to love is in essence the project of making oneself be loved," which leads to contradiction and conflict, "each of the lovers is entirely captive of the Other" wishing to be loved exclusively, but "each one demands from the other a love which is not reducible to the 'project-of-being loved.'" [47] In other words, when you ardently love someone, you want the security of your lover's unconditional requited love, but paradoxically; this complete security can only be assured if the lover is no longer freely choosing to love. An analogy to Sartre's analysis would be the idea of trying to keep a free bird in an open cage. If the bird chooses to remain, it has been conditioned to do so, knowing nothing else than life in captivity. The choice to remain is not a free choice.

Enduring relationships have a very different dynamic than passionate love affairs. They require honesty and authenticity, not just superficial seduction and flattery, (except in unfortunate situations of coercion or obligation). The consensus seems to show that what partners want most from each other is self-confirmation, or self-verification.[48] According to self-verification theory, "people choose partners who see them as they see themselves, thereby creating social environments that support their self views." [49] This is not the same as self-esteem theory. We do not necessarily choose to be with people who make us feel better about ourselves. It has been shown that people with negative self-views will choose partners who verify their negative self-view just as often as people with positive self-views will choose a partner that verifies their positive self-view. But this doesn't mean that those individuals who reaffirm their negative self-view are masochistic. They don't want to suffer or punish themselves, what they really seek is to feel understood and evaluated by their partner in a true and accurate way. For example, a woman who doesn't think of herself as physically attractive may choose a partner who downplays physical appearance, or a man who lacks confidence in decision making might choose a partner who makes all the decisions in their relationship.

Another theory is the Michelangelo phenomenon, [50] named after the well-known sculptor. He was said to have chipped away at a block of marble to reveal the "ideal," form that lay within. This theory explains how partners shape or sculpt each other's behaviors. It begins with the concept of "behavioral confirmation," in which case one of the partner's behaviors begins to align itself or to adapt to the other partners expectations. "In ongoing close relationships the confirmation process is likely to be rather powerful, in that over the course of extended involvement, the behaviors that begin as interaction–specific adaptations become embodied in stable dispositions and habits." [51]

These relationships are said to confirm the *ideal self*, centered on one's aspirations, rather than the *ought self*, which is centered on obligations. Employing an unconscious technique similar to Michelangelo's the partner affirms this ideal self by "sculpting," that is by eliciting behaviors and dispositions that are consistent with the ideal. This process is built gradually, sometimes in an active way; guiding the partner towards situations where the self can excel, sometimes passively; by providing the partner with emotional support and security, sometimes deliberately; offering information and advice, and sometimes inadvertently; as when unconsciously serving as a model for your partner. [52] Consequently, this support is seldom consciously acknowledged by the partner being "sculpted."

Moreover, the partner doesn't necessarily agree or encourage his or her partner to conform to some general or accepted ideal; rather, there is support for the person to be who he or she ideally wants to be. According to certain studies, "...individuals prefer that their partners elicit behaviors that are positive and congruent with their ideals rather than behaviors that are merely normatively desirable." [53] This situation reminds me of my relationship with my husband. I was raised in a family that was anti-social; we never received guests and rarely even ate together. I imagined my ideal self as socially active; a party-giver with an open-house policy, but to do this would mean overcoming my insecurity and social shyness. My husband, with an outgoing Latin temperament, a large family and many friends gave me multiple opportunities for realizing my ideal self.

The point underlying these theories is that the self is looking for recognition from his or her partner in order to obtain a verification of the ideal self, in a subjective, (who I want to be), rather than normative (who I should be) sense of ideal. The message your partner sends is a bit like looking into a mirror and seeing your ideal reflection.

Another important point to notice is that this attempt to sculpt one's partner is not always beneficial to the person being sculpted. "When partners sculpt one another toward their own ideals rather than the self's ideals – even when such sculpting is masterful and yields a lovely product—the consequences tend to be maladaptive for both personal well-being and couple adjustment." [54] This behavior is called the "Pygmalion phenomenon," (as in George Bernard Shaw's play mentioned earlier) since it is an effort to transform rather than affirm. It can be a form of mistaken or malevolent recognition of one's partner. Many people experience this feeling. It occurs when their partner is trying to 'make them over,' 'turn them into someone else,' or coerce them into maintaining an image they can't live up to or that they feel is a falsification of self. Individuals who persist in such relationships, feel frustrated and misunderstood since they do not feel recognized for their true self, by their manipulative partner.

These well-researched and documented theories concerning enduring relationships confirm common sense observations; that similarity between partners is much more likely to lead to mutual understanding and harmony. Studies show that when people are matched concerning such factors as occupation, age, religion, ethnicity, and education, they are more likely to enjoy long-term happiness in their relationships. [55] Experience, backed by research, confirms that we are attracted to and get along better with those who are similar to our own selves.

Up to now, I have discussed enduring partnerships without explicitly discussing marriage. Marriage which is practically a universal practice is more than an affair between two people. According to Levi-Strauss, in all societies studied, marriage is a major element of social structure. [56] The age at which you marry, to whom and how it's done, is largely dependent upon socio-cultural influences, legal and religious. Marriage has always been a socially recognized institution.

Many factors influence marriage. In many cultures, it is normal to freely choose your marriage partner whereas in others, the choice is imposed by a family or group decision. Marriage should not be thought of as limited to monogamous, heterosexual relationships that have followed a traditional pattern of meeting, courting and falling in love. It's interesting to note that as late as the beginning of the twentieth century in America, love was not high on the list for reasons to marry. "A survey conducted in 1903 revealed that young women were most interested in their potential husband's: strength of character (42 percent). Business ability came in second (25 percent), followed by respect for females (18 percent), and finally by love (17 percent). Men were also pragmatic, with 74 percent of their votes going to 'domestic tendency,' considerably more than the 45 percent garnered by love," [57] Over the last one hundred years, views have changed. In recent U.S. polls, love is overwhelmingly seen as important to marriage, around 90 percent, whereas financial stability weighs in at 30 percent. However, about 70 percent disagree that there is only one true love for each person, which obviously opens up the door for changing marriage partners when love is gone.[58] At least in the Western world, the concept of marriage, as well as the marriage ritual, has changed, and continues to change, as with the growing legal recognition of homosexual marriage

Whereas some people fight for the right to be legally married, others reject the importance of marriage. In some progressive liberal cultures, couples consider the institution of marriage obsolete (except perhaps for certain legal rights). People frequently have sex and live together before marrying, and given the high divorce rates, they have fewer illusions of a lasting relationship. Getting married is not the major life choice it once was. But according to sociologists, marriage still represents social recognition. This appeared in a recent article in Time Magazine. "Getting married is a way to show family and friends that you have a successful personal life. …It's like the ultimate merit badge." [59]

Apparently, researchers from very different perspectives have found "marital intimacy includes closeness; warmth; deep understanding of the other; sharing of ideas, information, and feelings; fostering reciprocal personal growth; feeling needed and making the other feel needed; and giving and receiving help and affection." [60] These are the same factors noted above for any enduring relationship. These elements are more important than sex. [61]

For any species, the frequency of sexual relations drops off quickly after the first encounters: with the introduction of new partners, it jumps back to its earlier level. Human beings seem to be no different. [62] With the passage of time, couples complain of waning libido, and although there are strategies to rekindle sexual interest, there is nothing that will be as sexually arousing as a new partner.

Just on pure speculation, from an evolutionary point of view, the lassitude we feel with the same partner, and the excitement kindled by a new partner, makes sense. Passing genes along with one particular person might limit the chances of survival. The more partners, the more diversity, and perhaps the more chances the offspring will survive. We know that for human survival it is important to nurture and protect an infant for at least two years. The two year period corresponds with the passionate bonding period, when couples feel intensely in love.

So in terms of recognition, how important is sex? Obviously it depends upon the couple. If sexual attraction was the primary motivation for entering into a serious relationship, the partners may feel disappointed and cheated by marriage when their sexual relations wane. It is very interesting what R. D. Laing had to say about recognition in general and sexual relationships in particular. According to Laing, if a person receives no recognition from their partner, there will be a feeling of a real emptiness and futility when attempting to fully commit to the relationship. Normally, the self gives and receives, and reciprocally needs and expects the other to give and receive as well. But some people are incapable of reciprocity. For them, relationships are 'a one-way street.' To make a difference to the other is victory, but to allow the other to make a difference to one's own self, is defeat. In this case, others are feared in case they might make a difference, thus weakening a sense of control. Laing applies this relational analysis to sexual relations between two partners. According to Laing, "…basic intentions in sexuality are pleasurable relief from tension and change in the other." However, "sex may be felt to be empty if the other is not dancing as well….. Any theory of sexuality which makes the 'aim' of the sexual 'instinct' the achievement of orgasmic potency alone, while the other, however selectively chosen, is a mere object, a means to this end, ignores the erotic desire to make a difference to the other." [63] One interpretation of the frigid woman, and impotency in men, is their refusal to give satisfaction to the other. Sexual satisfaction if it is to be meaningful is mutual gratification, and mutual recognition.

Do some people prefer to live alone? Are there those who have no need or desire for intimacy, or for recognition from the other? I would suspect that they are a minority, considering how important it is to have a significant other at some point in our lives. Some people become recluses, for example: an elderly person who has been widowed, a homeless individual suffering from paranoia, or some certain anti-social individuals, but even in these cases, there was probably an important initial caregiver who was influential in modeling their primary sense of self.

Certain psychological pathologies, such as autism, schizophrenia, or psychosis, can obstruct the need for recognition as far as emotional attachment is concerned. Some adults without any obvious pathology may not show signs of needing recognition from significant others. But even in these rare cases, most people retain some remnants of emotional attachment from their youth that have aided in constructing their sense of self.

We know that human exchange is essential to the psychic development of infants. Newborns, without affection or human tactile attention, even if nourished, may not even survive. The untouched newborn is not only psychologically damaged but may literally die as was shown in René Spitz's landmark studies, in which the mortality rates of emotionally neglected institutionalized infants was near thirty percent. The case of feral children is another perfect example of the devastating effect and irreparable damage that a lack of social contact and human intimacy can have during the important imprinting stage in early childhood. There are more than a hundred reported cases of these children. Confined by humans or brought up with wild animals, living in isolation without human care, love, social contact and language, they are never able to develop relationships or even the most basic social skills.

It is logically possible that some people consciously prefer non-recognition when it comes to interpersonal relationships at least on an emotional level. They will then seek recognition in some other way. Psychological studies concerning attachment relations in early childhood, concluded that what is important is not whether the self seeks recognition, but *how* the self seeks it. "Those who pour themselves into their work focus on beefing up the competence component of their self-esteem, whereas those who strive to win the devotion of others focus on the lovability component," says Swann.[64] Apparently, some people become 'thing' persons, looking for recognition through individual achievement and others become 'people' persons, who look for recognition by pleasing others.

Self-esteem researchers, such as Maslow, Carl Rogers, and Erikson, have found that relational components are vital for psychological well-being.[65] I think that most of us are a mixture of both "thing persons" and "people persons." It is not only a question of our nature but of the various circumstances we find ourselves in. In a professional crisis, if a man is losing his job, he may well forget to be loving and attentive to his wife, but in an emotional crisis, if his wife has fallen in love with another man, his work problems may seem unimportant or inconsequential.

In this discussion of significant others, I've been concentrating on intimate relationships such as our conjugal partners. I've said very little about family members and friends though they are clearly significant and strongly affect our social self. As James said, "a man has as many social selves as there are individuals who recognize him." [66] Among the individuals who recognize us, there is an undefined hierarchy of their importance, beginning usually with our immediate family, including our partner, extending to close friends, colleagues and co-workers, then to those with whom we share common interests, and finally to casual acquaintances. Their importance in our lives depends upon how we relate to them. A person can be a mother, wife, daughter, best friend and employer, all at the same time, presenting a different exterior facade, speaking, behaving, and dressing differently, according to the person being addressed and social situation. Our relationships, roles, and identities, are all inextricably linked. As Laing said, "A person's Own Identity cannot be completely abstracted from his identity-for-others. His identity-for-himself; the identity others ascribe to him; the identities he attributes to them; the identity or identities he thinks they attribute to him: what he thinks they think he thinks."[67]

Sometimes we behave differently with different people and sometimes we behave the same but are perceived differently, depending upon who is doing the perceiving. In the same situation, one person views you as lethargic, another as calm; one sees you as stressed another as dynamic. The parents of a baby might find their newborn docile and tractable, whereas their friends might find him dull or lethargic. An employer might consider an employee as efficient another employer might consider the same person officious; one friend may find your remarks understanding, and to another, the same remarks are condescending. How you are recognized by the other is not completely within your control. Some of our interpersonal relations are pre-determined, others are chosen.

Groups: Show Me the Company You Keep

When it comes to recognition, how we relate to significant others corresponds with how we relate to groups of persons, large or small. A group can be as intimate as our own immediate family and as comprehensive as the human species. Groups are a continuum of interpersonal relationships and intersubjectivity.

As with other animals, group membership is essential for our survival as a species. Group formation and fidelity within that group is instinctive, as it provides protection and insures propagation. In nature, animals have no trouble recognizing other members of their group. Wolves tend to "hang-out" with the same group of wolves all their lives and the same can be said for elephants, birds, chimpanzees, and many species, so why should it be any different for us?

For our ancestors, recognizing members of the group was essential, and exclusion from the group, to be cast out of the extended family, tribe or clan, and thrust into unknown territory or the hands and spears of the enemy was certain peril. Exclusion from the group and death were probably two nearly equivalent punishments in most prehistoric societies and early civilizations. In the Bible, the eviction of Adam and Eve from the Garden of Eden and the end of their privileged union with God is an apt allegory of our fragility when cast out of the security of a sacred group. Being expelled from Paradise, they became 'mortal.' Socrates was given the choice of drinking hemlock or being banished. He chose the former, banishment was not only a death sentence, but a humiliation and dishonor as well. Banishment and social exclusion have persisted through time as an extreme social punishment. Therefore, "if there is any truth to socioanalytic or sociobiological theories, then there must be some innate motivation to be included in the social group."[68] As we will see in the next section, our instinctive need to belong to a group, to imitate and resemble others and to reinforce our recognition as part of the group, finds its source in our ancestral hominid need for survival.

Group fidelity, like professional affiliation, implies inherent moral codes, and breaching the group code is dishonorable. William James noted the importance of honoring our social self, "club opinion is one of the strongest forces in life." [69] Two centuries before him, the philosopher John Locke made the same observation. He said that there is not "one in ten thousand who is stiff and insensible enough to bear up under the constant dislike and condemnation of his own club," and ...."to live in constant disgrace and disrepute with his own particular society.... This is a burden too heavy for human sufferance."[70] Even today, when a group member no longer conforms to the group's rules of behavior or no longer adheres to their ideology, the punishment is exclusion. The member is no longer recognized as a member, and he may be considered disloyal or a traitor.

One hypothesis for this need to follow group rules, even though they are sometimes burdensome is referred to by anthropological psychologists as "cost signaling." Members of a group behave in a way that 'signals' their cooperation and reliability. This is particularly observable in religious and cultural sacrificial traditions, following rules that are 'costly' in terms of personal pleasure and comfort. [71]

Being recognized as part of a group, is based on similarities and differences, from the purely physical or material to the purely ideological. Group membership may be a matter of fact or a matter of choice, imposed or consciously chosen, as in our relationship with a significant other. Sociologists have pointed out that there is a basic difference between being a member of a group and a member of some category. Sociologist Richard Jenkins writes, "Group membership is a relationship between members: even if they do not know each other personally, they can recognize each other as members. Membership of a category is not a relationship between members: it doesn't even necessitate a relationship between categoriser and categorized." [72] Categorization is imposed by the standards of our socio-cultural context. We are identified, stereotyped, classified, according to a large range of factors we have not chosen, such as gender, ethnicity, age, education, socio-economic level etc. This is something we may find disagreeable because how we are recognized is beyond our control. Being stigmatized is the major problem with categorization. To the same extent that one may enjoy self-proclaimed identification, "I'm proud to be an American, or Black, or a Muslim," most people also want to be recognized as a unique individual with the ability to choose.

Recognition in the form of categorization is something beyond our individual control and it can have important consequences for social acceptance. Some categorizations are value-laden while others have no effect on personal freedom. On a socio-cultural level, being Black, or Gay, does not have the same value neutrality as having brown eyes or preferring white wine. Throughout history and up to the present, the color of a person's skin, their sexual preferences, or economic class, have been used as a means to restrict rights, privileges and respect.

Fundamentally, personal recognition is based on being like or unlike, and this particularly applies to group formations. Conforming to others is probably one of the most fundamental methods of gaining positive recognition. Being a part of a group means sharing similarities with others, having something in common; even if it is as simple as being in group number one as opposed to group number two.

Conformity and group formation begins early in life; witness how quickly it becomes important for children and adolescents to fit in with others their age. Being normal is of the upmost importance, and young people, especially in modern societies, tend to conform in terms of activities, food preferences, fashion, entertainment, language, speech, and social attitudes. Any divergence from what is accepted by their peer group puts one in immediate danger of being ridiculed or ostracized. Since social rejection for young people is so traumatic, many young people are ready to sacrifice their personal ideals and thoughts in order to conform or fit in with a certain group. This growth stage in life sometimes causes adolescents to undergo enormous conflict with parents or other authoritarian figures, since they often give priority to what their peer group values as opposed to what they have learned from family or educators.

Often, the feature that makes people stand out from the general population is the same feature that bonds them to others like themselves. We might even say that when people share some distinctive characteristic that differs from the population as a whole, this characteristic is likely to create a more enduring structure for recognition, so that "the more individuals believe that they share central aspects of self, the greater the bond they experience with others who share those attributes (i.e., the more they care about and are influenced by those others)." [73] This psycho-social theory is confirmed by many of our popular clichés, based on the assumption that people are attracted to others like themselves, such as "birds of a feather flock together."

There are many reasons why young people identify themselves with a particular group. As in most explanations of human behavior there is the double influence of nature and nurture. Family affinity is a genetic survival instinct; individuals tend to give greater value to genetic relations in order to promote the future of their genes. If our genes cannot personally be passed on by reproduction to our children, we are inclined to assure that those who share our genes, our immediate family, survive and have offspring. Our siblings share half our genes, our half-siblings one fourth, cousins one eighth, and so on. This principle is known as Hamilton's rule, or kin selection. Grandparents look after their grandchildren, uncles and aunts their nephews or nieces, and close cousins are often supportive. One of the common social consequences of this behavior is nepotism, favoring kin over non-kin in professional affairs. As far as nature is concerned, recognition for our own family has its biological basis.

But this is not the only factor. There is more to family adherence than genes. Our primary caregivers and early educators, most often our family, have a very strong influence on our future choices for identification. Even if our first caregivers are not our biological parents, they will still have an enormous effect on our character, beliefs, values and eventual needs including our choice of group adherence. "A child may be committed to group membership long before she can describe what it means to belong to that group. She may have a strong feeling that she is a Roman Catholic, a Chicagoan, or a Girl Scout before she has a clear sense of what these entail." [74] This is why ideological groups, such as religions and political institutions, must initiate new members when they are very young. "Virtually all formal groups assume a role of educating the child to the meaning of belonging to the group. The affective experience of group membership is generally central and is a motive for the child to behave and believe with other members of the group."[75]

In the case of nature or nurture, our family is probably the most important group we belong to, whether we are conscious of it or not. "It provides its own messages ("Us Andersons never quit") and it serves as the translator of most of the other sociocultural influences – gender, age, social class, and so on" [76] A family or community continues to recognize an individual as a member, depending upon the similarity of shared interests, behavior, beliefs, goals, ideology, etc. The more family members have in common, whether it is a case of nature or nurture, the more these individuals will continue to identify with the family as a group.

We also know that family members don't necessarily stick together, but often grow apart. Parents sometimes disown their children and some children renounce family ties. Though many families remain in contact, some have quite distant and detached relationships. Certain individuals end up not conforming at all to their family's or community's lifestyle or belief system. The reasons why are varied and complex, since there are so many factors that influence people during their development. I was born into an American Catholic and Protestant family with rather conservative political views. I now have double nationality, am not religious and consider myself a liberal, (ex-hippy for that matter). In my case and many others, the pendulum swings. For example, conservatism gave rise to liberalism; the hippies gave rise to the yuppies. Conformity is but one path and recognition can come from being like as well as being different, fitting-in as well as standing-out.

Movements into or out of a group take place throughout a lifetime, as encounters and separations, life experience and a host of other factors come into play. Our group affiliations may be voluntary, involuntary and sometimes a mixture of both. Sometimes the individual chooses to abandon the group consciously, because of a rift in ideology or total disagreement with the group's actions or behavior, or indirectly because of a conflict of interests. If there is a dramatic change in one's personal life, moving to another country, losing a job, or getting a divorce, for example, a person may automatically shift from one group to another and become socially recognized in a different way. A citizen becomes an ex-pat, a CEO becomes one of the unemployed or a married person becomes widowed. A change in beliefs and life styles may result in changing group affiliation and contrarily voluntarily joining a group may cause a modification in our self-concept. A person might join the Freemasons, the Republican Party, Greenpeace, Alcoholics Anonymous, or any other of the thousands of established groups to find like-minded people in an effort to become more like the person they would like to be. Voluntary or not, being recognized as a group member, implies a redefinition of self.

We know how important group affiliation is for self-identity. According to psycho-sociological theories, group affiliation is necessary for self-confirmation or self-verification, as with attachment to significant others. This concept has been referred to as an "opportunity structure" or "lifestyle enclave." These terms refer to "microsocial environments wherein people insulate themselves to a degree from the remainder of society and are likely to receive validation for their values and goals." [77] Tight group formation is reminiscent of a couple in-love, because objective observers can be a threat to their self-sustaining idealistic bubble. But as in the case of significant relationships, group affiliation is not necessarily self-verification in the sense of self-esteem. Choosing a group is more important for self-validation and reassurance through in-group acceptance than being accepted by society as a whole. Many marginal groups, street gangs, mafias, cartels, even derelicts or vagrants, are cohesive and well-integrated amongst themselves while rejected by society at large.

For that matter, group validation can very well be in conflict with normative values, that is, values agreed upon by the social consensus. A person might be recognized in a positive way by other in-group members and negatively by those outside of the group. For example, a tough and cruel ring-leader may be recognized as a hero within his corrupt gang and as a social menace by society. A Wall Street millionaire may be admired and envied by likeminded traders, but seen as an arrogant egotist by those outside the milieu. The leader of a right-wing political party leader might be admired by his constituents, but seen as radical by the general public. This is why members of a group insulate themselves within the group in order to reconfirm their own value system and self-beliefs.

They are looking for stability and coherence in their self-view. As Elizabeth Pinel, and William Swann pertinently wrote, "Paradoxically, in seeking to identify with others, people are striving to be themselves." [78]

On a more philosophical level, I find that this need for group validation sometimes implies a 'group-reality.' What people believe to be real, whether or not it corresponds to reality, can have very real consequences as some delusional group movements have shown. For example, members of the People's Temple Agricultural Project believed in Jim Jones' utopian paradise which led to mass suicide. Similarly, the German belief in an Aryan master race and a Jewish international conspiracy to take over the world led to the Holocaust. But even for less delusional and destructive group beliefs, there is a socially constructed reality. This is easily observable in children's games, where the rules are made up as they go along. Anyone who breaks the rules, arbitrary as they might be, is eliminated. Sports are another common and socially acceptable example. Each sport has its own rules, vocabulary, hierarchy, and coherent structure. Various groups, on very different social levels, from local street gangs, to bourgeois elite country clubs, have their own way of speaking, their own codes of behavior as to what is acceptable or non-acceptable, and their own value system. Any divergence risks exclusion. When a member does diverge from the group's ideology, a new group may be formed, leading to sub-groups; a common phenomenon in the domain of religion and politics.

Inclusion for those within a group implies exclusion for those who are not part of the group, in other words, being a *we* implies a *them*. As mentioned above, recognition can be positive when interior to the group, while negative from outside the group. This dualistic aspect of group formation has very important moral implications. In their book, *The Essential Other, A Developmental Psychology of the Self*, Robert Galatzer-Levy, and Bertram Cohler express the following. "The attributions of undesirable traits to other groups, allows group members to believe they are good because badness resides in others. This central determinant of group dynamics, which first becomes apparent in school-age children, shapes much of the hostility in relations between groups of all kinds." [79] For members within a group, there is always the danger of irrational justification and possible self-righteousness. Throughout history, dangerously misguided social, religious, political and ideological groups have existed that have led to the most horrendous behaviors, including but not limited to racism, ethnic cleansing, forced conversions, witch hunts, and mass slaughter. These actions occur when group cohesiveness is achieved through hatred combined with the attribution of evil to the hated group, thus leaving the hating group purified and good.[80] This is a point I will elaborate upon in the final section on moral implications and mutual recognition.

Media: Spreading the Word, It's All about Me

There is probably no domain in which the search for recognition is more prevalent and easily observable than in modern media. Media as a means of communication and the mass transmission of information has not only progressively expanded throughout human history, but has recently exploded and imploded, with modern technology. We have only just begun to see the huge consequences of mass media.

Long ago, information was dispersed orally and spread quite slowly, both across space to distant lands and through time as tales were recounted and passed on from generation to generation. The advent of writing facilitated dispersing information, but there was still the problem of language and translation. As stories were passed on, they were undoubtedly modified and elaborated upon to the point of fabrication. Courageous men became formidable heroes, mutant vicious animals became monsters, inexplicable events became miracles, and (sometimes delusional) visionaries became prophets of God. There was no way to authenticate what was true.

As means of communication progressed and with each media innovation, such as the printing press, newspapers, photography and recording, radio, television, and the Internet, individuals have profited. Information travels easily and quickly, making personal recognition available to more and more people in less and less time. Journalists and reporters have always exploited the famous and infamous alike, aiding those seeking recognition as well exposing those trying to avoid it.

Most people are extremely flattered by media exposure. It's satisfying to hear, "Wow, I saw your picture in the newspaper," or "My God, I saw you on television!" In the world today with modern technology, media exposure is the key to mass recognition, and though some individuals suffer from overexposure, paparazzi and scandalous rumors, most relish the attention media brings. If it weren't for media, it would be very difficult for anyone to be recognizable beyond their own family or close community.

The Internet is undoubtedly one of the most extraordinary advancements in media ever invented. It practically assures instant global dispersion of information. The most exceptional feature of the Internet is that anyone, anywhere with access, can immediately reach an international public, practically uncensored (with certain exceptions such as China) and without the filter of media professionals. Journalism and news reporting has become democratized. It is mediated and transmitted by just about any member of the general public, such as instant eye-reports by ordinary citizens. Self-promotion through public means is becoming increasingly accessible and accepted. With the clever use of social networks and the media, and a bit of luck, one can attain popularity and success. However, if an individual is not careful or perspicacious enough, he risks negative exposure and may really "put his foot (or Twitter) in his mouth."

As far as personal promotion is concerned, Social networking using Facebook, You Tube, Twitter, MySpace, Instagram and Flickr, to name a few, has greatly facilitated those seeking recognition by a single group or on a large international scale. It makes the communication of activities, interests, thoughts, tastes, and opinions, easily transmittable to a selected group of friends (a new definition of friend will be needed since the advent of Facebook), followers or to literally the whole world.

Human behavior and Internet use has opened up a whole new subject of research for psychologists and sociologists. [81] But in my view, Internet communication is a goldmine for narcissists and exhibitionists, and ironically, for introverts or extremely inhibited individuals as well. I'm familiar with both. Several people I know, who are very shy and socially withdrawn, blossom in cyberspace. They find it easier to express themselves in a virtual world of friends and acquaintances since they have the physical comfort of distance, of not shaking hands or looking someone in the eye. They can reflect before they speak, take their time to feel sure about themselves before they venture into an opinion or give a point of view.

On the opposite side of the personality spectrum, many people love to share the minutiae of their lives and their daily activities, which they relate in stream-of-consciousness type thoughts, apparently believing that everything that concerns their life is of interest to those they know and even those they don't know. They have a perfect forum to express themselves. Judging from the Internet, it's no wonder that narcissism was being considered for removal from the American Psychiatric Association's DSM-5 (Diagnostic and Statistical Manual of Mental Disorders) as a personality disorder. Considering social networks, blogs, on-line journals, and instant text messaging like Twitter, a major portion of the population is narcissistic. Many people spend hours a day, nearly addicted to recounting something about their lives, as well as sharing pictures and videos of themselves, their family, friends, trips, parties etc. The Internet has become a public forum for what was once the fodder of intimate journals kept under the bed. Some people, who emit an hour by hour and minute by minute texting of activities, must be motivated by some kind of attention seeking. (In the U.S., young people who have cell phones send and receive an average of 88 text messages a day) [82]

For what is referred to as today's "me generation," anyone can become a micro-celebrity. Could this be as Jeremy Rifkin, author of *The Empathetic Civilization*, pointed out, our desire for fame? He talks about "the Internet's incredible power to inflate and amplify each person's desire for recognition-the fame factor." [83] Or is it simply a need for recognition, "Look at me!" "Listen to me!" Such behavior could be explained by a desire for fame or notoriety, or it could be simple attention seeking, a need that someone acknowledges your existence. In the spirit of Descartes, "I'm recognized, therefore I am."

Granted, some people sincerely want to share information, not necessarily about their personal life, but rather about something that is of potential interest to compatible individuals. In my discussion of groups, I pointed out that recognition involves seeking like-minded others. The Internet or other media technology has greatly facilitated group creation and group membership. Individuals can share information on anything from cute kittens to important social causes like raising money in response to a catastrophe, or a tumultuous political event like overthrowing an oppressive government such as the 'Arab Spring.'

However, taking part in a common cause is very different from the constant chronicles of narcissists. It is interesting that this public display of the private self renders people vulnerable for disapproval as well as approval. The search for recognition does not always result in a boost of self-esteem. The Internet is a public forum for personal information with obvious advantages, but it has also become a huge resource for those who take advantage of it to disapprove, humiliate, slander, insult, and bully others, leading to some very dramatic consequences. Privacy for those who wish to avoid public recognition is also put into jeopardy. I have sometimes had a 'friend' share some information or photos without my consent, which is probably only the tip of the iceberg, as far as privacy infractions are concerned. There is a delicate balance to maintain between making your life public and keeping it private. The Internet, just like any other technological tool, is vulnerable to wonderfully constructive use and horribly destructive misuse, and to positive recognition as well as negative recognition.

Another interesting aspect of the Internet is that it is relatively democratic. It is used by the common people as well as the rich and famous. Anyone and everyone can be heard and seen. It's a haven for influencing the masses, according to or in spite of one's desires. As far as popularity goes, it has enabled a total vulgarization of success, that is to say, vulgarization in the original sense of the term; relative to the common people, rather than filtered by an elite, cultured, educated or privileged arbitrator. The general public is the judge. What is important is the big numbers, the quantity of 'hits,' 'votes,' 'likes,' 'thumbs up,' and not the social status of the voters. Popular success is like any other commodity on the market, what counts is making a sale, not the identity of the buyer. Whether an individual is an unknown, or a famous celebrity, via the Internet, he or she can soar to fame or plummet to obscurity.

However this virtual public may have its downside, even for those who enjoy substantial statistical success. As Rifken pointed out, "the drive for fame reflects a new sense of existential aloneness and a desperate need to be recognized. The desire for fame is often driven by a fear of mortality and the need to gain at least a fleeting sense of immortality or, if not that, at least to know that one's existence is duly noted, recognized, and celebrated by millions of others." [84] Does financial success or extreme mass popularity assure happiness? The consensus is no, and in fact, for some individuals it is emotionally destructive. How many entertainment figures, charismatic public leaders, and well-known financial millionaires have plunged into drugs, alcohol, depression, even suicide? Being recognized on a global level, being idolized by the masses and having millions of virtual friends on a social network, cannot replace the affection, care, and understanding of even a single significant other. Recognition on a mass anonymous basis comes from an abstract objectified other rather than a concrete subject in the form of a significant, empathetic person. The result can be an existential emptiness that leaves one's ego feeling like an emotional black hole.

My intention is not to undervalue the positive aspects of a more democratic media system, especially as far as factual information is concerned. Openness, clarity, and multiple perspectives on important political and social issues have tremendous potential in enlightening people all around the world. Written and visual reporting of everything from disasters to political injustices can go a long way in sensitizing a vast and varied public, rendering individuals more empathetic to those less fortunate who do not share the same material comforts, or social freedoms as those in technologically developed countries. The current concept of *memes*, that is to say socio-cultural ideas that are passed on vertically from generation to generation, can be passed on horizontally with a rapid and efficient Internet system. As in genetic evolution, memes can be mutant, they can replicate with great rapidity, and they can be modified as they are reproduced. The question remains, are they good memes or bad memes? Messages of hate, discrimination, and uninformed prejudice can spread as easily as humanitarian efforts for the common good.

Animals: Recognition from our Fellow Earthlings

I feel it important to mention our fellow earthlings as a source of recognition. It is certain that they are not in the same category as material possessions, yet I'm not sure I could categorize them along with significant others. Animals are sentient beings, although we may not recognize them on the same level as self-conscious humans. People find comfort, companionship, affection, and yes, a strong sense of recognition from their pets, not only in the case of "man's best friend," but from other beloved domesticated and wild animals as well. I've always appreciated the company of my own pets and I am certain that they recognize me, if only to the extent that I'm the hand that feeds them.

I won't take part in the long scientific and philosophical debate on animal consciousness, though I personally find it quite fascinating. The extent to which, animals have a conceptual recognition of humans will continue to be studied and disputed for some time to come. Nonetheless, I think that scientists and philosophers agree that intelligent animals like mammals have fairly evolved complex brains similar to our own, and are conscious beings. In fact, in 2012, an international group of prominent neuroscientists concluded that many animal creatures, like humans, possess the neurological substrates that generate consciousness, which they officially wrote up in *The Cambridge Declaration of Consciousness*. Animals have the capacity for recognition, not only of objects and places, but members of their own species as well as other species, including humans. They have spatial and episodic memory, very highly developed senses, a certain capacity for problem solving (which some label as reasoning), use tools, can communicate their wants and needs, (although they lack symbolic language), exhibit intentional behavior, and quite importantly for this discussion, seem to show empathy, and depending upon how you define it, even morality.[85]

It is no wonder that people may recognize animals in the sense of respect. Some people depend upon them for the quality of their lives, from a cowboy's trusted horse to seeing-eye dogs. There are countless stories of tremendous fidelity and heroism concerning domestic animals. Some dogs are highly trained to protect and defend their masters and there is no confusion for a loyal pet when it comes to recognizing his or her master or the master's enemy. Thanks to their highly developed sense of smell, dogs are better than humans for tracking down individuals, criminals or lost children, or detecting illicit drugs.

Many animal owners, and animal activists, are convinced that animals are sensitive, thinking, feeling beings. These attitudes are sustained by numerous children's stories or Hollywood movies with talking animals, which have exploited our desire to humanize the animals we live with.

But on the other hand, there is a tendency to anthropomorphize animals, especially our own pets. People lavish their pets with affection and treat them to commodities like expensive foods, beds, play toys and even clothes. Ironically, the place where I saw dogs treated in the most human fashion was in China, where they also end up on certain dinner plates. Perhaps, this is in part due to the one-child policy. When the single child is grown and gone, affluent Chinese people can be incredibly doting pet owners. I've seen their dogs not only coiffed and dressed in fancy clothes and shoes but even pushed around in baby-strollers. Often, the antics and actions of people's pets are interpreted in a way that makes them seem more *intentional* and humanly goal directed than they probably really are. A friend recently talked endlessly about how smart his new kitten was, for example, it turned off the alarm clock so that he could get a late morning sleep, sat on his computer to keep him from working, and 'smiled' and bowed its head sheepishly when he caught it peeing in the living room plant.

People who believe their cat or dog (or pet snake) is 'pouting' because they are not being paid attention to, feels 'guilty' because they've done something wrong, or are 'sad' to be left alone, would be hard to dissuade. Animal stories support the notion that they have feelings or even sentiments. Dogs have been said to 'mourn' a lost master, as in the tale of "Greyfriars Bobby" the Skye terrier who faithfully attended his master's grave for 18 years.[86] There is obviously some dog-like cognitive connection between the master's absence and the place where he laid under the earth, but to define this as mourning in a human sense of the term is another matter. Though it is sure that animals recognize their masters as a source of care and comfort, and miss that care and comfort when it is no longer available, that is not the same as saying that they can conceptually recognize that their master is 'dead,' and will never return.

These points are not to mock or criticize pet owners, (well, perhaps a bit), but to say that people experience a sense of recognition from their pets, whether it is real or imaginary. As philosopher, Avishai Margalit observed, "as for respecting animals, this is clearly an anthropomorphic concept of respect. We do not grant any special respect to scallops and scorpions, not because they have no "achievements" but because we don't know how to "humanize" their achievements…..... When we speak about respecting an animal we are really speaking about respecting ourselves. When we worry about respecting a chimp that is being mockingly mimicked by onlookers at the zoo, we are really worrying about respect for ourselves." [87]

The idea that there is a recognizing subject in the consciousness of one's pet might be a case of anthropomorphizing, but by the same token, feeling that we are recognized when we are not, is rather common. There are situations in which we imagine other people recognize us when they don't. Some self-conscious individuals, whether from shame or an inflated ego, might mistakenly think, 'everybody is looking at me,' when in reality people aren't paying any attention whatsoever. This idea of feeling recognized when there is no real recognizing subject can be taken a step further. The recognition some feel in their relationship to animals, has a parallel with that of a gardener to her plants. They perk up and look happy when watered; wither and look forlorn without attention and I have heard more than once that you should talk to your plants if you want them to flourish. The anthropomorphizing of nature is a very important component in romantic thinking and writing, and no one is shocked to hear expressions like "the skies are menacing" or "the plants are thirsty." The whole principle in this kind of thinking is to give something inanimate a meaning in relation to the self. In this sense, we recognize our *self* in animals, nature, perhaps even inanimate objects, which is exactly why they are meaningful.

Chapter III

The Spiritual Self

For many, the spiritual self is the most important and omnipresent aspect of being human. It is also one of the most difficult to define, since spirituality takes on so many different forms, varying from culture to culture, generation to generation, and person to person. It can range from being dogmatically religious to "New Age" experiential.

Discussing recognition for the spiritual self may seem ironic, even verging on being an oxymoron. But it is such an important feature of what we consider the self, it cannot be ignored, and many people seek recognition for their spiritual self as part of their mortal existence as well as their anticipated immortal existence.

The Soul: Eternal Recognition

The spiritual self is what some might refer to as our 'soul,' but exactly what constitutes the soul is subjective, varied and difficult to define. There are historical, cultural and religious meanings referring to the spirit or soul.

Plato's philosophy of an immortal rational soul, followed by early Christian thought which abandoned the notion of the resurrection of a person's body in favor of dualism, and the concept of an immaterial soul that leaves the material body and continues into eternal life, are two such examples.

Many personal accounts have been written concerning spirituality or the soul, not to mention celebrated holy books and sacred writings. In most cases, the soul or spirit has been identified with the immaterial, transcendent essence of a person, and in some cases, any sentient being. In the major religions, the concept of spirit or soul is thought of as being independent from the body and thus immortal. Regardless of its connotation, whether traditional or modern, it is usually described in rather nebulous, vague terms that should be nonetheless immediately understood. Lecturer, author and psychotherapist, Thomas Moore, wrote in his book, *Care of the Soul*, "Soul is not a thing, but a quality or a dimension of experiencing life and ourselves. It has to do with depth, value, relatedness, heart, and personal substance. …….. When we say that someone or something has soul, we know what we mean, but it is difficult to specify exactly what that meaning is." [88] This sort of secular definition is typical when discussing the spirit or soul; it is something that should be immediately evident even though it's difficult to define. William James places the spiritual self at the top of the hierarchical scale, the bodily self at the bottom, and the various social selves in the middle. He describes what he considers the spiritual self as "a man's inner or subjective being, his psychic faculties or dispositions." Since these "dispositions are the most intimate part of the self," [89] we should be familiar with them as tacit knowledge.

For many psychologists as well as most contemporary philosophers, the soul or spirit is identified with the psyche or mind and therefore not necessarily disassociated from cognition, the brain or the physical body. James' psychological definition falls into this category since he describes the spirit as our "subjective being," that is, our active element of consciousness, the thinker as opposed to the contents of our thoughts, or it is the "feeler" as opposed to the feelings themselves. But James' spiritual self, the subject or empirical *I* also remains nebulous and vague. He says, "some would say that it is a simple active substance, a soul of which they are thus conscious; others, that it is nothing but a fiction, the imaginary being denoted by the pronoun I; and between these extremes of opinion all sorts of intermediaries would be found." [90] In James' essay on self-consciousness, he manages to circumvent a discussion as to whether this "central nucleus of the Self" is "a spiritual substance or a delusive word." For James, the important thing is that it is something that is *felt* in the same way as the body is felt. He deduces that at least for himself, any sense of the spiritual self is accompanied by some physical sensation. "*Our entire feeling of spiritual activity, or what commonly passes by that name, is really a feeling of bodily activities whose exact nature is by most men overlooked.*" [91]

Discussing the essential nature of the spiritual self or soul raises an enormous polemic that I can only treat superficially. However, since looking for recognition for the spiritual self depends upon the way in which it is perceived, this requires at least a brief digression in order to explain a few of the differences between spirituality and religious belief, both of which are concerned with the existential meaning of life on earth as well as life after death.

These multidimensional concepts, religion and spirituality, are often used in conjunction, but sometimes employed in opposition, and lack definitive consensus. [92] Often, spirituality is related to one's conception of the divine. There are numerous conceptions of the divine, ranging from a totally transcendent God, completely apart from the experienced world; to an immanent pantheistic God, who only exists in relation to the world to insure its unity and structure; to a transcendent cosmic reality that has no God-head. The following is a sample of the many representations of God.

Anthropomorphism: God as a person

Non-anthropomorphism God as "something Higher," the transcendent

Theism or pure transcendence: God as the unmoved mover

Pantheism or pure immanence: God exists in the unity of man and the world

Pantheism: immanent transcendance or transcendent immanence

Individual Pantheism: God exists in the deepest part of myself or I receive support from God

Ontological Pantheism: God as the ground for existence

Social Pantheism: God exists in our relations with others

Cosmic pantheism: God is found in nature or beauty [93]

With these considerations in mind, looking for recognition for the spiritual self depends upon one's belief system. It may be realized through religious practice, with specific traditions and rituals, ceremonies, moral conduct, sacred law, and organized worship. These practices vary from religion to religion; some have grave consequences, like human sacrifice, and others are merely symbolic, such as respecting holidays. On the other end of the scale, looking for recognition may be sought through more personal forms of spirituality based on more individualistic subjective views, with methods such as meditation, introspection, and looking for existential meaning or the divine within oneself. Another way of dichotomizing the methods of achieving recognition for the spiritual self is by saying they may implicate orthopraxy, (practice), or orthodoxy, (belief), or a mixture of each.

Since the spiritual or religious self varies from culture to culture and may evolve from one generation to the next, it seems undeniable that religion or spirituality reflects its socio-cultural context. A person who has no social interaction, no language, no sense of the other, such as feral children, will have neither a religious nor a spiritual concept of self, nor any concept of a supernatural being. It is certain that as society and culture evolve so do attitudes towards spirituality. This was obviously the conclusion during the nineteenth century, by psychologists, such as James, Freud, and Jung, or by Emile Durkheim, one of the pioneers in the sociology of religion, as he famously suggested, "God is society writ large."

It's tempting to speak of evolution when speaking of our conception of God or our spiritual self, perhaps not in the sense of progress but simply of adaptation and change. We have become increasingly diversified, individualistic, less family, clan or community oriented. Spirituality, which has gained popularity of late, is a more individualized expression of faith or belief in the transcendent or divine, though not necessarily in the belief of a monotheistic entity. In the last few decades the difference between religiousness and spirituality has become more polarized, a fact observed by contemporary psychologists. "The most egregious examples are those that place a substantive, static, institutional, objective, belief based, "bad" religiousness in opposition to a functional, dynamic, personal, subjective, experience-based, "good," spirituality." [94] This sort of normative judgment is reflected by the psychologist Gordon Allport's Religious Orientation Scale, upon which he based his distinction between mature and immature religious attitudes, which are either extrinsic, "what's in it for me," or intrinsic, a genuine and non-self-interested belief. In this sense, some people, sensing an interconnected, higher consciousness or a universal unity, claim to be spiritual, but not religious. And, there are some very religious people who seem to lack genuine spirituality.

I don't wish to polarize religiosity and spirituality, but in order to discuss a person's search for recognition from an "ultimate transcendence" (still using metaphoric language), I would like to present two different but not necessarily opposing spiritual goals. First let's consider the Judeo/Christian/Muslim traditional views of a monotheistic God and secondly, the Buddhist and related East Asian views of transcendence.

When James wrote about the spiritual self, he was referring to a more traditional religious monotheistic concept of spirituality. His views on religious psychology remain pertinent and have been reiterated by more contemporary psychologists. According to James, our incessant search for our social self ultimately becomes the search for an 'ideal' social self. As was discussed earlier, in all our social encounters, we are constantly judged by others who become important sources of recognition. These numerous others, varying in importance, come and go throughout our lifetime. We adapt and modify our self in relation to the recognition we receive, continually seeking our best possible social self, from the most reliable and sincerest possible judge. "This self is the true, the intimate, the ultimate, the permanent Me which I seek. This judge is God, the Absolute Mind, the 'Great Companion.'" [95] Being recognized unequivocally by an ideal spectator, who sees all and knows all, including our personal true self, is one of the greatest comforts of religious belief. What could be more comforting than to be assured that there is a higher judge than any of our human counterparts that can understand, forgive, and reassure? As R.D. Laing said, "It seems to be a universal human desire to wish to occupy a place in the world of at least one other person. Perhaps the greatest solace in religion is the sense that one lives in the Presence of an Other." [96]

The idea of an impartial ideal spectator or judge has been evoked in other 19th century sociological theories such as Durkheim's *conscience collective,* a collective social force that surpasses our individual existence and takes on a supernatural reality. For C. H. Cooly, it was the "social mind," a product of successive individual social encounters, or "looking-glass selves," compiled into a general social reflection. If the *I* is only a series of *me's* the self is inherently unstable and needs the presence of a "generalized other," as George Mead proposed, in order to give it coherence. Mead said that for an individual, "only in so far as he takes the attitudes of the organized social group to which he belongs toward the organized, co-operative social activity or set of such activities in which that group as such is engaged, does he develop a complete self ... only by taking the attitude of the generalized other toward himself, in one or another of these ways, can he think at all; for only thus can thinking – or the internalized conversation of gestures which constitutes thinking – occur." [97]

If as in Judaism, Christianity, and Islam, God is a *Deus humanissimus*, a personal God seen as humane, understanding, loving and caring, He is the ideal pure subject that sees, hears and knows all suffering. This Pure Subject, who resembles but transcends the humane subjects we encounter in life reminds me of what Martin Buber described as the "Eternal thou." For Buber, God, as the Eternal Thou is always present to us and we are present to God whenever we are in relation to another human as a Thou. The *I-Thou* relation between the individual and God is universal and primary as the foundation of all other human relations. "Every particular Thou is a glimpse through to the eternal *Thou;* by means of every particular Thou the primary word addresses the eternal *Thou*." [98] God, for Buber, can never be an *It*, since God cannot be measured, cannot be understood, or talked about as a sum of qualities, (as in some religions) and God cannot be sought because God is everywhere.[99] This often presents a problem, since according to Buber, there are many who wish to possess God as an *It*, as in institutionalized religion.

Martin Buber's philosophy of religion though adopted by many people who believe in a personal God, is not held by all followers of traditional monotheistic religions. Different believers seek recognition from God in different ways. They may seek it by respecting religious rules, by obeying God's commandments, by doing good deeds, through piety, charity, altruism, heroism, by a submission to God's will or by demonstrating complete faith and confidence in God's plan, even when things appear quite grim. God's recognition might be sought as a path to salvation and each religious denomination has its own interpretation as to how that salvation and eternal bliss in union with God is obtained.

The great comfort in being recognized for the spiritual self is that a person is recognized in an ideal sense for who he or she truly is. When we seek recognition for our material self, or multi-faceted social self, we know that there are dissimulations, guises, pretenses, façades, inaccurate images of the true self. However, God is omniscient and thus the only purely objective, non-self-interested, non-prejudiced, unbiased personal judge who is capable of knowing us as we are truly are. This true or authentic self, though clear to some people, is a mind-boggling much disputed concept for philosophers; a concept I will discuss in a following chapter. However, for people of faith, the concept of a true self poses no problem since it is defined as the spiritual self or soul as known by God.

In the case that God is the ideal spectator and judge, one of the most important ways in which the spiritual self communicates with God, rendering recognition and in some instances receiving God's recognition in return, is through prayer. As usual, I'll begin by citing William James, who said that the main reason we pray "is simply that we cannot help praying."[100] The reason for this is that though man is essentially social, the only truly adequate Socius, i.e., the "Great Companion," according to James, is in an ideal world, and prayer is therefore a necessary consequence of this human reality.

Prayer is certainly one of the most essential features of religion, and one of the most important expressions of the spiritual self. It is not only action but words, willful, deliberate expressions of our innermost thoughts. In a little known but wonderful book, *On Prayer*, (1909) written by Marcel Mauss, the nephew and disciple of Durkheim, Mauss' main thesis is that prayer is one of the central phenomenon, even the "essence" of religious life. Prayer is essentially social; even when individualistic, society influences its content and form; and it is evolutionary in nature, progressing from very rigid rituals to a more expressive individualism that may culminate in a sort of mysticism.

Another very comprehensive study of prayer was written by Friedrich Heiler, a German theologian and historian of religion. Heiler, believes in a very personal God, "a supersensuous, superhuman Being on whom he feels himself dependent, yet a being who plainly wears the features of a human personality, with thought, will, feeling, self-consciousness." [101] As for Mauss, prayer is social, "Since prayer displays a communion, a conversation between an "I" and a "Thou," it is a social phenomenon. The relation to God of him who prays always reflects an earthly social relation: that of servant or child or friend or bride." [102] Heiler, like Mauss, sees prayer as evolving from the primitive and ritualistic with an appeal to alleviate misfortune and suffering, to the mystical and prophetic prayer that places emphasis on illumination rather than intervention. To sum up his theological position, *"Prayer is, therefore, a living communion of the religious man with God, conceived as personal and present in experience, a communion which reflects the forms of the social relations of humanity."*[103]

For believers in a monotheistic God, the sense of an ideal tribunal that surpasses any social reference is an essential part of consciousness. But even those who are not religious "are haunted by this sense of an ideal spectator," and a need to be validated by an ever present "higher recognition," according to James. "Only a non-gregarious animal could be completely without it." [104] This higher recognition is what psychologists of this generation might refer to as our moral conscience. In this case, the source of our sense of moral consciousness is no other than the 'voice' of our parents or primary caregivers and educators, whether we consciously remember this voice or not. A personal God, to whom we ask for intervention, intercession, guidance and permission for action, to whom we confess, confide, give thanks, or devotion, and even adoration, greatly resembles the idealized authoritarian figure of our own parents, and looking for recognition from one or the other shares many of the same features.

A Soulless Spiritual Self

Spirituality in the Buddhist belief system is quite different from the notion of a spiritual self or soul in monotheistic religions. In monotheism, there is usually a relationship between a substantial *I* and an eternal *Thou*, between an individual subject and a personal God.

Before proceeding, I would like to mention several caveats. First of all, my familiarity with East Asian spiritual belief systems, such as Buddhism, Hinduism, Confucianism, or Taoism, is rather limited. My intention here is simply to point out a few major factors that put non-theistic beliefs in contrast to theistic as far as the spiritual self and recognition are concerned. Secondly, I'm currently restricting my discussion to Buddhism not only because it has become increasingly popular in the Western world, but also because it is a philosophy that can be integrated with other religious beliefs. Also, I'm fully aware that Buddhism is not officially considered a religion since there is no belief in God as creator. However, Buddhism, in its many various forms, is adhered to by millions of people and shares many of the same dimensions as monotheistic religions.[105]

Discussing recognition for the spiritual self in Buddhism is very paradoxical since its principle doctrine *anatta*, is antithetical to the concept of a soul. *Annata* is the doctrine that there is neither any substantial permanent self, nor any immutable eternal spiritual essence. The

Buddha, Siddhartha Gautama, the "Enlightened One," historically broke off from traditional Indian religion and Brahmanism, in which each person possesses an eternal soul, (atman) in union with a metaphysical cosmic counterpart to God, (Brahman). In Buddhism, especially in meditation, the mind and body make up an undifferentiated unity. This is quite unlike monotheism which presupposes a form of Cartesian separation of body and soul, the physical incarnating the immaterial, an idea which goes back to the Greeks. Buddhism is neither materialistic nor dualistic, but closer to pluralistic, claiming that the natural world is too rich and beyond our understanding to be described in any single way.

A major goal in Buddhist philosophy is to awaken to the fact of *anatta,* and to liberate oneself from the false belief or imaginary idea of a self. The concept of a *me* or *mine*, has no corresponding reality and is the source of all desire and suffering. The preoccupation we have with *me* leads to selfish desire, egoism, attachment, accompanied by feelings of pride, conceit, hatred, ill-will, etc. Whereas in Judeo/Christian tradition, the source of man's suffering is his pride and disobedience, in Buddhism the origin of suffering is desire.

In most cases, desire is antithetical to a spiritual self, and thus the desire for recognition for the spiritual self would be completely impossible. However, it might be mentioned that not all desire is bad in Buddhism. When desire is not selfish *tanha* but altruistic *chanda*, wishing the well-being of others, or improving the state of the world, one is exercising one's spiritual self.

Since there is no supernatural being to count on, every individual is on his own and totally responsible for his actions. Action is the literal meaning of the Sanskrit word *karma*. Most of us are familiar with the notion of karma as the continual cycle of birth, death, and rebirth, which is conditioned by the moral nature of our actions. Good actions lead to good results and evil actions to evil results, causing a person to inter into the cycle of reincarnation *samsara*. Future rebirths are determined by a person's moral actions, working her way out of the cycle by following the prescripts of Buddhist ethics. The only way out of this system of continual rebirth is by attaining the final solution called Nirvana.

Nirvana is the final and highest good in Buddhist philosophy. In lieu of a soul, the path to Nirvana is perhaps the key to the spiritual self in Buddhism. By leading a moral life, such as following the "middle way" and respecting the noble eightfold path, as well as embracing wisdom,(a profound understanding of the interconnectedness of the human condition and the true nature of reality, as through meditation and recognizing the four noble truths), a person may find her way to Nirvana. Nirvana, literally a "quenching" or "blowing out," represents the ideal of human perfection, a transformed state of consciousness which is free from the illusion of a *me*. What is extinguished in Nirvana, are the roots of evil, greed, hatred and delusion. However, as mentioned above, considering the doctrine of *anatta*, it is perplexing to envisage the nature of the spiritual self as it approaches the state of Nirvana, since the subjective self that reflects upon the empirical self has less and less of an empirical self to reflect upon. By the time Nirvana is attained, the entire self is only pure conscious awareness without content.

A spiritual existence is therefore a life in which one follows the path of enlightenment. It is realized through meditation, a controlled state of altered consciousness, in which one is conscious and aware of the here and now, but with a sense of calm and inner stillness. The transformative insight in meditation is that a person has no true essence and the conscious mind is a process like everything else in the universe. There is no mysterious 'I' or subject behind one's thoughts but only the thoughts and experiences themselves. This understanding is the key to eliminating all personal desire and any preoccupation with an ego.

I find this notion of a 'content-less' self curiously paradoxical. Given that mental processes are always changing and just an illusion; the *me* doesn't really exist. Add to this the precept that in Buddhism there is no mysterious *I*. In that case exactly *what* is being passed on in rebirth? Something, or some essence of the original spiritual self which was present in the beginning, must surely be sustained in the karma cycle in order for this same self to arrive at the state of Nirvana.

Recognition for the spiritual self in Buddhism is radically different from monotheistic religions in which the spiritual self is an individual soul in relation to God. There is no set of individual *me* qualities to be recognized. However, Buddhism does embrace intersubjectivity and we could infer a sense of recognition for the spiritual self, even though it would seem counterproductive to any sense of the Buddhist spiritual *non-self.* [106] I'll attempt to explain how.

Those who practice Buddhism, like all individuals, are born into a social nexus in which they are causally interconnected with other people. Buddhists are language users and thinkers who share concepts with their community; they share perceptions and ideas with those who are in their social construct. For followers of Buddhism, the purpose of withdrawing from society to isolate oneself and meditate is to avoid the influence of inter-subjective relations with others, to de-contextualize one's *self*, and to deconstruct one's identity in order to obtain a spiritual liberation. But, according to Buddhist teaching, one should not become a recluse and pursue a path of deconstruction unless emotionally healthy, and the way to emotional health is through empathy. As Allen Wallace, an expert on Tibetan Buddhism wrote, "The single most powerful practice for achieving such emotional health is the cultivation of a sense of connectedness with others. This is done by empathetically reflecting again and again on others as subjects, like oneself, with their hopes and fears, joys and sorrows, successes and failures. In this way, whether alone or with others, one overcomes the sense of loneliness and isolation."[107]

In meditation, the goal is to obtain a state of 'content-less' awareness, called *bhavanga*. In this case, it seems that consciousness would no longer be inter-subjective. But since meditative practices are primarily concerned with the four "measureless states" of loving kindness, compassion, sympathetic joy and equanimity, empathy and intersubjectivity should be vital to realizing a spiritual self. The practice of loving kindness involves developing an attitude of benevolence, friendship, and goodwill towards all living creatures. "Through compassion the meditator identifies with the suffering of others, and through sympathetic joy he rejoices in their happiness and good fortune. The cultivation of equanimity ensures that these dispositions are always balanced and appropriate to the circumstances." [108]

According to Buddhism, both compassion and wisdom must be cultivated in order to obtain spiritual enlightenment. In the practice of mindfulness, (the seventh element of the noble eightfold path), the person meditating concentrates first on her own body, feelings, and mental states, then on the other's. Attention is shifted back and forth between oneself and other in order to cultivate "*reiterated empathy*, in which one imaginatively views one's own psychophysical processes from a 'second-person' perspective." [109] A person's body is viewed from an imagined perspective coming from the other, so that one's presence-to-self is sensed not only from within but from without. Such practice leads to the insight that the second-person perspective of one's own being is just as real as the first-person perspective, and neither exists independently of the other. The goal is to experience one's own body and feelings rather than identifying with them. Through objective observation of one's feelings, "by observing the effects they have on oneself and others, one begins to recognize through experience those processes that are conducive to one's own and others' wellbeing and those that are destructive." [110] In this way, a multi-perspective view of the self and others, and inter-subjective relations are cultivated in the lived world.

What can we conclude about recognition for the spiritual self in Buddhism? If the spiritual self is *only* a content-less pure consciousness, it would be indistinguishable from any other pure consciousness, and since recognition is logically dependent upon discerning differences or likenesses, it would be non-recognizable in any sense of the term. However, before reaching the extinguished state of Nirvana, there seems to be another sense of the social-spiritual self in Buddhism, practicing loving kindness, compassion, sympathetic joy and equanimity in everyday life, a self that perceives it's interconnectedness with other sentient beings. The Dalai Lama, other High lamas, Buddhist teachers and well-known practitioners are individuals who are recognized for their spirituality as well as their social self as they coexist in the social world. As long as the self is part of the social world, there is some recognition for the spiritual aspect of that self, but there is obviously no recognition from a transcendent supernatural being as in monotheism.

Death: Recognition beyond the Grave

Following this discussion of spirituality and the immaterial aspect of our eternal self, it seems timely to consider the idea of recognition for our death. It may seem ironic and antithetical to speak of recognition for our death; it would appear that recognition, establishing one's identity and determining meaning would pertain to the living. However, our death is inevitable, and we might say the ultimate factor in confirming meaning in our life.

This final state of recognition is not only for believers in an after-life and eternal recognition from a personal or otherwise transcendent God. It is also recognition from the living, a final reckoning or summing up what our life has come to signify to others who remember us, and perhaps the world itself.

All throughout life, we recognize important events through celebrations and rituals, such as birth, rites of passage, marriage and finally death. Although losing a loved one is usually a time of great bereavement, it is also a time when we honor and remember the deceased. We show our recognition in a number of culturally determined ways, most of which consist of a ritual burial and mourning. They may include wearing special clothing, avoiding certain public activities, reading sacred texts, and delivering eulogies to name a few. Other ways we may continue to show recognition is perhaps by giving the name of a deceased to a newborn, dedicating works, keeping souvenirs, visiting the burial site, lighting candles, leaving flowers, and praying. Many of these traditions are related to our belief that the dead continue to live in another form after death, (a major reason people pray for the dead), and thus, many of them serve to perpetuate our recognition for their past lives among the living.

The way in which a person is shown recognition after his or her death, is often in direct relation to the way in which the person was recognized in life. People with large families and many friends have huge funerals; they are mourned by many, whereas the death of those who have lived out their lives in lonely isolation may not be acknowledged by anyone at all. Although, there are rare cases in which a once well-known individual ends her or his life in squalor and obscurity, most renowned people, royalty, the very rich and famous, as well as the infamous, make the front page of the news and are broadcast on television worldwide. (The funeral of Princess Diana was viewed live by more than thirty million spectators). They may be buried in famous cemeteries, have plaques, monuments, memorials, public buildings or streets named after them. Wonders of the world such as the pyramids or the Taj Majal were constructed in great part to commemorate the dead. Some graves attract millions of people whether a rock star (Elvis, Jim Morrison, Michael Jackson to name a few) or a political dictator like Mao Zedong who has a two-hour waiting line just to walk by his body in his Beijing mausoleum.

On the other hand, there are cases of people who were minimally recognized during their lifetime, but who gained recognition posthumously. A familiar case is with artists such as Van Gogh or Emily Dickinson, whose works live on, rendering them famous. It is also the case with prophets. Jesus or Mohammad had a limited following while they were still alive but they are currently worshipped by millions.

We feel an obligation to honor the dead, even those we don't know. We recognize all the deserving unknown heroes buried in anonymous graves such as the Unknown Warrior in Westminster Abbey, as well as other unknown soldier's graves around the world, or countless anonymous victims of war or genocide in museums or at infamous killing grounds. The death of heinous criminals, monstrous killers, despotic dictators, (Hitler, Mussolini,

Ceausescu, Osama Bin Laden, and Gaddafi to name a few) might actually be joyously celebrated. But more often, even when we disliked a person when alive, once he or she passes away we avoid criticism. Even those who don't believe in life after death abhor the desecration of graves or the public display of a dead body. Most often, we tend to recognize the dead regardless of who they were and of our personal belief system. This may be a sense of recognition that is more often spoken of in deference as, "respect for the dead," but respect is a major part of the concept of recognition. It does not necessarily indicate admiration, as a validation or approval, but rather a sense of considerate regard.

One of the most important characteristics that distinguishes humans from animals, even advanced primates, is that we are conceptually aware of our own death. At some point during our lives, we imagine our death and how life on earth will go on without us. Who will miss us? What difference will we have made? Most people leave a clearly recognizable legacy, a family, children, and grand-children, a living proof of their existence, those who have inherited their genes and those who have been influenced by their way of thinking. Other people leave a concrete legacy, such as an invention, a work of art or more abstractly, a contribution to society, with long lasting political or economic consequences. We recognize our self in what we are able to leave behind, and any legacy we leave, however small, will hopefully leave a trace of our existence through continued recognition. Falling into anonymity, forgotten by one and all, is death beyond death.

Long ago, before there was any system of external memory, that is, some form of written or recorded evidence, people who were dead and long gone were only kept alive in people's memories by oral narratives and perhaps by passing on some physical souvenirs. Once external symbolism began to be used, individuals could be described and commemorated in written texts and thus assured of a longer more accurate perpetuation of their memory. Long ago, wealthy people were remembered by having their portraits painted by talented artists. Photography followed, and decades later videos that recorded people's actions and their voices. Now, with computers, data gathering, indexing software and good search engines, we will be able to archive everything we've seen and done, and one day, external memory systems will be absolutely infinite.[111]

In Paul Auster's book *The Brooklyn Follies*, his main character who feared imminent death, wryly proposed a new enterprise called "Bios Unlimited." It would organize professionally written biographies of the nobodies, or the forgotten-ones in this world, to be cherished and read by their loved ones, to permit them to live on in written memory. His idea, which I found extremely clever at the time, will soon become a technological reality that is already taking on sci-fi dimensions. There are some web sites that are exclusively concerned with commemorating and remembering the dead. *The World Wide Cemetery* allows you to create a monument for a loved one. You can write a biography, post pictures, create links with other family members, and others may contribute eulogies or leave flowers. Other sites like *Legacy Locker* or *Entrustet* allow you to manage all your information on the Internet, to deal with your digital after-life so that others can have access to your digital assets and deal with your virtual persona on-line after you are deceased. Even more to the point concerning recognition is *Virtual Eternity.* This website is the virtual "gift of immortality" by helping you to pass on your legacy to future generations. It allows you to create a virtual clone, of yourself, a life-like avatar or "intellitar," an artificial representation of yourself that preserves and shares your personality, that looks and sounds like you, and that is programmed so that future users can actually converse with your avatar. Here, for a small fee, you have the future of personified immortal recognition, available not just for the rich and famous but for any ordinary person!

Though most of us do not look forward to our death nor plan it, there are some whose death is consciously calculated or unconsciously construed for receiving recognition. Most people who commit suicide suffer from a mental disorder, (drug abuse, depression, schizophrenia, etc.). But there are a few individuals who kill themselves for reasons that we might say are partially planned in order to receive some sort of recognition. It might be personal, done in revenge, or seeking attention from a disappointing lover, or as a self-sacrificial act. It might be a heed for recognition for a greater cause as with martyrdom, such as immolation, or other public demonstrations, or as a military, religious or other sacrificial suicide. In these cases, personal recognition is not necessarily the primary motive, but an implied motive just the same. For those who believe in an afterlife and a personal God, there is some personal recognition and even recompense for a sacrificial death. Some human endeavors, very dangerous professions, and extreme sports, are quasi-suicidal. The higher the risk, the more spectacular, and the more recognition the risk taker receives.

As was emphasized in the foregoing discussions of the material and social self, our existence as a unique person, comes through recognition from the other. Death is an inevitable event that plunges us eventually into non-recognition. It may take many generations, but those individuals who continue to receive recognition after centuries of time are so very few, that they are nearly deified, (or literally deified as in the case of Jesus Christ). For most of us, immortality on earth through recognition from our fellow human beings is so unlikely that our only hope for immortal recognition is spiritual, coming from a universal, infinite, eternal "Consciousness."

Non-Recognition: Getting Away from It All

Before concluding this section, what about the notion of non-recognition? Non-recognition occurs when a person fails to recognize others, or when a person is not recognized by others. In either case, non-recognition may be intentional or unintentional.

When a person fails to recognize another unintentionally, it might imply a cognitive problem, memory loss, or perhaps some confusion in identification. Instances of poor memory can be minor, such as forgetting a face, or when or where you met. Most of us have experienced that eerie and troubling feeling of not remembering a past experience, name, or place when we should be able to recall it easily. In a severe form, memory dysfunction such as Alzheimer's, dementia, or certain other disorders, affects the person who once knew you so well, a mother, brother, or a best friend, so that he or she barely recognizes you, or no longer recognizes you at all. Such non-recognition can be devastating, and for the person who has memory problems, the fear of relapsing into oblivion must be terrifying. Memory is the functional foundation of recognition.

In other situations, you might not recognize someone simply because they have changed so much that they no longer resemble the person you knew, growing older, taller, rounder, thinner, or balder. The changes might also be on a psychological level, such as drastic changes in someone's system of beliefs or values, their personality or character, leaving you with a feeling that you no longer recognize the person you once knew.

Problems of memory or accurate identification are quite different in terms of non-recognition from *intentional* non-recognition; refusing to acknowledge someone's presence, accomplishments, importance, and rights. This is a subject I will be developing at length in Chapter X of this book.

As for the second case, there are people who don't wish to be recognized. While researching for this book, when I talked to friends about my belief that recognition is necessary for identity and structuring the self, some declared indignantly that they neither needed nor wanted any recognition. Though I'm convinced that a minimum of recognition is necessary for self-construction, I understand their point of view.

Needing solitude or preferring privacy requires little explanation. Some might choose asceticism, avoiding recognition in any of the material and social senses I evoked earlier, Tibetan monks for example. Some people may not want recognition for certain acts or deeds, feeling they don't deserve it or they simply don't like attention. Some elderly people, those who have been morally injured by others, or disappointed in them, or people who have suffered loss, may deliberately withdraw from society, avoiding recognition. Their memories become selective, and isolation becomes an emotional defense, avoiding painful or stressful reflection. Excluding interrelationships protects their sense of identity as a fixed-self. Some people are loners, or free-spirits, and recognition from others has no value.

On the other hand, we know that total deprivation of recognition, like solitary confinement, is a severe form of punishment, and mentally harmful.

Continually renewed recognition is not the only way to stay psychically healthy nor is it categorically beneficial to one's sense of self. Temporarily "getting away from it all," is sometimes quite necessary in our stressful, over-saturated social existence. This is certainly the case with celebrities, entertainers, politicians, or anyone who is constantly in the public eye, hounded by journalists, paparazzi, and fans. It would also be the case for the infamous; criminals, wrongdoers, sociopaths, and social outcasts, fleeing from incrimination and criticism.

However, you don't have to be famous or infamous to feel the need to escape your social environment; bosses, colleagues, friends, neighbors, or even your significant others. This is a popularly known fact that has been treated extensively in psychological studies of modern social life styles; we all know it is stressful and tiring to keep up a consistent image. Sometimes some people want to just relax and be themselves, in the sense of not making an effort to maintain an established persona. Also, since people around us constantly influence the way we think or feel, often imperceptibly, we may want to get away in order to think clearly, one good reason for taking a vacation. Changing your environment can be helpful in relieving stress and obtaining a more objective attitude, and when you have time and space to reflect in isolation you can gather your thoughts in quiet reflectivity. This is also one of the main principles and goals of meditation.

I must say that I relish solitude and there are many situations in which I find recognition from my fellow human beings far from desirable. Being asocial, avoiding others, being happy without human company, is not necessarily like anti-social personality disorder, being hostile or feeling aggressive.

Often, this need to get away, is temporary, and followed by an equal desire to get back. Just as there is a psychological feeling of freedom and relief in non-recognition, there is a stabilizing comfort in being recognized, surrounded by people you know and who know you. I've known some celebrities who complain about their lack of privacy, but become somewhat destabilized when people don't recognize who they are.

Sometimes people want a radical change in their life, a desire to shed off a former identity. Getting away, moving to a foreign environment, a new town or another country where you are no longer recognized might be a way to break with the past. As mentioned earlier in my discussion of group recognition, isolation from the group was equal to a death warrant for our ancestors. The fear of exclusion from the group persists today and group separation can be an anguishing loss of identity, but sometimes no longer being recognized as a part of the group might be a choice, an intentional separation in order to remodel a new identity. It might even be a matter of survival, as in cases of political or ethnic persecution. Establishing different forms of recognition is a means to restructuring the self.

PART II

ORIGINS

In order to understand a phenomenon like recognition, it's helpful to consider where it comes from. In this section, I'm plunging with great trepidation into the roots of recognition, which necessarily involves the origin of consciousness. I'll be considering both the *phylogenetic* origin of recognition, by looking at how it has evolved, from australopithecines to modern humans, (Chapter IV), as well as the *ontogenetic* origin of recognition, or how it develops in a single individual, from infancy to adulthood (Chapter V).

There are passages in this section that are fairly scientific -- about as scientific as I can get-- so for those who have little interest in science, bear with me. But in an effort to be thorough in supporting my main thesis, the research of qualified experts is important. I hope these discussions will not be too complex for those who aren't familiar with the subject or too superficial for those who are.

Chapter IV

Back to the Beginning

Recognition is a form of consciousness, and a consideration of the development of recognition implies studying how consciousness came about. How can one study such developments in pre-historic humans? Consciousness is subjective, private, and immaterial, so what goes on in the consciousness of another can only be inferred. How can we get into the mind of the first humans when we have a hard time getting into the minds of our friends or loved ones? (My husband's for example). All we have to go on are fossils, artifacts, or other traces of human behavior. The challenge is awesome but so are the attempts to come up with convincing theories. The development of recognition, like consciousness, involves co-existence and interconnectedness, the domain of anthropology and evolutionary or cultural-historical psychology. These are fascinating fields which depend upon a multi-disciplinary study that includes biological evolution, primatology, archeology, neurobiology, and philosophy, to name a few. The following discussion involves a very curt summary of some of the most recent hypotheses in these areas.

Consciousness: the Understated Problem

Before discussing the evolutionary origin of recognition, I'll briefly discuss consciousness, though briefly is a huge understatement. I have read a lot on consciousness, from Descartes to Dennett, and humbly admit I still only understand a little.

Consciousness is what I consider the most important and mysterious subject in philosophy and science today. Presently, it is a greater mystery than the origin of the universe, which physicists seem to have worked out to some extent. As James said, the meaning of consciousness is something "we know so long as no one asks us to define it." [1] James presciently observed the explanatory gap that continues to beleaguer modern philosophers, "the 'chasm' between inner and outer worlds," that is, between the material-physical world and the immaterial-spiritual mind. [2] Explaining this chasm is what the philosopher David Chalmers calls the "hard problem," that is, "how physical processes in the brain give rise to subjective experience." [3] I must add that what is considered the easy problem, the physical or materialistic aspects of consciousness, is not so very easy. I admire the genius of neurobiologists who manage to somewhat explain the function of the brain, with its 100 billion nerve cells, 100 trillion connections and the mechanistic functioning of consciousness; the difference between the sleeping and waking state at the neuronal level; or describing focal attention, sense perception, hearing seeing, etc.

Though the easy problem is not entirely understood, the hard problem remains stubbornly unresolved. As Karl Popper puts it, "The emergence of consciousness in the animal kingdom is perhaps as great a mystery as the origin of life itself." [4] His friend and co-author, the neuroscientist John Eccles says it will remain enigmatic "as long as it is regarded as *an exclusively natural process in an exclusively materialist world*." [5] In other words, even if we succeed in explaining consciousness materialistically, we must also explain it on the subjective phenomenal level.

There are some brave and brilliant attempts to deal with, or simply deal away with, the hard problem, ranging from completely materialistic to mysteriously mystic explanations. On the materialistic end, there is Francis Crick, who sees conscious awareness as no more than an assembly of nerve cells, and the firing of neurons.[6] Others describe the brain like a digital computer, which only gives the impression of free will.[7] In our computer oriented world, the brain is treated more and more like an information processing machine and we increasingly use the computer as a metaphor for the mind.

But I agree with the philosopher John Searle's rejection of the very popular computerized idea of the brain. In his famous example of the "Chinese Room argument," Searle explains that consciousness can't be intrinsically computational, functioning like a programmed computer, because "nothing can be intrinsically computational. Computation exists only relative to some agent or observer who imposes a computational interpretation on some phenomenon." [8] In his book *The Rediscovery of Mind*, Searle insists that even though consciousness is a natural biological phenomenon, we also have subjective, qualitative states of consciousness that are intrinsically mental. He says that looking for a link between the two is like looking for a link between H2O molecules (physical) and liquidity (a quality).[9]

The last couple of decades have produced an enormous increase in neurological data, resulting in numerous neuroscientific theories on the relationship between consciousness, the nervous system and the brain. Neuroscientists basically assume that consciousness depends upon a special arrangement of matter in the brain and that our capacity for conscious awareness is an emergent product of evolution. As Chalmers said it "winks in," at some level of physical/neural complexity.[10] For neuralists like Gerald Edelman, "mind is a special kind of process depending on special arrangements of matter." [11] Edelman, with his theory of "re-entrant connections" to account for the emergence of conscious awareness, explains that the brain, as a part of the physical biological world, is more organic than computational and undergoes natural selection in an ecological habitat. This view seems to be supported by certain neurological discoveries showing that the efficacy and growth of synapses in the brain increase with mental use.

Another popular neurologist, Antonio Damasio presents a processual perspective emphasising the importance of "feelings" for conscious awareness, which seems to preclude that computers can't be considered conscious. He claims that "the realization of human consciousness may require the existence of feelings. The 'looks' of emotion can be simulated, but what feelings feel like cannot be duplicated in silicon. Feelings cannot be duplicated unless flesh is duplicated, unless the brain's actions on flesh are duplicated, unless the brain's sensing of flesh after it has been acted upon by the brain is duplicated." [12] Likewise, the neuroscientist, R. Llinàs, links the notion of fixed action patterns, or FAP's, ("instinct") into his consideration of feelings (emotional states), so that the origin of consciousness is linked to motricity, "cognition and consciousness *probably evolved from the emotional states that trigger FAPs*" [13]

Daniel Dennett has certainly taken the forefront in explaining consciousness. Dennett, like G. Ryle before him, denounces "the ghost in the machine," and Cartesian dualism. For Dennett, the conscious self is an illusion, no more than a series of multiple-drafts or narratives, with no central focus or continuity. We have information processing brains that produce consciousness through *higher order* representations of our *lower order* processes.[14] (I'll be getting into this self as a narrative illusion in more detail in the next section). However there are a number of skeptics who feel that Dennett and others are "explaining away" rather than explaining consciousness. [15]

This is only a glimpse of the prickly problem of defining consciousness or explaining subjectivity (questions that keep people like me from sleeping at night), which has already been a bit of a digression, although, I'll resume the subject of consciousness in discussing the social self.

Recognition: Binding, Attention, Memory

There are many unresolved arguments concerning consciousness, but some aspects are commonly agreed upon. First, that consciousness is not a thing or a state but a process. Consciousness is "a "stream of thought," or sense of continuity as James wrote, a view which is currently substantiated by modern neurobiology.[16] Furthermore, we rely entirely upon memory for this sense of continuity since conscious recognition involves discernment, how things are the same or different from what we have already perceived. To recognize is not just to perceive, but to *re-cognize* i.e., know again. It is a dynamic state, founded in the past, alive in the present, with a view to the future.

Secondly, since there are different levels of consciousness and memory, there are also different levels of recognition. Though memory is necessary for recognition, not all recognition or memory is conscious. We may even speak of pre-organic memory, such as a bar of iron that has had the *experience* of magnetization. On a simple organic level, geneticists describe the retention of programs designed for protein synthesis encoded in genetic DNA, in which "memory mistakes", known as mutations, have a tendency to persist.[17]

On a simple biological level, insects or animals with primitive nervous systems have a stimulus–response behavior relative to the environment, such as a slug that is sensitive to the pull of gravity and push of light. It has no neural means to perceive or recognize anything more complex, not even its fellow slugs. The much studied bee has a more complex stimulus. A bee must recognize another bee, as well as its intricate dance, and the direction in which it is pointed. It might be considered to have a very primitive consciousness, although as Eccles points out, "there is no reason to assume that the bees know what they do; their brains are so small and so stereotyped in organization." [18]

This elementary neuronal behavior is what the psychologist Merlin Donald calls "binding", a basic function of simple "Level One Awareness." In order to perceive complex things, to create a whole experience, the brain must "bind" raw sensation such as light rays and sound waves "to find patterns in space and time that reveal the existence of objects and events." [19] According to Crick, (a co-discoverer of DNA) and Koch, who collaborated on a theory of the neurobiological basis of consciousness, even the simplest acts of object recognition involve attention, conjoining two or more features in order to inter-relate them. This is pattern recognition in its most basic form. Thus, selective binding, as a by-product of attention, would be a useful adaptive process for any organism to perceive objects and events, such as moving through space, finding food sources and sensing predators. Without binding, attention, and simple memory, there is no recognition and without recognition, an organism cannot respond to what is presented to the senses. However, this recognition can proceed unconsciously, as in the case of insects.

Conscious Recognition: Moving Forward

The next level of consciousness, "Level Two Awareness," involves short term memory storage, or the ability to hold an image or experience in consciousness for a period of time so that an organism is no longer bound to the here and now in a simple stimulus-response function. This is the case with all mammals including humans. In order to carry out the simplest tasks such as mating, animals need to have short-term memory, the ability to carry around images and thoughts. They break with simple reaction to stimulus.

Even short term memory enables automatized action to take a load off of being conscious of the here and now, enabling consciousness to disengage itself from action and focus attention on other things. Atomatization enables us to accomplish several things at the same time, like driving a car and listening to music and having a conversation with a fellow passenger.

Higher primates and humans have a more sophisticated brain, higher consciousness and access to what Donald refers to as "Level Three Awareness." [20] This level involves long-term memory, the ability to voluntarily control and be aware of our actions. The result is "our remarkable capacity for conscious, deliberate rehearsal, review, and refinement of action." [21] Intelligent mammals as well as humans are capable of remembering elaborate event representations. This involves what Donald calls "episodic memory" or "episodic awareness." Animals are capable of remembering where they've hidden their food, where they might encounter danger or find protection, etc.

Humans have reached an even higher level of consciousness, one that goes beyond episodic. We have a much more sophisticated brain, memory system and level of awareness. We are not only conscious of our environment, but we are aware of our *self*. We are aware of other selves and on a meta-cognitive level, we are aware of being aware. This of course is the most important point for a discussion of recognition since humans are the only animal (with a minor caveat explained later) capable of recognizing their self. The fascinating question is how did we arrive at this level of consciousness?

Animal Consciousness and Recognition

But before continuing with a discussion of how self-conscious awareness developed in Homo sapiens, I would like to return to a discussion of animals and animal consciousness. It is an important issue for defenders of animal rights, loving pet owners, and those who like to point out how radically different we are from our fellow earthlings. As pointed out earlier, there is a lot we don't know about animal consciousness, sometimes feeling a strong empathy and recognition from our pets regardless of their lack of linguistic communication. Descartes infamously imagined animals as totally lacking any sensibility whatsoever, relegating them to the statue of insensible and insensitive automatons. Most philosophers and scientists today grant them more consciousness than Descartes, but since animals lack the symbolic language we have, they can't communicate descriptively (see below) and we can't be sure of just how conscious they are.

For animals as well as humans, consciousness remains a subjective experience. Thomas Nagel wrote a well-known essay on the subject in 1974, called "What is it like to be a bat?" He could have asked the same question about a cat, or a dog or a frog, but the poignant fact about a bat is that it *sees* by bouncing high-frequency sound waves off of objects and analyzing echoes. Though we know technically how a bat's brain functions, we clearly cannot have the subjective conscious experience of a bat.

It is the same case for having exactly the same subjective experience as another human being. No amount of information on how your optic nerve functions will enable me to experience how you see things. Though we can infer from animal behavior that they share many human cognitive perceptions and feelings, we can never know how they experience us or the world.

Studying animal behavior, we can conclude that animals consciously recognize other members of their group. They cooperate, imitate and even predict each other's behavior. However, animals don't have our level of awareness, that is, self-consciousness. There are some well-known experiments by Gallup [22] which come up often in discussions of recognition. They have shown that chimpanzees and orangutans recognize themselves in the mirror. In order to test their self-awareness, Gallup placed colored marks on the chimpanzees' foreheads while they were anaesthetized, and later put them in front of a mirror. Some quickly touched the mark upon seeing their reflection, showing that they were aware that it was their own body that was reflected. The same experiment did not work with gorillas, (or any other mammals). One very interesting explanation for this is that chimps and orangutans had to develop an elaborated representation of their physical self in order to maneuver their large body mass through the tree tops.[23] These arboreal primates are more preoccupied with their corporal selves than gorillas and have a better physical model of their bodily self. Another very important common sense observation, is that although these higher primates may identify a mark on their body in the mirror, it really only demonstrates that they recognize a reflection of their *physical* self. It doesn't imply that they have a concept of a narrative self, thinking of their past or future and capable of introspection. These are cognitive capacities we believe are unique to humans.

First Humans and Conscious Recognition

Why and how did humans develop such sophisticated cognitive abilities evolving into a recognizable narrative-self? Though Homo sapiens have only a 1 to 2 % genome difference with higher primates, the particular genes that are involved, such as the genes that control neuron division and expanding brain capacity, make an enormous genetic difference. Though there was no definitive missing link, no moment when self-consciousness suddenly arose, there was a continual expansion of awareness through time to result in not only quantitative but also qualitative differences between higher primates and humans.

It is probable that beginning with Australopithecus, some 4 million years ago, our first fully bi-pedal ancestors possessed Donald's "level two awareness" and episodic memory. They most probably had a slightly more developed cognitive level than the higher primates, with their pair-bonding, some social cooperation for obtaining food, caring for the young, and some symbolic signing. There was certainly some simple recognition just as with any mammalian group. Recognizing group members was important for security and survival.

Approximately 2 million years ago, during the transition period of Homo habilis, humans developed primitive stone tool-making which required cooperation and imitation for their fabrication. With a larger brain and skull, Homo habilis infants required an earlier birth in order to pass through their mother's relatively narrow pelvis, which was essential for the mother's bi-pedal ability to run. This probably led to less mobility for the group in order to care for the helpless young, and thus more dependence on tools for defense in a fixed territory.

Homo erectus represented a major shift. As the brain attained 80 percent of its present size, tool making became more complex and fire was controlled, and seasonal hunting and long distance migration became the norm. It was the beginning of a period that Donald calls mimetic culture. "Mimetic skill or mimesis rests on the ability to produce conscious, self-initiated, representational acts that are intentional but not linguistic." [24] Mimesis is not simply mimicry or imitation, which animals do quite well. Though mimesis is not necessarily conscious, there is a more developed use of memory, re-enacting, re-presenting and therefore, *re-cognizing* events and relationships, not only for external communication, but also for representing acts to oneself. This could include survival actions like skinning animals, trapping fish, making fires, caring for infants. Mimetic behavior is intentional, even if it is pre-linguistic and pre-symbolic. There is a sharing of attention, such as pointing and following another's gaze, actions that are lacking in the higher primates. A group member might point out a dangerous animal, gesture to others the need to climb a tree or hide in a cave and be attentive to the fact that everyone follows him to safety. This communication of intentions is a break with cognitive egocentricity.

Mimesis also implies more complex social integration, both through conformity and coordination, doing things with others and like others in the group. This was also the beginning of specialized individual functions, when certain group members adopted certain roles, such as hunters, gatherers, fire-keepers, or leaders. Individuals probably worked in isolation but for the community. Therefore, they had to *carry* or maintain a sense of a common goal in their minds even if they had no self-awareness. Though they may have lacked symbolic language, there was surely some communication of emotion through vocalization and facial expressions. This period saw important advances in human recognition, if not for the individual as a *person*, which requires descriptive language, then certainly for sharing symbolic meaning.

Mimetic behavior must not be underestimated for social bonding, which is a strong foundation of our incremental intelligence. The primatologist Frans de Waal points out how higher primates imitate one another in the learning processes. [25] Body mapping starts out very early in life. For example, if an adult repeatedly sticks out its tongue, an infant monkey or human will soon imitate. This has been partially explained in neurobiology by the presence of "mirror neurons," discovered in the lab of Giacomo Rizzolatti in 1992, in the brain of the rhesus monkey. They are a subset of neurons in the frontal cortex that respond in the same way, whether the monkey observes another monkey performing an action (grabbing for food for example) or when the monkey carries out the same action itself. [26]

Yawns, laughter, smiles are all contagious. Our bodies react spontaneously to others, we tense up when someone else is in danger, gasp if someone starts to fall, move our body watching someone else dancing. We continue to be able to recognize the way others feel without any verbal language, such as growls and furrowed brows which show anger, or screwing up the face in disgust, showing acceptance by smiling or affection by cooing and giggling. These primitive reactions along with other body language are of great psychological interest since they represent our true inner feelings.

This unconscious mimetic behavior is also called synchronicity, since we synchronize our movements to match others. "We involuntarily enter the bodies of those around us so that their movements and emotions echo within us as our own," says de Waal. [27] We smile when others smile, cross our arms when they cross theirs, begin to clap our hands when they clap theirs. Humans probably began very early to move in rhythm, marching, pounding, rocking, etc. As Merlin Donald says, "rhythm is a uniquely human attribute; no other creature spontaneously tracks and imitates rhythms in the way humans do, without training."….. "It is the quintessential mimetic skill," since it can involve any part of the body, vocal or visuomotor.[28] Analogously, one of the reasons marching bands, rock concerts and discotheques are so popular is that masses of people rhythmically bond together.

Mimesis seems to be an essential basis for empathy, which comes from the Greek word *empatheia*, or *Einfühlung* (feeling into) as proposed by the German psychologist Theodor Lipps. Unconscious, empathetic merging is very probably a very important precursor for recognizing others as well as the self, and could serve as a theory for the development of self-consciousness. It is very likely that we are not first aware of our own intentions and subsequently attribute those intentions to others, but attributing similar intentions to ourselves and other is co-learned. [29] Nicholas Humphrey, a Cambridge psychologist argues that our ancestors needed to be able to predict other's behavior, and in order to do that they began observing their own inner processes to acquire an "inner eye."[30]

In her book *Braintrust,* the Canadian-American philosopher Patricia Churchland discusses the interrelationship between mimetic behavior, group affiliation and empathy and how they promote social adhesion. Mimicry is important because it helps each of us recognize the other as being like or unlike our self. If the other is like me, I can better predict his or her behavior, and "feeling that someone is trustworthy is a positive, oxytocin-related, bonding emotion." [31] I'm reassured and my stress level falls, leaving me feeling less anxious and more secure. Mimetic behavior is conducive to both better survival as well as social harmony.

Self-Recognition: Language and Thought

The transition period from Homo erectus to Homo sapiens is rather mysterious, but it is certain that there was a major cranial enlargement and a change in the vocal apparatus about 200,000 years ago. We're still unsure of when Homo sapiens became capable of speech, (for example, did Neanderthals have a vocal tract?).[32] However, by about 50,000 years ago, the transition from erectus to modern humans was complete. In fact, biologically, man hasn't changed in the last 40,000 years!

It is interesting is to consider the important changes, physical and psycho-sociological, leading to our present consciousness. As mentioned earlier, there is no way we can positively know the level of consciousness of Upper Paleolithic Homo sapiens, but judging from archeological findings, we presume that their culture resembled that of the early Stone Age. We know they made clothing, had methods for transporting heavy objects, had more advanced tools and weapons, constructed shelters, and decorated themselves and their environment. They had an enriched social life, with rituals marked by dance, masks and costumes and buried their dead with some ceremony which indicates an awareness of death. They certainly would have begun to figure out basic causality, birth, death, the seasons, climate, as is the case with certain hunter-gatherer societies, like the !Kung Bushmen.

This is the beginning of Donald's "Level Three Awareness" that he calls Mythic Culture. In mythical thought, which is often tied to religious beliefs, "the mind has expanded its reach beyond the episodic perception of events, beyond the mimetic reconstruction of episodes to a comprehensive modeling of the entire human universe. Causal explanation, prediction, control, --- myth constitutes an attempt at all three, and every aspect of life is permeated by myth." [33] According to Donald, the initial use of language was not necessarily just for social organization: it was initially invented for creating conceptual models of the universe and integrative thought which could compare experiences of concrete episodes, or happenings, in order to extract general themes. Stories were supplied to explain why the sun rose every morning, why there was rain or drought, how babies were born and why people died.

However, it's not just the beginnings of language, but its predecessor, symbolic thought, that is so mysterious and important. Symbolic meaning most likely developed in mimetic culture through pre-linguistic gesture, such as waving to attract attention, smiling, shaking the head in disapproval or bewilderment. But all symbols were arbitrary in the beginning. Why would shaking the head back and forth mean "no" and up and down mean "yes"? Meanings, like bowing the head, putting the hands together as in prayer, giving a thumbs-up, would be consolidated by use within each respective culture. Donald proposes that these symbols were invented according to the needs of the current mental models for creative projects and collective enterprises. But we can't simply say that *perceptual* mental models correspond to episodic cultures, as for the higher primates and early human beings, whereas *conceptual* models correspond with symbolic thought. Mimetic culture had both elements. It involved reference and meaning, referring to things in the world as well as expressing relations, with modifiers like "higher," "closer" etc. In conclusion, "where humans differ from apes and other mammals is not so much in their possession of signs and symbols but in the types of mental models they construct." [34]

Another very interesting theory concerning the birth of symbolic language appears in Julian Jaynes' book, *The Origin of Consciousness in the Breakdown of the Bicameral*

Mind, one of the most fascinating works on consciousness that I have ever read. Jaynes' rather radical thesis is that language and even writing *preceded* consciousness as late as 3,000 years ago. Though his conclusion is controversial, since we usually see symbolic language and conscious thought as coinciding, much of what Jaynes wrote is profound, and credible. For Jaynes, as with for Donald, pre-historic group-life necessitated some form of communication, initially gesture, for basic survival; protection, organization, maintaining peace, caring for young, etc.[35]

During the Pleistocene era, 70,000 to 8,000 years ago, there was a huge climatic change, migration out of Africa to Eurasia, the Americas, and Australia. In northern climates, where there was less light, vocal calls became more important than visual gestures for communicating intentions. The first vocalizations, Jaynes believes, would be relational, using modifiers, for example to indicate that danger was close, or distant, as was noted above with Donald's mimetic man. Then humans invented words for commands, to aid in hunting or making tools. Only later did nouns begin to be used, as for naming animals, which corresponds with the epoch's visual expressions like the elaborate cave-wall drawings. Finally, during the Mesolithic era, 10,000 to 8,000 BC, there was the advent of names. This corresponded with the formation of larger communities, more stable populations, longer life spans, and more fixed relationships. By inventing names, people could be kept in mind and referred to in their absence or after their death. This would correspond with the formation of recognizing individuals, that is, personal recognition.

The Danish psychologist, Preben Bertelsen, in *Free Will, Consciousness, and Self: Anthropological Perspectives*, describes the period from 40,000 to 20,000 BC with its explosion of cultural artifacts, advanced tools and utensils, sophisticated tents and huts, and decorated graves as an emergence of a "de-centered mode of life." [36] The development of art implies for Bertelsen, that man began to "experiment with the creation of meanings." This would require the brain to have a generative function, that is, the ability to take things apart and recreate.

During the Agrarian revolution, around 10,000 BC, a more "individuated mode of life," had begun. Within the structure of villages, there were indications of social stratification, bigger homes and graves for the wealthier people and chiefs. With urbanization, beginning around 4,000 BC, we see a true shift in socialization, with more division of labor, class stratification, and the formation of political, military and religious powers. Community life would never be the same. It became irreversibly more specialized, stratified and individuated. Therefore, life began to take on different meanings to different individuals, with different mental models on how to behave and what made a good versus a bad life. A whole new stage of mental development unfolded, with personal consciousness and self-reflection, "the realization that each individual has a distinct 'inner' life which is distinct from one's own." [37]

Jaynes also saw Agrarian culture and urbanization as a transition period: social roles were defined, with more skillful workers and artisans, as in ancient Natufian culture. But for James, "Natufians were not conscious." They were still signal-bound with stimulus-response manner.[38] This theory clearly conflicts with Bertelson as well as most anthropological psychologists. However, Jaynes presents a quite original argument. Individuals at that time, heard auditory hallucinations, their own *unrecognized* voice or the recalled voice of the chief or God-King. Each worker "had within him the voice of his king to assist the continuity and utility to the group of his labors." [39] This is not so far-fetched if we think of consciousness in terms of self-awareness. People at this time were conscious, but lacked reflective self-consciousness. (Some very "unaware" people I know lead me to suspect he's on to something). Jaynes imagined the birth of consciousness for reasons similar to Bertelson's, but at a much later time, between 2,000 and 1,500 B.C. In essence, human consciousness was due to vast geological catastrophes and mass migration, and the intermingling of people from different cultures with their different gods, leading individuals to conclude that something inside others was different from themselves. "It is thus a possibility that before an individual man had an interior self, he unconsciously first posited it in others, particularly contradictory strangers, as the thing that caused their different and bewildering behavior. In other words, the tradition in philosophy that phrases the problem as the logic of inferring other minds from one's own has it the wrong way around. We may first unconsciously (sic) suppose other consciousnesses, and then infer our own by generalization." [40]

This is the same conclusion that was remarked earlier while discussing mimetic behavior, and attributing intentions to others and the self. It was through observation of others, that persons turned their observation inwards. We essentially recognized other people before recognizing our *self* as a person.

Another well-known evolutionary psychologist and anthropologist, Robin Dunbar, in *Gossip, Grooming and the Evolution of Language* holds a complimentary theory. [41] He proposes that the increase in brain size and intelligence in primates was due to the increased size and complexity of their social group. In pre-symbolic times, this was done through grooming, in order to maintain friendships and establish hierarchies. The more complex human societies became, the more demands upon memory, for understanding, analyzing, and organizing more numerous relationships. Since one couldn't get around to grooming everyone, language emerged. Human "social intelligence" hypothetically developed when humans began living in groups, since natural selection favored higher intelligence. When a cohesive group was necessary for finding food, shelter, and marking territory, the more socially intelligent groups survived. Dunbar came up with a number of 150 for the reasonable limit of possible human relationships, whereas for other primates it's about 50. This is about all humans can handle in terms of storing social information. (It will be interesting to see if human's brain capacity for social networking will be able to extend itself with the advent of Internet and virtual friends).

The reason I've been emphasizing the emergence of symbolism and language is that we have come to consider language and thought as two sides of the same coin, and necessary for human self-consciousness. I believe that symbolic language is essential for recognition in existential terms, for constructing a self. John Eccles points out four levels of language, with only the higher two being uniquely human. Level one is simply *expressive*, (cries, calls, laughter, etc.). Level two serves a *signaling function* in which a sender communicates something to a receiver (barks, chirps, moos, meows, and now 'tweets'). These first two levels are used by all animals as well as humans. Level three is *descriptive*, telling about experiences; this includes a huge variety of statements that can either be true or false. This is an important point for recognition since it implies the possibility of deceit, or intentionally appearing to be other than what you are. The fourth level is *argumentative* and requires the ability to think rationally.[42]

It is important to note that the difference in levels is qualitative and not just quantitative. There is a real biological difference in the human brain, whose asymmetric economy has allowed it to almost double its cortical capacity.[43] Eccles proposes that our brain has evolved to develop special linguistic areas in the cerebral cortex where we might find the deep structures of universal grammar encoded in their micro-structure. As Noam Chomsky has pointed out, all children are equally equipped to speak a language with an innate structure of the brain that he calls a language acquisition device, now known as an LAD.[44]

Distinguishing different levels of language is important for discussing recognition because symbolic meaning is only possible in the descriptive and argumentative level. Self-representation may have begun in mimetic pre-linguistic culture, but in terms of creating a personal self-concept, descriptive language was necessary. We can only recognize our individual psychic self by means of a self-narration, a descriptive story of who we are.

In summary, there is general consensus on the development of human consciousness. Our brain development, as well as our consciousness was gradual and incremental, and in direct relation to our growing social integration. As Donald concludes at the end of his book "We are collective creatures even to the texture of our awareness." [45] Our individual mind and thoughts about our self and the world are dependent upon a community of minds. Meaning only comes through others; this includes meaning in the exterior objective world as well as our interior subjective feeling of meaningfulness. It is through being recognized by others that we came to recognize ourselves.

Chapter V

From Infancy to Self

When does a newly born human individual begin to have a sense of recognition, or even more importantly, start to recognize his or her *self*? As with considering the origin of recognition for the human species, speculating on a growing child's need for recognition involves the birth of consciousness. Is the newborn infant as James said, a "blooming, buzzing confusion"? Or as Locke said, a *tabula rasa*, just waiting for the imprint of experience to produce conscious awakening?

In fans means incapable of speech. Before infants can express themselves verbally, what we know about their consciousness can only be inferred or deduced from studying their behavior. Though an infant's consciousness is more accessible than prehistoric humans, we can only conjecture how it is subjectively experienced. To answer questions concerning an infant's developing mind, we need to enter into the prickly thicket of developmental psychology, and though psychology is relied upon to explain and predict behavior, it is not a hard science with irrefutable laws. However, factors such as the influence of the primary caregiver and the social environment, genetic predispositions, emotional development, and the child's evolving sense of identity, have been researched extensively with convincing conclusions.

The Selfless Infant

Does the newborn have *self*-consciousness in terms of personhood? The experts nearly unanimously say no. An infant's awareness is restricted to bodily functions, sucking, rooting, grasping, and clinging, with simple or complex reflexes that are stimulus bound, a period that Margaret Mahler, a pioneer in child psychology, once called "normal autism." Although infants spend much of their time sleeping, during wakeful periods there is a continual attempt to achieve homeostasis through tension reducing actions like urinating, defecating, regurgitating, sneezing, coughing, etc. The infant confuses such actions with the mother's ministrations and conscious experience is either pleasurable/good, or painful/bad. This period is called *symbiotic* since there is a complete fusion of the infant with the mother, and no differentiation between the *I* and the *not-I*. However, during the first few months, the infant gradually starts to distinguish between inside and outside. Very interestingly, she starts to recognize and respond to faces in eye-to-eye encounters, which evoke the familiar social-smile, but external satisfaction still comes from some *part-object,* usually the mother, that satisfies the infant's needs, "albeit still from within the orbit of the omnipotent symbiotic dual unity," says Mahler.[46]

Similar to Mahler's analysis, the psychoanalyst Heinz Kohut, who was trained in neurology like Freud, had a theory that parents served as what he called "selfobjects," an amalgam of self and not-self, that help regulate the infant's psychological organization. Kohut attributes the maintenance of the infant's homeostatic balance to the continuous and reciprocal interactions with selfobjects rather than to its solitary efforts to reduce tension as for Freud.[47] There is a dyadic, back and forth relationship between the infant's undeveloped *self* and the primary caregiver, which is very important for establishing his or her sense of self. The primary caregiver recognizes the infant by responding to gestures, needs, and displays of emotion, and thereby plays a very important role, even to the extent of the infant's evolving brain structure which is responsible for socio-emotional development.[48]

There have been extensive studies that demonstrate that "the vast majority of the development of axons, dendrites, and synaptic connections that underlie all behavior is known to take place in early and late human infancy," [49] and maternal behavior is an important part of the external environmental that mediates genetic differences.[50] Consequently, the first years of life are extremely important for early imprinting.

This symbiotic or selfobject stage as presented by Mahler and Kohut, corresponds to the psychologist Ulric Neisser's "ecological self." The ecological self has a certain kind of self-consciousness but it is restricted to perceiving the self in its local environment. Newborns, he says, most certainly have some sense of *physical* self as they exist in the environment, even if they have no sense of a *conceptual* self. (And so do animals by the way. They too are aware of their body within the environment. For example, they don't try to go through objects, like fences or furniture, but around, over or under them!) Up until the age of about 5 months, before an infant's consciousness begins to split from the initial symbiotic relationship, there is very little sense of recognition in terms of a conceptual self. Until the age of 3, it is not so much "the sense of *who* I am, but *that* I am," [51] as Mahler said. But from about 8 months on, cognitive progress is extraordinary.

The Mirror Stage: Recognizing a Self

The period of infancy from about 6 to 18 months was identified as the "mirror stage," by Jacques Lacan in 1949. This notion of mirroring, which is obviously important for recognition, has been analyzed by several well-known psychologists, sometimes in a metaphorical sense, as in imitation, and other times in a literal sense, as an actual mirror reflection according to the psychologist Malcom Pines.[52]

Beginning with biological mirroring, the infant seems to be pre-adapted to respond for human interaction, such as the social smile mentioned above.[53] Caregivers intuitively interact with their babies with exaggerated expressions and high-pitched baby-talk, an apparent cross-cultural practice. "By reflecting back imitatively, mother is acting as a psycho-biological mirror, an active partner in the infant's developing capacity for social relations and the beginning awareness of self-representation and object-representation." [54] The mother is not acting consciously in her reflective behavior, it comes quite naturally. Parents usually react joyously when their babies imitate them properly, encouraging them to continue their imitative behavior. There is an evolutionary reason for this. Mimetic behavior for our hominid ancestors aided survival. A baby that can imitate well is a sign of a normally developing frontal cortex, which is very important for social mammals such as our selves. Successful imitation shows that the infant is on the right development track with a normal social brain and signals the presence of a social capacity to learn and behave appropriately.[55]

It must be remembered that reflective behavior is not only visual; it's also in the way a caregiver touches or holds the infant. Otherwise, it might be argued, congenitally blind infants would not have this important reflective imprinting. In any case, there is a sort of gestural dialogue between the mother and baby which constitutes initial mutual recognition. It has been suggested by several well-known psychoanalysts such as D.W. Winnicot and Kohut that a positively responsive mother, smiling, tender and loving rather than depressed and indifferent, is important for the infant's emotional well-being,[56] which corroborates our common sense.

Another characteristic of this imitative mirror stage is when the caregiver and infant *share* the same experience, a sort of dual imitation as in vocalizing together, smiling and gazing at one another. The psychologist Daniel Stern calls this "state-sharing" and argues that in terms of mirroring these are moments of great importance for having similar experiences, a first form of intersubjectivity by sharing mental states.[57] If we compare this to the development of consciousness in Homo sapiens, this stage corresponds with Merlin Donald's mimetic person. Katherine Nelson has pointed out that this imitative sharing which is pre-linguistic, like mimesis, "enables learning to produce forms modeled by others and form an internalized model so that it may be recalled (mentally or in action) and used for future productions, transformations, and recombinations." [58] At this level, neither the infant, nor Donald's mimetic man have arrived at a level of symbolic language, but this is an important preliminary step. At this point in awareness, says Nelson, for the infant, "there is only one perspective on the world, his or her own. There is only one reality, that of the directly experienced world." [59]

Another very important early development closely related to state-sharing is joint attention, which occurs at about 9 months of age. When an infant cries or gestures to get her caregiver to focus on some object, such as a bottle, a cookie, or toy, she most likely solicits a response. Both mutually mirrored imitation and joint attention -- pointing for example -- imply a shared reality, the first step to symbolic communication. This is a huge cognitive leap with existential consequences that some (with exceptions) claim to be a uniquely human capacity. [60]★

During the first year of development, there is not only an increasing distinction made between the self and the other, but also the notion of what is called "object permanence," the awareness that objects continue to exist even when out of sight. For example, a small child expects that a toy that disappears under a blanket will reappear. The sense of a self as something permanent and continuous begins to emerge at this stage as well. By the time a child is one year old, she can associate two events, quite importantly, her own behavior and another person's reaction.

This leads to *anticipation*, an important element in recognizing the other as one who fulfills expectations. Higgins and Vookles point out four major types of anticipation, the first involving a positive reaction, such as satisfaction in the form of food and joy, as with receiving a comforting bottle or playing peek-a-boo. The second is the absence of a positive reaction leading to disappointment and frustration and even anger, as when Mommy refuses to give a cookie or stops playing. The third, a negative reaction in the form of distress or fear, such as reacting to a jealous barking dog, and finally, the absence of a negative reaction, as when Mommy makes the dog stop barking, which results in a feeling of security and reassurance. [61] This cause and effect association is important for recognizing outcomes as well as the affective reactions of others which in turn, aids in recognizing the *self*.

Awareness in the form of anticipation at around one and a half years, leads to the child's recognition of himself as an *agent*; that is, that certain behavior produces certain results from the other. This is what is considered a higher order form of recognition since the child can recognize a relation between relations. For example, if Johnnie throws his food, Mommy picks it up. If Mommy yells, this makes Johnnie cry with sadness. If Mommy laughs it makes Johnnie smile with pleasure. The child "can now represent *self-other contingencies*" and can thereby "learn the interpersonal significance of their self-features.

Their self-features now have *psychological significance.* (…) Because children's self-features can now have this new psychological significance, they can experience new emotions such as pride, joy, shame, fear of punishment, and feelings of abandonment and rejection." [62]

Considering this new stage of recognition, I find Ulric Neisser's theory of the development of self, very pertinent.[63] The young infant has only an "ecological self", but her awareness soon deepens into what Neisser calls an "extended self," and later on to an "evaluated self." The evolution of Homo sapiens has prepared us to extract information from the environment as well as to anticipate what might happen later. Imagination, in the form of anticipating the not-yet, is enormously important in our development. "The infant who starts out by living only in the present soon begins to master the past and future as well," says Neisser.[64] In this way, the infant's consciousness extends from the actual to the possible. Before full self-consciousness, the infant's goal-directed behavior, such as crying for the bottle or reaching for a toy, concerns a self with wants even though he or she doesn't know *who* it is that wants. Babies have motives without knowing they have them.[65] But as pointed out before, the baby begins to recognize feelings expressed through behavior, such as mother's scolding or smiling. "It is reasonable to assume, then, that we are born able to see the intentions of other people." [66] But this is not a surprising assumption, since most animals can do the same.

For Neisser, it is important that the baby's ecological self is the target of the caretaker's display of emotions, as well as her intentions. "The infant sees not only that his mother is loving but that she loves something in particular--and that something is his own ecological self." [67] If the mother's reaction to his throwing food on the floor is by scolding him, she is not only angry, but angry with *him*. If she smiles, she is not only amused, but amused with *him*. Even if the infant cannot imagine the feelings of others he can certainly see them. A baby doesn't think of himself as having emotions, but since the emotions of others are quite visible, it is not long before the analogy is made, that if the other is angry, or loving, perhaps I have those feelings as well. "If such insights occur, they would reverse the classical principle of "empathy," which maintains that we attribute feelings to other people only by analogy with our own conscious experience. Perhaps, on the contrary, we attribute feelings to ourselves by analogy with the perceptible feelings of other people." [68] This is exactly the same conclusion that was pointed out earlier concerning the origin of self-consciousness in prehistoric humans. Though it seems counterintuitive, we first attributed consciousness to others and then discovered ourselves as being conscious as well.

When it comes to mirroring in a literal sense, there has been extensive attention paid to the stage when children come to recognize themselves in a mirror. The aforementioned mirror tests carried out by Gallup on chimpanzees have also been used with children. (As a reminder, when a child is asleep or distracted, a spot of colored paint is put on his forehead. Upon seeing himself in the mirror, he tries to remove it.) The consensus seems to be that mirror self-recognition appears at about 18 months of age. This is what Lacan referred to as the "specular image," a great step in conscious awareness. The growing infant now has a self that he recognizes as an object for the other. As Merleau Ponty commented, "Par l'image dans le miroir il devient spectateur de lui-même. Par l'acquisition de l'image spéculaire l'enfant s'aperçoit qu'il est visible et pour soi et pour autrui." [69] (By means of the image in the mirror, he becomes a spectator of himself. Through the acquisition of the specular image, the infant sees that he is visible not only for himself but for the other.)

Bear in mind that self-recognition in the mirror does not indicate that the child necessarily has a concept of self, as was observed earlier concerning chimpanzees. In fact, there is evidence that when chimpanzees were raised in social isolation, they were not able to behave in a self-directed way even after extensive exposure before a mirror. They needed 3 months of group experience to show any self-recognition.[70]

For Margaret Mahler, this self-recognition stage comes when the infant has broken from the symbiotic, fusional stage with the mother and becomes aware that she is different from the other. She calls this process "separation-individuation." When infants begin to crawl and then walk, they start to wander away, take a distance from the mother, even though they prefer her to stay within eyesight and remain accessible. Somewhere around 15 months, the mother becomes more than a home-base to go back to; she is a person with whom the baby shares her discoveries of the world. [71] Toddlers continually bring things that they have found interesting to share with their mother. "Look mommy, a flower, a ball, a worm."

The young child, who can now express herself verbally through words and gestures, realizes that what she finds interesting or what she wishes does not always correspond to the mother's interests or wishes. Mahler adds, "What a blow to the hitherto fully believed omnipotence; what a disturbance to the bliss of dual unity!" [72] In her observations, Mahler also found that "recognition of mother as a separate person in the large world went parallel with awareness of other children's separate existence, their being similar yet different from one's own self. This was evidenced by the fact that children now showed a greater desire to *have* or to *do* what another child had or did—that is, a desire for mirroring, for imitating, for identifying to an extent with the other child." [73]

Social interaction becomes more and more important to the child. Increasing awareness of self occurs at the same time as there is more awareness of other children who are basically seen as being either similar or different. [74] Little children are more attracted to other little children than to adults. Another thing that occurs during this stage of comparison between children is a phase the psychologist Charlotte Buhler called "transitivism." [75] The child who hits will say that he has been hit, a child who sees another fall will cry. There is a sort of merging of the self with someone else who resembles and behaves like the self. I believe this is evidence that we begin forming empathy quite early in life, recognizing our own self in the behavior of others.

Shame: The *Look* of the Other

This new awareness of self as seen by the other coincides with a sense of shame, a very important feeling for self-consciousness. Before 12 months, the infant has an almost complete absence of shame.[76] Babies lack inhibitions. According to Mahler, the young baby in dyadic union with its mother, feels nothing but positive recognition. Then at about 15 or 16 months of age, his egocentrism becomes "particularly vulnerable to the danger of deflation." When the infant becomes aware of himself, he is capable of shame. If "shame arises from a disturbance of recognition," [77] the opposite is also true; it is because he feels ashamed, that he becomes aware of his *self*.

As mentioned above, the toddler, showing lots of interesting things to mommy, anticipating satisfaction and approval, is suddenly confronted with "unexpected noncooperation of the mirroring object," i.e., the mother or caregiver.[78] Facial expressions of disgust and contempt are distinct and universal, and easily understood by the infant. "Shame is originally grounded in the experience of being looked at by the Other and in the realization that the Other can see things about oneself that are not available to one's vision." [79] In situations where the child feels ashamed, he and the mother are out of tune, causing the infant to avert the look of the mother, a reaction "to escape from this being seen from the one who sees." [80] Whereas a look of contentment and satisfaction has always brought reassurance and pride, a look of contempt or disgust brings embarrassment and shame.

Infantile narcissism is always being the center of attention with an eternally approving caregiver. Shame is essential for the child to be able to separate and differentiate himself from his mother, a necessary step in curbing this infantile narcissism. But it is also essential that the infant receives some acknowledgement of his shame. Usually by reaching up, looking for a hug or a kiss, in an "attempt to reaffirm both self and the ruptured relationship, to feel restored and secure," according to Kaufman, the infant is immediately reassured by the mother or other disapproving caretaker.[81] Ideally, shame is acknowledged and internalized and the self is accepted both by the caretaker and consequently the infant himself.

On the other hand, adult narcissism is largely due to the child's inability to internalize and accept shame, or the disapproval of the initial caregiver. It is the failure of what is called "affect auto-regulation." Generally speaking, with too much attention from the caretaker, adoring, doting, completely projecting her ideal self on the child, the child cannot regulate between the ideal and real self. The shameful state is deregulated and bypassed, and not admitted into consciousness, inhibiting emotional growth. Shame needs to be recognized by the caregiver as well as the child, in order for him to develop a positive belief in self.[82]

The other extreme wherein the caretaker displays, continual discontent, unavailability or lack of empathy, also has negative affective consequences, resulting in "shame rage" or "narcissistic rage," and the inability to accept narcissistic injury as an adult.[83] Needless to say, shame regulation and the development of pathological narcissism is a complex affair, but the point I want to emphasize is that recognition from the caregiver plays a vital role in regulating adult narcissism.

On a philosophical note, the importance of shame was pivotal for Sartre's existential theory of consciousness. The unreflective self, like the infant in fusion with the mother, is only conscious of objects in the world, including other people. What Sartre calls *le regard*, or the *look*, coming from another person, causes the self to reflect on itself as an object for the other and consequently as an object for itself. "It is shame or pride which reveals to me the Other's look and myself at the end of that look," says Sartre.[84] Whereas, Freud said that during primary narcissism, the infant had the sense of being at the "center of the universe," for Sartre, when I or anyone experiences shame; it causes "a crack in my universe." [85] Sartre takes the concrete shame felt by the infant in the presence of an unsatisfied caregiver as an analogy for existential shame, that is, of being an object in the presence of the "Other" with his freedom to "look" at me. "Shame is the feeling of an *original fall,* not because of the fact that I may have committed this or that particular fault but simply that I have "fallen" into the world in the midst of things and that I need the mediation of the Other in order to be what I am." [86] His analysis reminds us of the Biblical Fall, when Adam and Eve, after disobeying God and tasting the fruit of knowledge of good and evil, knew that they were naked and hid in shame.

Theory of Mind: Discovering How Others Think

The next important stage for recognition in the evolution of a child's consciousness occurs at about 4 years of age. It involves what is called a *theory of mind*. When a child is able to take the perspective of another person, and realize that another can have opinions, views, desires, feelings, etc., other than her own, philosophers refer to this as a theory of mind. Psychologists have standard tests for measuring this capacity. For example, a child is shown a package of candy like M & M's that contains pencils. If the package of candy is then shown to another child, the first child is asked what the second child believes is in the package. At about 4 years of age the child will correctly reply, "M & M's," showing that he can take on another unknowing person's perspective. Children under 4 will more likely say "pencils," since they feel their point of view is the only viable one.

There has been some fascinating research in social cognitive neuroscience, led by Rebecca Saxe, at the Saxelab at MIT demonstrating the neuroscientific explanations for a theory of mind. She demonstrates that there is a direct correlation between thinking about others' thoughts and "a group of brain regions in the human cortex that selectively and specifically underlie the mechanism." [87] Once again, we can see that consciousness of our own thoughts and consciousness of another person's conscious thoughts seems to have coevolved. It seems that our brains are wired for intersubjectivity.

Theory of mind is very important in terms of our relationship with others and for seeking recognition. The child's need for recognition is reinforced when she realizes that the other has different opinions and viewpoints from her own, an effort must be made in order to influence the other to think about her in a favorable way. Upon becoming conscious of the other's feelings and desires, even without an articulated concept of consciousness, a child starts to modify his or her behavior in order to solicit a certain response, positive or negative. It is the beginning of willfully creating an image as well as developing the skill of manipulation. This cognitive advancement corresponds with the birth of the fully developed "evaluative self" according to Neisser.

Developing a Narrative Self: Learning to Tell a Story

Another important development in a child's self-consciousness is the gradual construction of a *narrative self*. Up until the age of 3, the child still has no definite sense of a continuing *me*. There are still only two concepts of time, the present and not-present and very young children often confuse their own memories with those of others.[88] Jessica might say to her mother, "Sophie bite Michael on the arm," when in fact she meant, "I bit Michael on the arm." Children under 3 years may recount sequences of events but not true narratives, which necessitate not only describing a series of temporal events but also a meaningful continuity. Randall might say, "We eat noodles for lunch, Nate hit Melissa on the head, our teacher showed animal pictures, Melissa likes noodles," with no particular order. However, around 4 years of age, young children begin to have a better sense of the connectedness between the past, present and future. Events take on a causal dimension. "When the teacher showed pictures of animals, Nate couldn't see and he hit Melissa on the head so she moves. She cried. At lunch we all eat noodles and Melissa was smiling." Language which has been constantly improving is now used to construct a narrative self.

Katherine Nelson points out how this stage in development is reminiscent of Donald's mythic man, for whom myths were not individual but social and cultural enterprises.[89] Narrative is essential for the growing child's consciousness of self, just like it was for prehistoric humans. To point out another analogy, the mimetic culture was a precursor to mythic culture, just as imitation and role playing is a precursor to narration. When we observe small children we can see the importance of imitation, playing mommy or daddy, nurse and patient, policeman and thief, adopting opposite roles and constructing various narratives. This is an important aspect in learning how to understand the viewpoint of the other. The sociologist, psychologist and philosopher, G. H. Mead elaborated upon the importance of play for developing an organization of the self in his well-known book *Mind, Self and Society.*[90]

The growing child is born in a specific social-cultural structure which will greatly determine the way his personal self-narrative is constructed. Different cultures emphasize different life experiences, and the child's parents or caregivers will reflect and pass on their social-cultural views about what is important and meaningful. This is one reason why a search for recognition is culturally dependent. Children learn how to reminisce and construct stories about themselves or about others through their relationships, not only with parents and other family members, but also from a myriad of other influences, from television cartoons and Sunday bible school, to gathering twigs in the Savanna and bathing in the Ganges. Cultural values influence how parents and significant others speak to young children about the past, what is important to remember and how to understand other's feelings as well as their own. The way in which children grow up and how they seek recognition will vary from culture to culture, according to the social-cultural values.

What people accept or reject, praise or criticize is culturally relevant. One general consensus is that in collectivist societies, such as East Asia, Africa, Latin America or Southern Europe, there is more emphasis on interpersonal connectedness, social obligation, conformity, group harmony and a shared identity. In more individualistic societies, North America, Australia or Western Europe, there is greater emphasize on individuality, self-actualization, personal uniqueness, the value of being different and self-assertion.[91] Obviously this will influence the child's sense of recognition; which will be sought and gained by fitting-in, or standing-out, or sometimes a mixture of both, depending upon the circumstances. Psychologists like Mahler, and those who adhered to her theory of separation-individuation, consider that a part of healthy normal development is to separate from and relinquish any emotional dependence upon primary caretakers in order to become autonomous, independent individuals. This is certainly a Western ideal, and it is perhaps true that "Mahler took a common moral precept and made it into a psychoanalytic theory." [92] However, complete autonomy and independence is not necessarily normal or an optimal goal in all cultures.

As children develop, between 4 and 5 years of age they usually learn what is expected of them and what is valued from significant others. Expectations and values are increasingly internalized as self-guides and these self-guides become a part of the child's narrative self. You often hear children admonishing themselves, their playmates or dolls, using the same tone of voice and words used by their parents. "No, no, don't hit. I told you it's not nice to hit," or "First you have your nap, then you can play." What we call the "voice of conscience," is in great part the voice of our parents, or perhaps in a Freudian sense, the voice of the father heard by the oedipal child. [93] Authoritative voices continue to be heard, rehearsed and repeated, though sometimes in later life the authoritative figure has been transferred to a significant other, a boss, leader, or God.

Even as this narrative self becomes more developed, when young children describe themselves, they don't usually talk about what they think or feel. Their principal self-concept still concerns their physical self. Ask a young child to describe herself and she will probably say something about her age, body, height, hair color, etc. When children are of school age and begin interacting socially, they start acquiring social skills, making friends, getting along, as well as being rejected. They are exposed to new values and ideologies, experiencing new expectations and added responsibilities and share an expanded reality. In order to adapt to this reality, developing children increasingly monitor themselves and begin to make social comparisons, not only being like or unlike other children but being better or worse.

Recognition becomes a challenge, not just a given as when they were younger. It is not just assumed like certain physical features, such as being thin, or red-headed, but intentionally sought through behavior, like being friendly or funny. It is indeed interesting to see the different manners in which growing children seek recognition, whether by being well-behaved, obedient, compliant, or by being difficult, disobedient, and corruptive. Attitudes and behavior, whether conformist or non-conformist, being alike or being different from others, are methods of attracting attention, seeking recognition and developing an identity.

Following childhood, there are the tumultuous adolescent years, when loyalties and values are in conflict. There is a new preoccupation with the physical body. Is it maturing too soon or too late? Adolescents are particularly physically self-conscious during puberty, with their bubbling hormones and uncontrollable desires, encountering inevitable prohibitions to curb them. Their preoccupations become, "Am I attractive, pretty, handsome, desired, virile, or popular?" It's a time of questioning and confusion, especially since pressures for conformity and performance from peer groups and family often conflict in their demands and expectations. There is a great need of recognition, but the dilemma is, from whom? This could be called a second period of separation-individuation, breaking away from the parents in order to find a self-identity. But the wandering away is ideally followed by rapprochement, creating new more complex bonds with significant others in order to find reassurance.

However, a young adult's need to be recognized as an autonomous individual -- with his own personality, desires, goals, and values -- is predominately, a Western ideal. When grown children don't receive recognition as responsible independent individuals, there is deception, frustration, and even heartbreak. In cultures that are less individualistic, there is less pressure on adults to be recognized as autonomous and independent. But even taking cultural differences into consideration, adults who never receive recognition from their primary caretakers -- not only orphans but those who are emotionally and affectively estranged -- may continue to suffer greatly, regardless of the recognition they might earn from friends, partners, coworkers or countless admirers in later life.

Up to now I've only discussed the infant's and child's evolving need of recognition. In the field of psychology the emphasis is usually placed on the influence that parents have on the child rather than the other way around. However, every relationship is an exchange and I believe that parents also depend upon their children for a sense of recognition. How this recognition manifests itself varies from culture to culture and from family to family. The spectrum is wide; some parents demand displays of respect, strict obedience, with an adherence to the same beliefs and values as their own. I know that in some societies, children are practically indentured and filial recognition is imposed. In Asian culture, honoring and respecting parents is unquestioned as an important virtue. In Western culture, it is equally possible for parents to be lax or indifferent when it comes to gratitude, filiations or loyalty. In some families, parents who hear "I never asked to be born," might expect little in return from their children, affectively or otherwise. When parents abandon their children at birth or when they're young, regardless of which culture or society they're in, recognition from their offspring can be neither desired nor expected at all.

Parents often raise their children in a fashion that was similar to the way they were raised, but parents sometimes raise their children in a way that makes up for deficiencies in their upbringing. A father may expect his son to take over the family business; a mother might want her daughter to take advantage of her inherited good looks. On the other hand, parents may encourage their children not to make the same mistakes, to diversify professionally, or not marry too young. There are many cases of parents wanting their children to fulfill their own fantasies and ambitions, satisfy their parental needs or unconsciously provide them with immortality. Through projection, they expect f their children to reflect their personal expectations, but such expectations can never be perfectly fulfilled. Children are neither clones, nor a Lockean *tabula rasa*. They are equipped with their own unique genetic predispositions and no child can be perfectly educated or programmed to behave in any specifically determined way. The complexity of influences creating the consciousness of any individual goes far beyond the will of his or her parents.

There are probably some common patterns concerning what parents most often expect from their offspring in terms of recognition, though I'm not sure what they are. Family traditions might be extended or broken, and the importance of recognition perpetuated or diminished. However, personally, I don't know any parent who doesn't appreciate some form of recognition from their children, if only a thank you, a small favor or thoughtful gesture.

Summary

The evolution of our need for recognition, both *phylogenetic*, the development of the human species, and *ontogenetic*, the psychic development of an infant, shows that recognition is an essential need for our sense of self from a scientific point of view. Perhaps we don't need science to prove to us that humans need recognition from fellow humans in order to be human, but it reassures me that well-founded science corroborates what seems perfectly evident in actual experience. As the psychologist J.M. Baldwin wrote in 1894, "my sense of myself grows by imitation of you, and my sense of yourself grows in terms of my sense of myself. Both ego and alter are thus essentially social; each is a socius, and each is an imitative creation." [94]

PART III

THE *SUBJECT* OF SELF RECOGNTION

In the last section, I looked at the origin of consciousness and recognition from the point of view of anthropology, as well as evolutionary and developmental psychology. Since I've been arguing that recognition is essential for a construction of self, what I mean by self needs more explanation. The self has become a modern preoccupation; how to evaluate it, change it, be true to it, improve, enhance or simply be satisfied with it. But what is the self? It is a concept that has captivated great historic thinkers as well as contemporary writers. Let's examine some of the paradoxes and consequences of this complex concept as it relates to recognition.

Chapter VI

The Self: Seeking a Definition

In this section, I'll discuss selfhood, the very important notion of self-consciousness, and contemporary views on what we call the empirical, social or narrative self, as well as some cultural differences concerning these concepts. I'll take up the important subject of self-evaluations, including what is popularly referred to as self-esteem, the importance of self-knowledge and the notion of a true or authentic self.

The Self: A Brief Historical Background

Early thoughts about the nature of self, beginning with the Greek philosophers were inextricably linked with ideas of the spirit or soul as the immortal aspect of man. For Socrates the real true self was the soul, a spiritual unity, whereas for his student Plato, man's spiritual self was divided into having both a rational and irrational duality. For both philosophers, the Delphic oracle's command to "know thyself" was a moral duty, involving the mental or cognitive aspect of this mind/soul. Aristotle however, distinguished the soul from the mind. For him, the mind is what constituted our essence or identity; it was higher than the soul and less united with the body.

This relationship between the mind, soul and body became a preoccupation for Christians. Since they believed in life-after-death and the continuation of a personal identity, Christians had to explain how this could be possible without the continuation of the body in the afterlife. The solution came in the form of dualism; an immaterial, immortal soul existing in a material mortal body. The concept of self as an immaterial soul, along with the inextricable relationship between the self and God, was of the utmost importance throughout the Middle-Ages. The material aspect of the self, including bodily desire, pride and vanity, or any selfishness related to the physical self was suppressed, whereas devout obedience and self-denial were encouraged.

René Descartes famously broke with Christian ideals in his *Discourse on Method,* in 1637 when he declared that the objective world, even our own body, could be an illusion, whereas our existence as a thinking being was necessarily true. With his *cogito ergo sum,* "I think therefore I am," he not only asserted dualism, a theory we have been grappling with ever since, but the priority of our cognitive existence. Without being aware of how radical his claim really was, he declared that the ego that was the source of certainty and not God or nature. Consciousness became the essential feature of the mind, distinct from matter including one's body and brain. Descartes' famous dualism has persisted to this day. The original source of a non-material, independent, conscious self comes from religion not science or philosophy, and it is largely because of religious beliefs that it is difficult to challenge the idea of a spiritual self as a theoretical truth.

With dualism, the workings of the mind had become the seat of the self, and probing its nature became of utmost importance in understanding it. John Locke is often credited with providing our modern theory of self and identity. In his *Essay Concerning Human Understanding*, (1690) Locke presented the idea of the self's mind as a *tabula rasa,* "blank slate" and rather than being furnished with innate ideas, the mind was a product of experience and education. This was a daring vision of the self as being constructed, i.e., a person not only *makes* himself but is also *made* by the social environment.

There was a fundamental rise in individualism in the 17th century and the simple criterion of memory in constituting the self came under attack, particularly by Hume. Almost every philosophical discussion of the self quotes Hume, and I feel compelled to do likewise. Hume famously wrote, in *A Treatise of Human Nature*, (1740) "For my part, when I enter most intimately into what I call myself, I always stumble on some particular perception or other, of heat or cold, light or shade, love or hatred, pain or pleasure. I never catch myself at any time without a perception, and can never observe anything but the perception." This view eerily anticipates certain 20th century theories of the self as a totally fictional, *substance-less* concept. Hume, willfully or not, seems to have done away with the existence of a soul altogether!

On the other hand, Immanuel Kant, one of the most important philosophers of modern times, perhaps in an attempt to explain the continuity of self, posited the idea of an empirical self, or "me" and a pure transcendental "I." In Kant's theory, I can be conscious of myself as the object of my consciousness (the empirical *me*) and I can be conscious of my consciousness, (the transcendental *I*). Put more simply, I can think about me. He was not implying that we have two selves but one self from two points of view in a "unity of self consciousness." His transcendental "I" though a unifier, was non-substantial and didn't exist in the world like other objects, including our own body. Kant, like Hume, was an extremely prescient philosopher. This entire dichotomy of the self as subject, the *I*, and the self as object, the *me*, has been taken up by modern philosophers and sociologists, as we will see.

Two other great thinkers, who had an enormous influence on how we consider the self, are the philosophers Hegel (1770-1831) and Sartre (1905-1980). They are also perhaps the most important for my discussion of recognition. Hegel, probably best known for his famous master/slave theory, emphasized the social context for the construction of our self. Sartre's famous theory in *Being and Nothingness*, famously characterized the self as the *pour soi*, the "for itself." Consciousness was always filled with content, like for Hume and insubstantial like for Kant. It was Sartre's famous theory of "the look," coming from the other that is essential in constructing our self-consciousness.

Another huge influence on our understanding of the self comes from Freud and the discovery of the unconscious. Our consciousness, which was so self-evident for Descartes, became a "fathomless uncertainty" with

Freud. Self-knowledge rather than being an immediate given, would necessitate a voyage to the inner depths of our repressed unconscious mind. When Freud is correctly translated, his famous ego loses its pejorative selfish connotation often associated with the word today. In German, the *es*, *ich* and *uter-ich* are literally the "it" "I" and "above I." The "above-I" is not just a conscience, but the internalized words and thoughts of the other, parents or authoritative figures. Freud, like Hegel and Sartre, proposed a theory leading to what we now consider the social–self.

William James most clearly articulated this concept of the social self. James had an enormous influence on all subsequent self-theories, at least as far as occidental philosophy and psychology goes. Not surprisingly, I began this book by citing James. He famously analyzed the self as a "stream of consciousness," emphasizing the concept of the self as both subject, the "I" or thinker, and the object, "me" as thought. James' "me" is analyzed into several types, the material self, social self and spiritual self, as was pointed out in the beginning of this book. Quoting James, "The total self (is) partly known and partly knower, partly object and partly subject. . . we may call one the Me and the other the I . . . I shall therefore treat the self as known as the me, and the self as knower, as the I. . . ." [1]

The self as subject, the *I*, unifies the self as object, the *me*, by amalgamating previous thoughts in the stream of consciousness, hence the importance of memory and what we call a continuous self. In other words, it is your present *I* which thinks about your past self as a *me*, which is constituted by your actions, interactions, thoughts and feelings, in a reflective flow.

The major shift in self-conception in the 19ᵗʰ century went from a search for a unified real self, to 20ᵗʰ century theories of the self as multiple, conceptual, embodied, social and perhaps fictional. Philosophers tended to concentrate on the self as subject, as a unified stream of consciousness, whereas, social psychologists tended to concentrate on the self as object, the social, narrative, autobiographical self. The latter sense of self is more pertinent for my discussion of recognition, but examining consciousness in the first sense is equally provocative, especially in considerations of self-knowledge, authenticity and intersubjectivity.

The *Me*: The Empirical, Social Self

When discussing the empirical or social self as introduced by James, two names that come up again and again are Charles Cooley (1864- 1929) and George Herbert Mead (1863- 1931). Though they were practically contemporaries and very similar in their thinking, Mead's theory seems to come logically after Cooley. Cooley is famous for what he called "the looking-glass self," which is important for a subject of recognition. His thesis is that our self-concept is constructed by how we are reflected by the other. The empirical self is always interactional and implies the other's presence. "Persons are not separable and mutually exclusive . . . they interpenetrate one another, the same element pertaining to different persons at different times, or even at the same time." ² Cooley did not separate the empirical self into material, social and spiritual as James did, but in a sense, the self still had multiple influences; we are consciousness of other selves being conscious of us. Cooley said, "A self-idea of this sort seems to have three principal elements: the imagination of our appearance to the other person; the imagination of his judgment of that appearance, and some sort of self-feeling, such as pride or mortification." [3] Cooley used the metaphor of an orchestra to describe the mind as social and an organic whole. It is a system in which individuals are active parts; "everything that I say or think is influenced by what others have said or thought, and, in one way or another, sends out an influence of its own in turn" [4] Cooley was really quite radical in his claims since he thought of the individual and society as united, not separable phenomena, but simply collective and distributive aspects of the same thing. Here we can see clearly how recognition of the self and the other are inextricable.

Mead's theory stated that "no sharp line can be drawn between individual psychology and social psychology." [5] He described his position as "social behaviorism." Our self-consciousness is dependent upon society. There is no self at birth; the self arises only in social interactionism, principally through language. "The whole (society) is prior to the part (the individual), not the part to the whole; and the part is explained in terms of the whole, not the whole in terms of the part or parts … from the outside to the inside instead of from the inside to the outside, so to speak." [6] For Mead, the self was indeed like Locke's *tabula rasa*.

But Mead differs from Cooley in subtle ways. Mead reiterated James' distinction between the self as subject and self as object, between the "I," self as knower, and the "Me," as known and perceived through the eyes of the other. Mead's *me* is perhaps less passive than Cooley's looking-glass self, in that we adopt the "role of the other," in a more objective way, one which includes the collective view of the social group. "The individual experiences himself as such, not directly, but only indirectly, from the particular standpoints of other individual members of the same social group, or from the generalized standpoint of the social group as a whole to which he belongs. . . . He becomes an object to himself only by taking the attitudes of other individuals toward himself within a social environment or context of experience and behavior in which both they and he are involved."[7]

This is perhaps a more objective viewpoint than Cooley's. By taking on the role of the other as representative of the social group we have a more distanced and general perspective. In order to avoid postulating a sort of chameleon type character who changes with each other person's single objective viewpoint, Mead proposed that we see ourselves from the viewpoint of the "generalized other." The *I* as consciousness of being, is continuously creative in conceptualizing the *me*, which I might add, is constructed through recognition by "others in general."

A striking case example which illustrates Cooley's and Mead's social theories of self occurs in a non-fiction book called *Black Like Me*, by John H. Griffen, a Caucasian born and raised in Texas who was interested in racism. He conducted a personal experiment under the care of a doctor who darkened his skin in order to pass for a black man in 1959. In one passage from his book he describes his feelings. "I felt the beginnings of great loneliness, not because I was a Negro but because the man I had been, the self I knew, was hidden in the flesh of another. If I returned home to my wife and children they would not know me. They would open the door and stare blankly at me. My children would want to know who is the large, bald Negro. If I walked up to my friends, I knew I would see no flicker of recognition in their eyes. . . . I had tampered with the mystery of existence and I had lost the sense of my own being." [8]

This perfectly illustrates that how our self-concept is inferred from how others see us.

As a social behaviorist, Mead saw social action as the source of self, especially as mediated by language. We see our-selves as objects beginning in infancy, in a pre-linguistic "conversation of gestures." For Mead, the development of language is the crucial step. It is through language that we come to know ourselves as the other knows us. As was pointed out in the last section, just as the young infant makes no distinction between the self and the other, young children make no distinction between the mind and the body. They conceive of their self only in physical terms, as a body. It is shortly before pre-adolescence that the child begins to distinguish two selves, the self as a subjective *I* and the self as *me*, an object for the other, (which is one reason most adolescents are so self-conscious and concerned about what others think). It is through language and conversation, a social act, that people learn to converse with themselves, and this in turn, becomes our constant inner dialogue. Thought is born from social interaction. When thinking, one takes on the role of speaker and listener, "out of language emerges the field of mind." [9] By declaring language as an essential factor in constructing our self, Mead pointed the way to our modern concept of self, which is often referred to as the narrative self.

A Narrative Self: The Story of Your Life

In the section on origins, I discussed how our development both as a species and as an individual person, is largely dependent upon social recognition. A growing consciousness of self involves social experience, memory and language. The popular theory today is that the self is a narrative construction. According to Ulric Neisser, the concept of narrative is "one of the more prominent currents in late 20th-century intellectual life." [10] Recent psychological analysis shows that "narrative does not merely capture aspects of the self for description, communication, and examination, narrative constructs the self." [11] In other words, who you are, and what constitutes your identity, is your personal story as you recount it to yourself and as it is recounted by others.

Creating narratives probably began about 35,000 years ago with Homo sapiens, evolving from the episodic to the mimetic and finally mythic culture. Self-consciousness, literally consciousness of a self, and narration developed simultaneously.

As we saw earlier, infant's consciousness sharing begins with joint attention, then mimicking, and finally language. At about the age of three, young children are able to relate several events in a reliable sequence. [12] However, according to Nelson most of the narrative productions of 3- to 5-year-olds still lacks a "temporal perspective, the mental as well as physical perspective of self and of different others, and essential cultural knowledge of the inexperienced world. It is these aspects, not the simple sequencing of episodic events that incorporate the power of narrative for both personal and cultural growth." [13] Children begin to develop a theory of mind, the understanding that others have different thoughts and feelings and a different perspective on the world than one's own, at about 4 years of age.

Recognizing the others' perspectives and interior motivations is related to intentionality, an age when children do more than simply mimic adults, they see others as motivated, in the sense of having motives, and adopt what Daniel Dennett called the *intentional stance* towards the world. [14] Theory of mind and true narrative, the sequencing of events, motivation, intentionality, etc., are all merged in cognitive development and the beginnings of a constructed self. However, as we will see, the way children learn to narrate is very different depending upon their cultural environment.

The idea of a narrative self has its roots in a very old philosophical idea that was evoked earlier. When Descartes said "I think therefore I am," his notion of thinking was not simply sentience, that is, being conscious of an outside world, but experiential self-conscious thinking that included both memory and language. (My cat may think as a sentient being, but she is not simultaneously affirming a self). Inherent in Descartes' idea of the thinking "I," was a coherent unified self with a sense of identity.

A well-known paradox in philosophy is to explain how things can change and yet retain their identities. It was famously posed by the ancient Greek philosopher Heraclitus who gave the example of a river with its constantly changing water, "No man ever steps in the same river twice." When we speak of self-identity, we confront a similar problem. How is it that people can change yet retain the same identity? To what extent can a person change his physique, memories and thoughts yet still be the same person?

In classical Cartesian dualism, you have a self that remains the same due to its unchanging, unifying, immaterial soul. Then this immaterial soul was questioned by Hume and many subsequent philosophers, leaving us with a questionable unified-self. According to the philosopher, Paul Ricoeur, one solution for explaining how the self remains identical, is by postulating the narrative self. [15] On the other hand, Dennett, who also sees the self as "a center of narrative gravity," comes to the contrary conclusion, that because the self is only a narration it is fictive, a totally insubstantial fabrication and illusion. [16] It is more or less agreed that self-narration, our life-story, aids us in constructing a coherent unified self, but this is not always so simple. Ironically, our self is perhaps both constructed as well as *de*constructed through recognition from the other. Even Ricoeur conceded in *Temps et recit*, that narrative self-identity was as much a problem as a solution, [17] and we will immediately see why.

The philosophical implication, from Descartes to Dennett, is that the self that most of us are concerned with, the self we want to understand, modify, defend, enhance, even immortalize, is the empirical narrative-self. This is the self we recognize and want recognized, the self that is constructed by our life story, our experiences, our relationships thoughts and feelings. There have been many philosophical thought experiments, (as well as silly Hollywood movies) to exemplify that our *real* self is what goes on in our mind. You can imagine transforming the way you look, (like various characters in books or in films who suddenly wake up in the body of a different gender, age or even species) without changing your *self*. And though the narrative self is not *all* there is to the self, as we will see, it is the narrative self that is of human interest. This is the self that has been chronicled by historians, described by creative writers, and is the focus of many contemporary philosophers and social psychologists. It's the empirical narrative-self that is psychoanalyzed and is the subject of the ever growing self-help industry.

It is through life stories that we learn about others and it is through telling our story that we learn about our self. We learn to tell stories as children, taking cues from our parents or other adults. And as children, we gradually began to learn the difference between true and fictional stories. Fictive comes from the Latin word *fingere*, which means to form or fashion; it's a creative enterprise that we all share in common. I am the main protagonist of my self-interpreted story, just as you are the main protagonist in yours. As J. Bruner said, "A self is probably the most impressive work of art we ever produce, surely the most intricate." [18] This is a creative process that is always accomplished through social interaction and within a cultural framework.

The reality of a person's fictive narrative self plays out in a community of other selves with their own fictive narratives. It is not a private enterprise since its significance is dependent upon the community and how they recognize me. "When I interpret myself in terms of a life story, I might be both the narrator and the main character, but I am not the sole author. The beginning of my own story has always already been made for me by others and the way the story unfolds is only in part determined by my own choices and decisions," says the philosopher Dan Zahavi. [19] This observation is consistent with the German phenomenological tradition of Hegel, Husserl, and Heidegger, who all acknowledged the importance of the historical context within which we construct our lives, its meaning coming from the relevant past and present. We cannot escape the influence of the "we-community" in shaping our lives.

Fictive or Real: Is Anybody in There?

The question posed by scientists and psychologists alike, is to what extent our narrative self is a fiction and to what extent is it grounded in reality. We all have an idea from the time we are very young, between true stories, the stuff of autobiographies and historians and made-up stories, the stuff of prevaricators and great novelists. But the difference between true and false, real and imaginary, is not as clear-cut as we may think.

We all know that memories, the essential ingredient in constituting a narrative self are fallible. They can deteriorate involuntarily or be confounded unconsciously. Our memories are not accurate records of what actually happened, they are rather continual reinterpretations and reconstructions, often based on our present priorities and future goals. We are excellent fabulators in that we modify or elaborate upon past experiences according to our listener, making sad experiences sadder, exciting ones more exciting. The way we tell things may be conditioned by wishful thinking, delusions, or the desire to conceal or impress. What we say to others or even imagine saying to others often becomes part of our inner speech. As the psychologist Bernard Baars pointed out, most of us spend more time each day talking to ourselves than talking to other people. [20] What we say to ourselves can become so convincing that the experiences we narrate to ourselves or others become our real memories. Thus, the narrative self is based upon a dynamic, ongoing interpretation of memories. In recreating our stories, which can change over time, we are simultaneously recreating ourselves, and those selves will be a mixture of truth and illusion.

The fictional quality of our narrative self, which is acknowledged by philosophers and social psychologists, has also been analyzed by modern scientists in their search for a material correlate of the narrative self in the brain. However, their findings do not resolve the problem of determining a fictive vs. true narrative self. As noted earlier, when discussing primary levels of consciousness, there is a sense in which memory is scientifically speaking, quite real. Our genetic coding is a sort of resolute memory with fixed chemical instructions. But on a neural level, memories are redistributed in many different areas of the brain. "These areas work together in varying ways to produce different kinds of memories; and memories are ever changing because they are reconstituted in different ways each time one remembers." [21]

John Kotre, in *White Gloves*, explains that as we remember our personal past, we may shift from levels of specific events to general statements about who we are. Kotre proposes that we have what he calls "the interpreter" in the left hemisphere of our brain, "that monitors and synthesizes activity throughout the brain and tries to make sense of it." [22] There are two elements in the interpreter's remembering, archival storage and self-mythmaking. "The remembering self, both as keeper of archives and as maker of myth," he concludes, "fashions a remembered self. *I* establishes *me*." [23] This is why it is absolutely necessary, according to Kotre, to learn to tell stories about ourselves.

The neuroscientist, Michael Gazzaniga, known for his research on split brain patients, (epileptic patients whose corpus callosum separating the two hemispheres of the brain has been severed) has also located what he calls the *interpreter*, in the speaking center of the left hemisphere, which interprets data that the brain has already processed. "There is a special device in the left brain, which I call the *interpreter,* that carries out one more activity upon completion of zillions of automatic brain processes. The interpreter, the last device in the information chain in our brain, reconstructs the brain events and in doing so makes telling errors of perception, memory, and judgment. The clue to how we are built is buried not just in our marvelously robust capacity for these functions, but also in the errors that are frequently made during reconstruction. Biography is fiction. Autobiography is hopelessly inventive." [24]

Gazzaniga firmly believes that our life is a fiction, but none the less, "it feels good and we are in charge of it." (One might ask, to what extent we really *are* in charge of it, which I will be looking at later). The interpreter, with its running narrative, "is the glue that unifies our story and creates our sense of being a whole, rational agent. It brings to our bag of individual instincts the illusion that we are something other than what we are." [25] In order to keep our narrative cohesive, "we have to learn to lie to ourselves." [26]

Gazzaniga's conclusion in 1998, corresponds closely with my favorite existentialist philosopher, Sartre, in 1956. We are masters at self-deception and what Sartre called *mauvais foi,* (usually translated as *bad faith*). However, Sartre's dilemma was to explain how we are able to lie to ourselves, that is, in what way we manage to simultaneously be the liar and the lied-to. Might this question one day be resolved by modern neuroscience?

In light of present knowledge, even if we grant that there is a materialistic correlate to our narrative memory system, this doesn't resolve the problem of reconciling a fictive self with a social reality, nor of distinguishing real from false memories. But, given that proof is not the most important issue for my present discussion, as well as being almost impossible to determine, we can look at other aspects of memory in constructing a self.

We conspicuously modify and reconstruct our memories, but how and why do we do so? According to some theorists, this selective memory process can be compared to what is described as "presentism." [27] This is what professional historians sometimes do when reconstructing the past, that is, they interpret it in terms of the present. This is not some kind of insidious manipulation but rather a way of rendering history more pertinent. What has meaning in the past is only relative to what is meaningful today. Likewise, autobiographical memories, or self-narratives, are reconstructed by individuals in light of their present self. [28]

One recent study shows that a person's current goals function as a control process in what is called a "self-memory system," that modulates the construction of memories. This system is responsible for the way memories are encoded and retrieved according to Conway and Pleydell-Pearce. [29] As Dan McAdams put it, "The life story is an integration of the reconstructed past, represented mainly as chapters and episodes, and the anticipated future, represented mainly as goals." [30] Mark Freeman in *Narrative and Consciousness: Literature, Psychology and the Brain,* also believes that "when we are trying to make sense not just of an event but also of some significant period of the personal past— some chapter, as it were—we do not seek to "recapture" what was, in its openness and indeterminacy." Rather "we interpret the past from the standpoint of the present, seeking to determine how it might have contributed to this very moment." [31]

These 21st century theories are reminiscent of Sartre's radical claim that we choose our past, not the "brute fact" of what occurred, but the meaning we give to it in light of our present and future projects. [32] Ever since writing my doctoral thesis on Sartre, I found this claim has been borne out by family members, friends and probably myself as well. Our life stories are frequently modified, memories are lost, forgotten, downplayed, others become more vivid, important and defining. Our memories change constantly it seems, depending on our present lifestyles, objectives and goals and most importantly for my present discussion, in terms of how we interact with others and who those others are.

We consciously and unconsciously rewrite our past, at least partially, and often there is no definitive way to determine when memories are true or false, real or illusory. Deciding whether or not an event really happened, is the very challenge judges and juries must face every day. As far as our personal identity and selective memory is concerned, the reality of what we remember is certainly less important than the way memories influence our decisions, behavior and goals. Or maybe, it is the other way around; our present behavior and goals influence our memories. In either case, the falsification of our memories is not so much conscious manipulation as an unconscious attempt to synthesize a self, or more precisely to create an identity. And, I would add, this adaptive memory function is very much influenced by our present sense of recognition from others.

Identity: Who Am I?

> "But if I'm not the same, the next question is, Who in the world am I? Ah, THAT'S the great puzzle*!*"
> *Alice in Wonderland, Ch. 2*

What are some of the sociological and psychological theories concerning personal identity?

Dan McAdams, in his "life-story theory of identity," believes that it's "an integrative configuration of self-in-the-adult-world." In the same tradition as the psychologist Erikson, for whom self and identity are not the same thing, McAdams claims that "young children have selves; they know who they are and they can tell you. But they don't have identities." Identity begins to form in adolescence or young adulthood. [33] One reason that young adolescents are often so troubled is that as developing adults, they are in the process of creating and asserting their identity.

Remembering Heraclitus' river and the problem of reconciling change with identity, (how does an ever changing river remain the same?), it is important to note that self-identity doesn't mean numerical identity, i.e., being one and the same. Self-identity is the perception of a continuous but evolving *self-as-process*. In light of James' account of the empirical self, and his "stream of consciousness," the self has the characteristic of continuity, integrating both how the self has remained the same as well as how the self has changed, connecting the past, present and future.

Our selective memory, as was explained by the theory of presentism, reflects our general need for continuity. According to recent research, the fact that our present beliefs and attitudes affect our recollections has a couple of major implications for self-identity. First, people find support and justification for their present self, and second, since consistency is exaggerated, people perceive themselves as basically coherent and stable. [34] According to William Swann, "Stable beliefs and the feelings of continuity they engender are as integral to our mental well-being as air is to our physical survival." [35] Having a sense of continuity means understanding that events and experiences have a cause and effect relationship; intuiting a coherent connectedness, and making sense of our lives and reality. We need to be able to feel in control of our lives, to count on things, from the sun rising every morning, to finding our keys where we left them the night before. This need for predictability and coherence is part of our hard-wiring. According to Karl Popper, "One of the most important of [the] expectations [that children are born with] is the expectation of finding a regularity…. This "instinctive" expectation of finding regularities . . . is logically a priori to all observational experience, for it is prior to any recognition of similarities . . . and all observation involves the recognition of similarities (or dissimilarities)." [36]

It is tempting to embark upon an epistemological discussion of whether or not this "instinctive" expectation would qualify as *a priori* knowledge, (coming before experience as for Kant), or if this expectation is *inductive*, (a result of experience, or "constant conjunction," as for Hume). Either way, the important point is that recognition of differences and similarities is necessary for the concept of recognition.

Continuity and coherence are essential ingredients for recognizing our self, recognizing others, and even recognizing what is real. Swann says that, "The sense of continuity associated with stable beliefs, … reinforces our conviction that we understand reality--social as well as physical--and can determine our relation to it. Depriving us of this special form of competence fosters a feeling of incoherence and meaninglessness that poses a colossal threat to our sense of self." [37]

When this feeling of continuity or coherence breaks down, or is radically different from what we expect, the result is what the psychologist Heinz Kohut called "disintegration anxiety." When our sense of self becomes fragmented, when we no longer recognize ourselves, or when we are not validated by others, our self-concept is threatened, and we feel like things are falling apart. Rollo May said that "such anxiety is described on the philosophical level as the realization that one may cease to exist as a self." [38] This kind of anxiety is comparable to what is more popularly known as an identity crisis. This is what happens when we no longer recognize ourselves, when our core belief system, predictable behavior, or the way we are perceived by others is no longer consistent with our past. Our identity becomes incoherent. Avoiding this unfamiliar self, is one reason some individuals remain in unfavorable or even destructive situations, (abusive relationships, harmful work environment). Some people will forfeit positive change and a chance to improve their circumstances, rather than risk inconsistency in who they believe themselves to be, or how they think they are perceived by others. Even if that perception is negative (such as being viewed as undeserving, weak, or incompetent), the potential loss of a stable view of themselves is too threatening to effect a change.

Another closely related theory is called "diachronic disunity." [39] This is the positive side of disintegration anxiety. Some people, who feel a discontinuity in their sense of self, will consider this an affirmative identity shift. When someone says "I've really changed," or "I'm not the same person anymore," it may be with pride and a feeling of positive resolution. In such a case, an essential feature of their former identity has changed so radically that at least metaphorically, they no longer recognize themselves. Think of "born again Christians," reformed drug addicts, or people who have "come out" about their sexual preferences. Galen Strawson has argued that diachronic unity is actually a healthy, positive and common human experience. [40] In some cases, radical change is threatening and destabilizing, as in disintegration anxiety, and a person's present outlook, future goals and how they are recognized by others is less fulfilling. In other cases, radical change can be seen as a constructive self-transformation with a more fulfilling outlook and positive sense of recognition.

Because this theme of continuity and coherence or identity-structure is important for self-recognition and recognition from others, let me go one step further and discuss a related theory called "cognitive deconstruction." Cognitive deconstruction has been defined by Roy Baumeister as, "the attempted rejection of meaningful integrated thought." [41] What constitutes meaningful thought involves discussing meaning, a daunting subject. Philosophers have been pondering the concept of meaning for centuries, (although you might find a fifty- page book on the "meaning of life," at your local bookstore). But without going into content, we can say that functionally speaking, meaning is relational, dependent upon a structured context. The number 8 would have no meaning if there were not a number 7 or 9.

Words only have meaning in a system of communication. Isolated sensations have no meaning, but once they are linked, distinguished and associated with other sensations they may become meaningful. Baumeister wrote, "When people use meaning, then, they link their immediately present events, experiences, and concerns across space and time to other events, experiences, and concerns, as well as to broad abstract contextual structures (such as religious beliefs). Interpretation is a matter of taking the immediate event and integrating it into a broader structure, such as placing it in a context, relating it to general principles, evaluating it against general attitudes, inferring the existence of stable traits and tendencies, and so forth." [42]

Continuity and a certain duration of time are often correlated with meaning. For example, a meaningful experience is one that relates to other experiences and fits into a general life scheme or contributes to a fundamental project. A meaningful relationship is one that probably lasts for some time and contributes to your personhood. These distinctions can also be attributed to the way in which we construct our *self*.

In a deconstructed meaningless state, "instead of being aware of self as an integrated entity symbolically constructed as part of an ongoing network of relationships, commitments, institutional ties, ambitions, projects, and enduring traits, one is aware of self only as a physical thing (a body) or as a jumble of short-term feelings, desires, and behaviors." [43] When one is in a cognitively deconstructed state, there are some notable indications, such as:

1) living only in the present by avoiding long term or committed relationships or projects
2) being relatively passive and not acting responsibly
3) thinking in a closed minded way by avoiding complex or creative thought
4) being uninhibited, or unaware of one's actions or their consequences
5) a lack of emotions and empathy, which involves being aware of one's own and other's feelings; exactly what cognitive deconstruction attempts to avoid. [44]

There may be various methods of cognitive deconstruction, or escaping from the self, such as drugs and alcohol, isolation or meditation (which seeks ego dissolution). We might also add that certain psychological pathologies such as schizophrenia are severe cases of cognitive deconstruction. But keep in mind that not all methods of escaping the self are necessarily cognitive deconstruction. Some forms of escapism are simply temporary efforts to avoid physical or emotional pain, or any other negative situation.

Creating an Image: Minds and Mirrors

The above conditions, "diachronic disunity," "cognitive deconstruction" and "disintegration anxiety," whether voluntary and active, or imposed and passive, are breakdowns in self-coherence. They all imply non-recognition and are counterexamples to what we seek; a validation or confirmation of a unified, coherent, meaningful self, and the freedom and control to construct rather than destroy our lives. The most common way of confirming our identity is through social recognition. This is why creating an image, both exterior, and interior, physical and mental, is so important.

Cooley exploited this metaphor quite appropriately in his theory of "the looking-glass self." An image is what you see when you look in the mirror, an image is what you reflectively see in your mind. An image is what you project to others. This image and identity formation was at the heart of James' social-self, and from a certain perspective, a good part of the first section of this book could be interpreted as a discussion of the various ways people go about creating an image and forming an identity. As we all know, modern society is obsessed with images; how to build, enhance, maintain, protect, or alter one's image. When you consider the thousands of self-help books saturating the market, with advice on how to achieve goals, influence people, make friends, earn money, or find happiness, even though the methodology and particular objectives might differ, image and identity are major factors in the recipes for success.

How do we qualify our image in relation to our identity? One qualification concerns self-consciousness. We may be conscious of our self as projecting an image, which has been described as "impression monitoring." [45] Those who are highly self-conscious, maybe even pathologically obsessed, are said to be high in self-monitoring; whereas those who are unaware of the image they are projecting are low in self-monitoring. [46] The reasons we may be highly self-monitoring and concerned with our image can range from narcissistic pride to extreme shyness, but overall, there is a conscious concern about what other people think. Those who are low self-monitoring will claim or act as if they don't care what others think. This might be from total security and inflexibility in one's sense of self, with an "I'll say what I want or do as I please" attitude, or an extreme absence of theory of mind, -- the inability to see oneself from the other's point of view -- as is the case with very young children, or people with certain mental problems, like dementia or severe autism. We can interpret impression monitoring as a *need for* or a *rejection of* recognition.

Another very important qualification concerns authenticity; any image we create may be considered as authentic or inauthentic. An authentic image is consistent with the way a person believes herself to be, whereas an inauthentic, image is hypocritical or dishonest. Self-presentation or "impression management," though once considered negatively as inherently deceitful and manipulative, has regained interest by self-presentational theorists such as Shlenker who stated, "The impressions people attempt to create can be true or false and consistent or inconsistent with their self-concept….. Under internal as well as external control and can manifest socially desirable or undesirable motives. They can come about because of high moral standards or perfidious intentions. There is nothing intrinsic to the concept of impression management that dictates that is must involve dissimulation." [47]

We typically think of inauthentic or hypocritical behavior as unethical, for example, a politician who gives the impression of having strong family values in order to acquire conservative votes, while privately cheating on his or her partner. But inauthentic behavior is not necessarily reproachable, such as a young man who acts callous and tough to keep face with his neighborhood peer group, while being a sensitive loving caretaker at home. On the other hand, people can act to impress others and be true to their image, a politician might truly be ultra-conservative in private life, or a street-kid truly tough and insensitive. We often try to impress others, exaggerating our behavior, such as consciously showing our competence, kindness, understanding, or on the contrary, our incompetence, rudeness and lack of tolerance. Impression management is making an effort to be recognized by others in a certain way. It is not intrinsically authentic or inauthentic, good or bad.

Similarly, a major concern in social psychology and self-presentation theory has to do with the relationship between one's outer image and one's inner identity, especially in the case of inconsistency. One well-known sociologist, Erving Goffman, used theatrical terms in discussing such behavior; we are "actors" who are "playing roles," in various "settings." [48] His theory fits in well with the idea of a fictive self, but is hardly an unfamiliar way of considering human behavior. In fact, etymologically, the word person comes from the Latin word *persona* and refers to the masks once worn by stage actors. *Dramatis personae* designate characters in a story or play. As we all know, the actor metaphor has been used for ages, as with Shakespeare's often quoted "All the world's a stage, And all the men and women merely players."

If we insist that people are often playing a role, the implication is that there is some sort of authentic, true, or real self behind the role that is played. We all probably know people who appear to play a role, preachers being preacher-like, politicians being politician-like, acting and speaking as if following a script, incarnating the cliché of a preacher or politician. They want to be recognized as whatever they believe themselves to be. When Sartre criticized certain people of *mauvais foi*, i.e. *bad faith*, he was pointing out that many people unconsciously avoid the anxiety of accepting responsibility by playing a role, acting as expected, in automatic, unreflective perhaps exaggerated ways. His famous example was the waiter that moves and speaks mechanically; "he is playing at *being* a waiter in a café." [49] Of course what Sartre was criticizing was not so much outward deceit and hypocrisy, as a sort of inner-deceit; people being fixed and thing-like, unreflective, doing what they pretend they have to do, in accordance with their role. Sartre famously declared that such people were essentially denying their freedom and responsibility to do otherwise, since for Sartre, "each person is an absolute choice of self," and is "responsible for everything." [50]

Obviously, the way we act with others is sometimes influenced by the image we want to project or how we wish to be recognized, which consciously or unconsciously, depends upon our motives. These motives might be deceptive. We might deliberately put on airs, or keep a low profile, projecting a particular image to obtain an important job or seduce a potential romantic partner. We may or may not be conscious that we're exaggerating our gestures, being selective in our speech, or choosing particular clothing with the intention of making an impression.

Sometimes the impression we are trying to make or the image we wish to create is not natural, but we rationalize that "it's for a good cause." From a negative standpoint, calculating how we project a particular image can come across as covert manipulation to get what we want. Kenneth Gergen, in *The Saturated Self, Dilemmas of Identity in Contemporary Life*, sees "strategic manipulation" as a first phase of relational behavior in the developing modern society. "The individual increasingly and distressingly finds himself or herself playing roles to achieve social gains." [51] There is an implication here that the person has an essential self that he or she is betraying in order to achieve certain ends. However, Gergen sees the evolving post-modern phase as one in which the individual abandons the idea of a fixed identity and true self, giving way to what he calls the "pastiche personality," a "social chameleon, constantly borrowing bits and pieces of identity from whatever sources are available and constructing them as useful or desirable in a given situation." [52] In this case, the rewards of a good life, professional success and social popularity, etc. are managed through adaptability rather than bulldozing ahead to achieve personal goals. This is perhaps self-serving behavior, but it does not necessarily exploit others.

Today, individuals often adopt an identity that is "mutable," less fixed and stable. [53] Seen from a positive point of view this is being flexible and adaptable, but viewed negatively it's a case of flip-flopping or lacking convictions. This modifiable self, corresponds more closely with Hume's "bundle of perceptions," James' "stream of consciousness" or Sartre's "authentic person," who is at least conscious that his or her *self* is a matter of choice rather than a fixed entity.

In line with what was pointed out earlier about impression management, even if deceitful, such behavior is not necessarily unethical. Deceit is a survival tactic used by many creatures in the natural environment; human individuals have often resorted to dissimulation in order to protect themselves, like the tough kid out on the streets who is kind to his mother at home. But as we all know, manipulative and even non-manipulative people may confuse self-protection with self-interest. There are countless examples of such "confusion," to put it mildly, especially in the political or business world. As with the ideologically conservative politician mentioned above, is he protecting his private life for the sake of his family and ideals, or to insure a political victory? Whether or not deceit can qualify as being ethical and in which circumstances it may be condoned or justified is a huge philosophical question that I won't elaborate upon here, however, I will take up the concept of authenticity and its relevance to recognition shortly.

Although many of us may play roles or consciously try to make impressions from time to time, the way we present ourselves most of the time is natural, habitual, and automatic. We are usually unconscious of the image we are projecting, more absorbed in our actions than observing our self as acting. Presenting an inauthentic or false image is probably rare. Most of the time, our image is consistent with what we believe ourselves to be, and in cases of seeking recognition, the motive is probably simply the need for self-validation or self-verification, rather than manipulation. Playing a role or projecting an image authentically, is quite common, what William Swann calls "identity negotiation." "Once people form self-views, they usually make deliberate efforts to "act the part." Their actions, in turn, will influence how others respond to them, which will then influence their own responses, and so forth. This process of mutual give-and take is called identity negotiation." [54]

Let me add that most people who appear to be acting are perhaps literally playing a role, but they are usually playing themselves. They are unconsciously motivated by a need to confirm who they are by seeking validation from others. Some self-presentation studies have shown that people will exaggerate their behavior, especially if they think they may be misunderstood. They want to rectify not dissimulate their image. However, I know many dramatic individuals, who dwell on their unhappiness, suffering, or misfortune, much more often than their pleasure and joy. It is an unconscious attempt to getting a confirmation of their feelings. Complainers come to mind. In my own experience, whatever you suggest to a constant complainer is systematically rejected. People who are chronic complainers are not looking for solutions to their complaints but a sympathetic ear, understanding and an implicit validation of their suffering.

Chapter VII

Cultural Differences: We Mustn't Generalize

I would like to return to the second part of my question concerning the narrative self: to what extent is it grounded in society and conditioned by a social reality? This question is related to the philosophical dilemma of freedom and responsibility. How much influence does our socio-cultural context have in constructing the self and how much can we attribute to free will? If we selectively choose our memories and reconstruct our past, to what extent is our choice a *free* choice? If my insistence on the importance of recognition is justified, our choice of self is greatly determined by our social-cultural context. As Dan McAdams pointed out, writing on identity and narrative, "Life stories mirror the culture wherein the story is made and told. Stories live in culture. They are born, they grow, they proliferate, and they eventually die according to the norms, rules, and traditions that prevail in a given society, according to a society's implicit understandings of what counts as a tellable story, a tellable life." [56]

Considering that narrative styles and our self-concepts are greatly conditioned by cultural and social contexts, this is a propitious time to say a word about cultural differences. People around the world do not seek recognition in the same way or for the same reasons; motives, values and goals differ from culture to culture. I'm most familiar with Western lifestyles and belief systems, since I was born and raised in the United States. However, I'm sensitive to cultural differences, having lived more than half my life in France and five years in China, with family, friends and colleagues from various cultural backgrounds. In addition, my philosophical and psychological studies have taught me that conceptual formations and perspectives, which determine how we think and behave, vary greatly from one culture to another.

In Western societies, North America, Australia, and Western Europe, there is more emphasis on individuality, self-actualization, personal uniqueness, and rewards for self-assertion. In Eastern societies, East Asia, Africa, as well as Latin America, and Southern Europe, there is more emphasis on interpersonal connectedness, social obligation, conformity, group harmony, and shared identity. [57]

There have been numerous studies on the differences between East and West in parent-child relationships, education, cognitive functioning, social customs, values, etc. During a child's early years, memories such as homes lived in, family members, places visited, special days, become encoded so that they may be subsequently retrieved through a process of "co-construction," between children and their parents. The child learns how to discuss things from the parent's example, and child-parent conversations are instrumental for the child's understanding of ongoing events that will construct their long-term personal memories. [58] In parent-child conversations, does the parent emphasize grandmother's big house and expensive cars or does the parent point out how kind she was to get up early and fix breakfast every morning? The facts and opinions that parents emphasize the most will be the ones that are the best remembered and the most influential in later life.

There has been extensive research on this subject by Qi Wang, a professor of human development. Wang's findings are especially revelatory in showing the crucial role that parents play in shaping the way in which memory and self-identity are established and maintained. Wang found that Euro-American mothers, by focusing on the child's preferences and predilections, were "socializing their children into a sense of self as an autonomous being with distinctive and unique characteristics. They also are modeling to children the culturally desirable form and content of autobiographical memory in building one's unique individual identity." However, Wang adds, "By placing past events in a more social-relational context, Chinese mothers are modeling to children the construction of personal stories that give prominence to social interactions and collectivity.......In this way, Chinese mothers focus on socializing their children to be in harmony with others and to view the self as part of a social community." [59] For example, when discussing a school camp outing with his or her child, a Western parent will ask more questions about what the particular child experienced or accomplished, "How did you like riding a horse?" "Did you win a prize?" An Asian parent will inquire more about the group as a whole, "Where did your class go first? "Did you all enjoy the walk in the forest?"

Other studies have shown two different conversation styles when speaking about past events; high-elaborative mothers describe experiences more extensively and with more detail. They prompt their children to do the same by posing many open ended (what, where, when, why) questions. Conversely, low-elaborative mothers talk relatively little about past events and provide fewer details when discussing the past. These mothers tend to pose pointed, Yes-and-no questions with single correct and incorrect answers. Western mothers tend to be more high-elaborative and Eastern mothers more low-elaborative conversationalists. Taken together, these studies indicate that children raised in interdependent versus independent cultures are exposed from an early age to distinctive narrative environments that reflect different general values and meanings when it comes to personal memories. Western, independent cultures help children organize their memories in ways that distinguish them as unique and autonomous, while Eastern, interdependent cultures reinforce social values, such as moral behavior, connectedness and responsibility toward others. [60] The result is that the children end up with different self-concepts. Western children are more positive in their self- evaluations, with more embellishment of personal qualities, attributes and emotions. Eastern children describe themselves in a more neutral way, describing situations and behaviors, and emphasizing the group. [61]

In terms of recognition, these findings are important. Growing up in Western, independently oriented cultures will probably encourage children to seek recognition for descriptive attributes, whereas in Eastern, collectivist oriented cultures they will seek recognition more in terms of roles. Though this is a generalization, it explains to some extent individual cultural differences when discussing a need for recognition.

I must add though, that times are changing. China and other Asian countries are evolving dramatically; the lifestyles and values of the West are fast encroaching on the East. The one child policy in China, for example, is definitely influencing parental education. By the same token, certain Eastern values are being integrated into modern Western lifestyle. For example, the huge popularity of social networking, portable phones, and other devices demonstrates our desperate need to stay connected. What is happening to the American ideal of independence and autonomy when we can't seem to live five minutes in pure isolation, without making contact (tweets, texts, email) with others?

There is a delicate balance between generalization and cultural relativism, and a constant danger of losing perspective by favoring one view over the other. There is a great deal that all human beings have in common, and there is a great deal in which they differ. For example, most cultures are alike in that they include the family unit as essential for constructing the self. However, from culture to culture, there are different emphases within the family unit ranging from interdependence, to intergroup hierarchy, to interfamily autonomy. The implicit assumption has been that there is a universal need or desire to define one's self, as both belonging to and differentiating from others. [62] But the balance between these needs and how they are accomplished may differ greatly.

In addition to these apparent cultural generalizations, the question remains, is there an ontological difference, as to the very meaning of self between cultures?

Takie Sugiyama Lebra has observed that there is a basic ontological difference between East and West, on the very nature of being. [63] In the East, people value what she calls the "Shinto-Buddhist submerged self," and in the West, people value the "Cartesian, split self." There are two axes in Lebra's analysis; a horizontal axis with Culture at one end and Nature at the other, and a vertical axis with Being at the top and Nothingness at the bottom. Western culture would be located in the quadrant of Culture and Being; with a goal of "self-objectification," dividing the experiencing *I* and the experienced *me*. In the West, self-knowledge is the goal of existence, with an emphasis on causation and permanence. Eastern culture would be located in the quadrant of Nature and Nothingness; freedom from self, connectedness with others and nature, with an emphasis on co-occurrence and impermanence, as in Buddhist philosophy. Based on Lebra's analysis, it is easy to see how the Cartesian ontology would give rise to the Western concept of self as separate, individual and independent, and the Shinto-Buddhist ontology would lead to the Eastern concept of self as collectivist, co-extensive, and interdependent. Self-construction is a universal goal, but the very concept of self, the process towards constructing the self and its eventual structure are related to a person's socio-cultural context.

The question of our self-construction is unresolved. It is a reformulation of the famous nature vs. nurture question or the dilemma posed by psychological determinism. We believe ourselves free subjects, interpreting and even reconstructing our memorable experiences, yet we must acknowledge that we are conditioned or at least strongly influenced by our socio-cultural context. These two very basic ontological visions of the self have an influence on how we choose or need to be recognized.

Chapter VIII

The Evaluative Self, How do I Rate?

Most of my prior discussion concentrated on how we perceive ourselves, but in this chapter, I'd like to turn the discussion towards how we judge ourselves. Our character, personality, and our temperament are important in evaluating our self and others as well as establishing an integrated self-concept and a concept of other selves. Others may recognize us as being worthy or unworthy, good or bad, moral or immoral based on our behavior which is considered an expression of our personality, character or temperament.

If we refer to personality assessment, certain traits are more desirable and praiseworthy than others, regardless of socio-cultural context. Let's consider the "Big Five" personality model, [64]

1) extroversion
2) agreeableness
3) conscientiousness

4) emotional stability
5) intellect or openness to experience.

Most people would probably judge others or themselves favorably if their characteristics are measured on the positive side of this scale. Certain personality traits are considered commendable, such as being capable, compassionate, friendly, kind, generous, trustworthy, and creative. Those we judge negatively include being incompetent, selfish, negligent, irritable, cruel, and unwise. Other traits are judged variably depending upon the social context, the particular situation, or the consequences of behavior. Being emotional, serious, clever, bold, sensitive, aggressive, liberal, religious to name a few, can be viewed positively or negatively. For instance, to be effective, soldiers need to be insensitive, doctors unemotional, certain athletes aggressive, or Wall-Street traders bold. A crook can be clever and a politician can be religious or liberal which some see as a good quality and others a fault.

Personality traits are evaluated in light of a social context since they concern interaction between the self and others. Being kind or trustworthy or being cruel and deceitful involves behaving in a certain way towards other people. Even qualities such as creativity, open-mindedness, curiosity, and imagination exist in a meaning-structured reality which implies a social reality. Human values exist in an evolving human world.

Self-evaluation is of major interest in modern society. It is often discussed in relation to the popular concept of self-esteem. I contend that a need for recognition cannot be equated with a need for self-esteem, although our behavior and how it is evaluated, are important for both these concepts. This is why the concepts of egotism and narcissism, and their apparent opposites, altruism and empathy are important for a discussion of self-appraisal and recognition. Both self-esteem and recognition are morally neutral, but most people would agree that their "dark side," is acquired through self-interested behavior, based on egotism and narcissism for the purpose of self-aggrandizement, whereas their "bright side" is attained through social interest, based on altruism and empathy with goals that are consistent with a community spirit. However, even though egoism, narcissism, empathy and altruism are value-laden concepts, I don't believe they are *necessarily* good or bad in a moral sense.

Finally, what about authenticity? Being your true self whether as an egoist or altruist is generally considered a quality. Is it consistently a value? Although being authentic seems obvious to many people, I will argue that authenticity is an extremely ambiguous and problematic concept.

Self-Esteem: An Overrated Goal

The need for recognition is often equated with a need for self-esteem. This is a misconception. The two concepts are interrelated and a desire for recognition can arise from a need to confirm or enhance one's self-esteem, but current thinking in psychological theory claims that our need for self-validation, self-knowledge, or simple recognition, takes precedence over a need to feel good about ourselves. I believe self-esteem is a consequence of recognition and not its primary motivation.

Healthy self-esteem is important but the insistence on its significance has been exaggerated and overrated. The torrential wave of self-esteem advocates in the 1980's had a profound influence on our way of thinking and educating our young in the Western world, especially in the U.S. Their influence is still being felt. This movement has provoked an inevitable backlash of criticism pointing out weaknesses in emphasizing self-esteem. There are two sides of the self-esteem movement; the negative side that leads to egoism, narcissism, and even aggression and a positive side, with all the desirable characteristics most of us aspire to; feeling accepted, loved, well adjusted, and satisfied with our life and relationships.

In 1658, Thomas Hobbes said, "Proper self-esteem [is] a state of mind that ought to be. Those, moreover, who estimate their own worth correctly, do so on the basis of their past deeds, and so, what they have done, they dare to try again. Those who estimate their worth too highly, or who pretend to be what they are not, or who believe flatterers, become disheartened when dangers actually confront them."-- *De Homine (1658) Ch. XII, no. 9*

Hobbes was prescient in remarking that self-esteem is something that "ought to be." Today, especially in America, we consider it on a par with other assumed inalienable rights of "life, liberty, the pursuit of happiness." But Hobbes also noted that as a motivating factor, it can lead to problems if it is too excessive. These reflections have remained pertinent.

What is self-esteem and why do we need it? One widely accepted definition of self-esteem is called the "dual model" or "two factor" theory, which is (a) based on a sense of competence, power, or efficacy, and (b) based on a sense of virtue or moral worth.[65] The Rosenberg Scale is a well-known and widely used measure of global self-esteem comprised of 10 items that focus on general feelings and attitudes toward the self, without referring to any particular personal attribute, (e.g., "On the whole, I am satisfied with myself"- "All in all, I am inclined to feel that I am a failure"). If you want to know how you feel about yourself, (as if you didn't already know!), take the test, it's available on Internet.

This scale taps into the two general factors of worthiness and competence. It is interesting that in the two-factor theory, Americans seem to stress competence because it emphasizes individuality and success, whereas Asians tend to stress the role of worthiness, since they are generally more group-oriented and make greater use of interpersonal relationships. [66] In his book, *Self Esteem Research, Theory and Practice*, Christopher Murk has developed a structural definition, "*self esteem is the lived status of one's competence at dealing with the challenges of living in a worthy way over time.*" [67] There are quite a few 'loaded' concepts in this definition. Competence, challenges and worthiness are all relative terms that depend upon the individual, the circumstance and how these concepts are interpreted.

If we take for example competence and challenges, we can see how self-esteem is relative to an individual's expectations. An athlete may experience low self-esteem if he runs the 100 meter in more than 12 seconds whereas someone who is handicapped may gain great self-esteem from taking a few coordinated steps. William James is often quoted for his formula defining self-esteem; he said it depends upon the "ratio of our actualities to our supposed potentialities; a fraction of which our pretensions are the denominator and the numerator our successes; thus, Self-Esteem = success/pretentions." [68] Thus for James, self-esteem is the relationship between what a person aspires to and what a person accomplishes. He gives an example; *"I, who for the time have staked my all on being a psychologist, am mortified if others know much more psychology than I. But I am contented to wallow in the grossest ignorance of Greek. My deficiencies there give me no sense of personal humiliation at all. Had I "pretensions" to be a linguist, it would have been just the reverse."* [69] A person's aspirations are to his or her values. James valued his proficiency in matters of psychology, someone else might value their knowledge of fashion, yet another their ability to break into a house without getting caught. We might even say that a terrorist receives a boost in self-esteem from his cohorts (and the God he believes in) for having blown up a crowd of innocent bystanders. Nothing in the notion of self-esteem implies that it must be for something worthy in a universal sense. Some nefarious individuals throughout history and even living today have felt or continue to feel very good about themselves for some very atrocious acts.

One question is; why do some people have high and others low self-esteem? It is not always related to one's general situation; there is no direct socio-economic correlation. The wealthy and famous can have low self-esteem just as the poor and anonymous can have high self-esteem. Where does self-esteem come from?

It has been argued that global self-esteem is not a consequence of our situation. It is affective rather than situational, not just a matter of competence or other personal attributes. Those with high self-esteem like themselves and generally feel good about who they are, whereas people with low self-esteem dislike themselves or feel ambivalent. Global self-esteem involves feelings like 'I'm good' or 'I'm bad,' 'I can' or 'I can't,' rather than specific abilities. [70] Even James wrote, "There is a certain average tone of self-feeling, which each one of us carries about with him, and which is independent of the objective reasons we may have for satisfaction or discontent." [71] In other words, positive qualities do not lead to self-esteem, but self-esteem leads people to believe that they have positive qualities. When it comes to evaluating personal attributes, it is the emotional factor that influences our judgments. For example, most parents love their children not because they're cute and delightful; parents find them cute and delightful because they love them. This is apt to be the same case for self-love. [72]

Freud believed that self-esteem emerges early in life, before there is any evaluative cognitive ability. Alan Sroufe from the University of Minnesota carried out extensive research on problematic mother-child relationships. He came to the conclusion that positive and sensitive caretaking leads to better adjusted children, which comes as no surprise, though he places no particular blame on the mother when children are maladjusted. [73] John Bowlby, remarked that "An unwanted child is likely not only to feel unwanted by his parents but to believe that he is essentially unwantable, namely unwanted by anyone.

Conversely, a much-loved child may grow up to be not only confident of his parents' affection but confident that everyone else will find him lovable too." [74]

Positivity is important as a contributor to self-esteem, but sensitivity is more important, even if the attention is negative, making a good case for the importance of recognition. Children cannot count on insensitive caregivers, who provoke a lack of self-confidence since they interpret the child's actions and feelings as inconsequential. The need for recognition from the caretaker is so important that children will sometimes deliberately misbehave in order to be noticed. [75] The psychoanalyst Daniel Stern has commented, "Up to a point, it is better to respond badly than to be nonresponsive." Research has shown that an abusive or punitive mother may be better for a child than one who is not responsive. [76] The psychoanalyst Ernest Wolf came to a similar conclusion. "An ambiance of responsiveness is as essential for psychological health as a plentiful supply of oxygen is essential for physical health." The caregiver's responsiveness to the child should be appropriate but whether it's positive or negative is not so important. [77] Nathanial Branden, the self-esteem advocate, seems to agree. As he wrote in his book '*Honoring the Self*' "A child has a natural desire to be seen, heard, understood and responded to appropriately. This is the need for *psychological visibility*." [78] As far as psychological research and theory is concerned, it seems that recognition, at least in the developmental stage is more important than encouragement or praise for creating healthy self-esteem.

The basic belief behind the whole self-esteem movement was that low self-esteem was seen as a major cause underlying our personal and social problems. Branden, one of the foremost proponents of this movement once wrote, "I cannot think of a single psychological problem--from anxiety to depression, to under-achievement at school or at work, to fear of intimacy, happiness, or success, to alcohol or drug abuse, to spouse battering or child molestation, to co-dependency and sexual disorders, to passivity and chronic aimlessness, to suicide and crimes of violence--that is not traceable, at least in part, to the problem of deficient self-esteem." [79]

Though Branden tempered this extreme view in other texts, it was taken to heart by the general public, always on the lookout for a panacea to personal and social problems. This view was reflected in public policy, notably in relation to our education system in the United States. During the 1980's the *California Task Force to Promote Self-Esteem and Personal and State Responsibility* was established with the mission of exploring the causes of low self-esteem and finding methods for improving it, with the hopes of alleviating problems such as welfare dependency, teenage pregnancy, academic failure, drug problems, etc. Its results have been challenged as far from successful in remediating such problems. [80]

The danger in overemphasizing the importance of self-esteem is particularly evident in the manner in which it has infiltrated the American education system. While there is nothing wrong with encouragement, unmerited praise is not constructive. Though children love praise, it should be merited. In fact, "parents may unwittingly deflate their children's self-esteem by implicitly or explicitly denying their limitations." [81] Therapist Paul Watchtel pointed out "when the parent's perceptions are actually disjunctive with the child's evolving sense of his own reality, then what he experiences is that who he thought he was is simply not good enough. He senses in a dim way that the parents need him to be someone he is not, and whatever real attributes he has will be experienced as insufficient and unimportant." [82]

Some school curricula have been watered down so that children will be less likely to fail. In some systems, students are laden with praise and in various school competitions, everybody wins a prize. The theory supporting this policy is that children who feel good about themselves will do better. But the criticism is that "instead of teaching them how to read, they're teaching kids to feel good about being illiterate." [83] Here is another comment that appeared in Newsweek magazine, "Think of Halsey Schools [in Woodland Hills, California], where the word "bad" is never spoken, where everyone gets an award every year, where kindergarten students learn to count by being handed pictures of objects and told how many there are instead of figuring it out themselves. Ask yourself: wouldn't it be nice if life were really like this? And what's going to happen to those kids when they find out it's not?" [84]

There have been arguments for and against the general importance self-esteem. Some feel that maintaining self-esteem takes precedent as a motivational force in our lives; others feel that self-confirmation is more motivating, even if it means we sacrifice our sense of self-esteem.

Views conflict and both are correct, depending upon the circumstances and the individuals involved.

Arguing for the priority of self-esteem, we can begin with Nietzsche, who said, "I have done that', says my memory. 'I cannot have done that,' says my pride, and remains inexorable. Eventually – memory yields." [85] In other words, people distort their past in the service of maintaining self-esteem. It might seem like human nature has programmed people to want to feel good about themselves, even if it means compromising the truth. People might lie to inflate their self-esteem, not only to others but to themselves, a major factor in the concept of *mauvais foi*, i.e. *bad faith*. People love compliments, approbation, and positive feedback, and will concentrate on the positive and conveniently forget or downplay the negative, which is important for emotional resilience. Severe depression is the exact opposite, seeing only the negative and ignoring the positive. According to some clinical studies, self-esteem is more important than self-knowledge and being realistic. "People are so hypersensitive to threat potential that they will even neglect self-threatening feedback that is fictitious and seemingly harmless. They are so intolerant to negativity that they will neglect it regardless of whether it is consistent or inconsistent with self-knowledge. And they will mobilize recall in the service of the implicit goal of deflecting negativity and stabilizing a positive self-definition." [86] However, it seems to me that in this case, such extreme ego protection is more like narcissism than healthy self-esteem.

There are some basic errors with the idea that self-esteem is so important. People do not always monitor their self-presentation nor do they always want to think well of themselves. They do not always feel that they merit praise when they perform well. In fact, some people become anxious or distraught if they receive what they consider undue praise. Secondly, some people prefer not to think about themselves, they would rather forget themselves than know themselves. They are more concerned with others. And thirdly, many people are consumed by their work, projects or activities.

Psychologists generally agree that most people look for consistency and unity in their self-conception. It's our way of controlling ourselves and rendering the world more predictable. We constantly try to confirm our self-views whether they are positive or negative. This view is similar to Leon Festinger's (1957) who formulated the theory of *cognitive dissonance*. He claimed that people will try to establish harmony and consistency among their opinions, attitudes, values etc. The psychologist Gordon Allport also concluded "An impartial and objective attitude toward oneself is held to be a primary virtue, basic to the development of all others. There is but a weak case for chronic self-deception with its crippling self-justifications and rationalizations that prevent adaptation and growth. And so it may be said that if any trait of personality is intrinsically desirable, it is the disposition and ability to see oneself in perspective." [87] Despite the emphasis on self-esteem, critical analysis concludes that self-knowledge or self-verification is more important. I see recognition serving this latter purpose as well, which is reminiscent of the Delphic oracle, "know thyself."

Self-esteem is recognition for our attributes, our social self, our *me*, that is constructed though socialization.

Whether these attributes are accurate or not is irrelevant, and whether our self-esteem originates from infancy or is incremental makes little difference. We judge ourselves by our attributes and accomplishments. Our personal accomplishments can raise our self-esteem without the approval of others, but in order to have meaning, our private accomplishments depend upon a socially constructed reality. You can take personal pride in anything you achieve, but no achievement, happens in a vacuum. It's only perceived as an achievement relative to expectations within a social system.

Self-esteem can be falsely inflated or deflated, and doesn't necessarily correspond with reality, as in the case of narcissists or clinically depressed people. It is primarily an affective state; it involves how one *feels* about oneself. This doesn't mean someone can't be mistaken about *feeling* recognized. All emotional feeling is phenomenal, or in the mind, and it doesn't necessarily correspond with what is reality. However, in the case of recognition, I believe that there is a symmetrical notion that implies objectivity. It is cognitive as well as emotional. Though recognition can be confused with self-esteem, I believe that recognition has a more existential nature. Unlike self-esteem, recognition involves reciprocation; it is received from and given to the other. This mutual recognition between reflective subjects is what I consider the foundation of humanity.

The Social-interest / Self-interest Divide: Altruism vs. Egoism

As I said earlier, there is nothing inherently ethical or unethical about self-esteem. People can feel good about themselves whether it's for doing good things or bad things. Seeking recognition can be motivated by self-serving reasons or in the service of others. Someone may want recognition for how much money they make and how many cars they have in their garage, or for how much money they contribute and how many people they help by donating their spare time.

Selfishness and narcissism as opposed to empathy and altruism are two seemingly contradictory attitudes; the former considered negative and unworthy, the second positive and virtuous. But are they mutually exclusive? Generosity can be narcissistic, a form of coercive recognition, "I did something for you and now you owe me respect," just as acting selfishly can simultaneously serve others. It has been suggested, and I tend to agree, that the divide between selfishness and altruism is a bit of a red herring. [88] The contrast between self-serving behavior and serving others may be more of a gray area than a black and white division; doing something for oneself, may benefit others, and there is no real need to separate such actions. When it serves both purposes, it's called cooperation. As humans, we both cooperate and compete, and as a social species, we never would have progressed without both elements. Perhaps the real issue isn't whether or not altruism is motivated by selfish reasons, such as alleviating distress or getting personal pleasure from helping others. If everyone profits from individual actions, the moral worth of the motivation is less important. The fact remains, that we do judge people based on their motivations or intentions.

Altruism: Good for Goodness' Sake

Altruism, a term coined by Auguste Comte in the 19th century, is a fundamental component of many ethical systems. There has been a lot of recent research on altruism lately; its anthropological beginnings, how it ties in with genetics, its role in social evolution, and what chemicals are triggered in the brain when we perform altruistic acts, all pointing to its importance for our survival. For example, John Eccles, the neurophysiologist pointed out the instinctive behavior of self-sacrifice common to insects and animals, which he calls 'pseudaltruism,' [88] Frans de Waals has suggested that pure altruism may have evolved from a more primitive "*self protective altruism,*" as when a mother dog attends to her squealing pups in order to get a little rest, while also assuaging their distress. [89]

This is different from what we might call true altruism. True altruism is not an action carried out with the anticipation of reciprocation. True altruism is intentionally exercised *for* the other, regardless of any personal gratification. The pleasure that comes from altruism is "an unexpected by-product" as Rifken pointed out. [90] True altruism, on a grand self-sacrificing scale, is relatively rare, which is why the media makes so much out of stories of exceptional heroism or great acts of generosity, turning ordinary people into celebrities and celebrities into highly respected humanitarians. Generally speaking, true altruism earns true recognition.

On a daily basis, spontaneous altruistic acts are common. Most people will concur that it's very satisfying when you promote the welfare of others in even small, rather inconsequential ways. There is always a feel-good feeling when you give directions, help someone who has fallen, or retrieve a person's lost object. Nothing replaces personal recognition, even if it's a smile and "thank you." Contributing to charity, anonymous gift-giving, humanitarian work, and other benevolent actions promote our self-esteem as well as esteem from others. To improve human lives is extraordinary for our sense of self-worth. Fortunately for humanity it makes us feel good to help others, otherwise our species never could have survived and evolved. Altruism is an indisputable part of our human nature and more important than selfishness and competitiveness for the human species. It is no wonder that it is at the root of most ethical and religious systems.

On the other hand, some people are falsely generous, and perhaps unconsciously or consciously "do onto others *so that* others will do onto them." They morally oblige the beneficiary of their generosity to be grateful. This is closer to narcissism than altruism, practically obliging recognition, and engenders more resentment than admiration.

Egoism & Narcissism: The Modern Epidemic

In the first section of this book, I discussed various ways in which we look for recognition, our physical image, and work, group association, significant others, networking, etc. In a sense, we can say that recognition is essentially selfish, since it is necessary for developing a concept of self. Self-welfare, self-concern and self-care constitute forms of selfishness that assure our survival. Few people would denigrate health and happiness as being selfish goals. Thinking of ourselves doesn't have to exclude thinking of anyone else, and it does not necessarily result in a lack of regard or respect for others. However, it is evident that some people are excessively selfish and have an unreasonable need for recognition. A persistent and exaggerated need for recognition is what is popularly known today as narcissism.

Narcissism, as most of us know, comes from the Greek myth of Narcissus, the young man who fell in love with his own image reflected in the water. It is a well-known symbol throughout history, but Freud's famous essay written in 1914, familiarized the world with narcissism as a personality disorder. The current generation, at least in the occidental world, has recently been labeled the "me generation." We seem to be surrounded by narcissists in varying degrees, (Facebook, You Tube, Twitter, and other Internet platforms have revealed their omnipresence), and we have all probably behaved in a narcissistic way at one time or another in our lives.

A little narcissism is healthy or normal and would probably be the equivalent of possessing high self-esteem. But, excessive narcissism is the "dark side" of self-esteem. Though we all use similar defense mechanisms to protect our ego, the neurotic, uses them to excess, spending so much time and energy protecting the ego that it is at the expense of constructive character development and functional social relationships, a difference of quantity more than quality. A pathological narcissist's self-views of perceived self-importance and uniqueness are unrealistically high; narcissistic people overestimate their intelligence and attractiveness. They are preoccupied with defending a grandiose self, and most of their social behavior is used for this end. Social relationships are basically self-enhancement opportunities; it's more important for narcissists to be admired than liked and they have a hard time committing themselves, since they are always looking for a better deal.

However, it is sadly ironic that narcissists are often repugnant and offsetting, pushing others away, when they actually depend upon others for boundless recognition, thus validating their importance. They overly rely on social sources of evaluation, and constantly need to confirm their self-image. Today's me-generation narcissists feel a constant need to be in connection, via their mobile phones or some social internet connection. They need a continual hit of dopamine by being "liked" or invited, or simply acknowledged by others. Even though they believe they are great, they need other people to confirm it. Though they believe that they have very positive self-esteem, they actually lack confidence. Very often, unsure that they can develop the necessary skills or establish satisfying relationships, they compensate by putting other people down. In this way, they depend upon the other's inadequacy to feel good about themselves. Those who constantly denigrate other people are not hard to miss. They pervade every level of the social hierarchy.

The source of narcissism has been confirmed by a majority of psychodynamic theorists to be the result of problems stemming from interpersonal relationships during early childhood. Kohut and Kernberg are both well known for their research in the psychological development of narcissism. In a nutshell, the consensus is that because significant others were either un-empathetic or insensitive to the growing child's need of approval, the narcissist grows up looking for the approbation he or she missed as a child. Or as Kernberg said, because parents were cold and rejecting, the growing child concentrates on certain core aspects of his self that were once valued by the caregiver. Later, as an adult, he will deny any perceived weaknesses. Regardless of the source of narcissism, there is a clear lack of self-knowledge and underlying self-worth that causes the narcissist to depend excessively on others for a sense of self.

Narcissism, judging from recent literature on the subject, is a very common personality disorder in modern occidental culture, especially in the United States. If we consider self-absorbed people focused on success, who exploit others in their intimate relationships and are insensitive to the needs and desires of others as narcissists, then there is a serious epidemic in modern society. In America, recent data has shown that one out of ten people in their twenties and one out of sixteen of those of all ages have experienced symptoms of Narcissistic Personality Disorder by 2006. [91]

There are several correlating factors for this increase, including an emphasis on hyper-individualism -- as noted with the self-esteem movement -- a growing sense of entitlement, and the facility with which we can falsify our image, such as plastic surgery, Internet avatars, performance enhancing drugs and easy access to financial credit enabling us to buy an appearance of success. Many of these issues are addressed by Jean Twenge, and Keith Campbell, in their book *The Narcissism Epidemic, Living in the age of Entitlement*. As they say, "understanding the narcissism epidemic is important because its long term consequences are destructive to society. American culture's focus on self-admiration has caused a flight from reality to the land of grandiose fantasy." [92]

I would further add that on a collective level, patriotism, when it takes the form of chauvinistic nationalism, is a form of narcissism. In the United States for example, if you don't defend America's exceptionalism, believing that America is categorically "Number One," or the ultimate defender of freedom, justice, equality, and human dignity, blessed by God, you are somehow un-American.

In any case, the need for recognition that I've been emphasizing throughout this book, is in no way a defense of narcissism. If not already sufficiently clear, I hope to confirm my position in the last section with a discussion of *respect-recognition*.

Authenticity: The Paradox of a True Self

A discussion of authenticity serves as a bridge between the evaluative-self and my next section treating recognition's the moral implications. In terms of self-recognition, we would usually like to be recognized for who we believe we truly are. Our true self involves the paradoxical concept of authenticity. Although it is considered a quality and a virtue, a clear definition of authenticity is not so evident.

As pointed out earlier, the empirical *me* has been described as essentially fictive, while the transcendental *I* is an enigmatic, mysterious, and perhaps superfluous concept (what the philosopher Gilbert Ryle famously referred to as the "ghost in the machine"). If the self is an unsubstantial, fictive, socially constructed work-in-progress, what implications does this have for the attribution of authenticity, and the corresponding concepts of free will and personal responsibility? Though I'm not sure that recognition is the only way to supply an answer, it is at least relevant and important in finding one. As I've been arguing so far, being recognized by the other is important for our sense of self, as well as constructing a meaningful existence. Is this a spontaneous and independently free endeavor or is it a matter of social-cultural influence and social conditioning, or is it a bit of each?

In a sense, maintaining a transcendence of the ego, or a subjective *I* was vital to certain philosophers in order to confirm our autonomy as meaning-bestowing and world-constituting subjects. They were hoping to show that we are not just empirical *me's*, like passive beings caught in the causal material world chain, or like corks bobbing along in a river of influential others. However, as Sartre pointed out, this doesn't necessarily require a transcendental subject that is not part of the world, especially if we reflect upon the universal feeling of *anxiety*.

Both Heidegger's *angst* and Sartre's *angoisse*, are concepts that they purport to be proofs of our freedom. Anxiety, unlike fear, has no particular object. It is that feeling we have in face of our possibilities; our awareness that we always have a choice, we can always do, or at least think otherwise, and that we are free subjects responsible for creating meaning in the world. In *Being and Time*, Heidegger said anxiety is the most fundamental disposition, "*that in the face of which one has anxiety [das Wovor der Angst] is Being-in-the-world as such.*" [93] However, such angst is not a constant state. Life would be unsustainable if it was. Most of the time, we consider ourselves a part of the world, *vorhanden*, just another anybody, *das Man* following rules, adopting determined meanings. We are usually more concerned with how to pay our bills than feeling anguished by the fact that we are existentially free not to.

Sartre too pointed out that anguish, though not a frequent feeling was necessary for authenticity. It's the opposite of *mauvais foi*, taking our self for a thing, an "in-itself" as he said, with no free choice and in denial of our ultimate freedom. Our existential freedom comes exactly from the fact that consciousness as nothing, *no*-thing, can be *any*-thing.

Thomas Nagel, in his book *The View from Nowhere*, has more recently made a similar claim. We are a particular person somewhere in the world, but when we reflect, becoming aware that we are aware, we step back again and again, until we realize that we are nowhere. Nagel, reminiscent of Heidegger and Sartre says that "It is a problem that faces every creature with the impulse and the capacity to transcend its particular point of view and to conceive of the world as a whole." [94] Even if he doesn't use the word anguish, Nagel does talk of "the feeling of amazement that is part of the philosophical thought- a strange sense that I both am and am not the hub of the universe." [95] We feel responsible for ourselves, our situation and our world, but at the same time totally out-of-control, like impotent pawns of destiny. Most of us, at one time or another, experience that dizzying feeling of cosmic-depression or existential-nothingness, when we feel no more meaningful than a grain of sand on the ocean floor or a speck of dust in the universe.

Free choice, anguish, and self-identity are recent concepts in the history of man. Remember that our individuated mode of life began about 10,000 years ago, and urban life really only began about 3000 years ago. We have rapidly gone from a socially limited, tight-knit, intimate communal life with relative stability, to modern civilization and urban life, with our ever increasing mobility. Our social status is no longer a given but easily altered. We can now change homes, families, neighbors, and intimate relationships. Bonds are often created and broken, narratives are less easily maintained. Our possessions are replaced constantly, outmoded and renewed. Even our physical self is modifiable. All this adds up to increasing choices and increasing freedom. As Preben Bertelsen said, "the new requirement, the new mode of life, is to be sincere to oneself, to one's own values, one's own life project. The demand made in the modern era of individuation is a demand for authenticity." [96]

Authenticity never used to be a question, at least in the modern Western world with increasing freedom of choice and individualism. Recently, it has become a pre-occupation and the ultimate human goal. The humanistic psychological tradition, as advanced by Abraham Maslow, suggested that once we moved up the pyramid of basic needs, from physiological, to security and safety, to love and belonging, to success, status and self-esteem, we progress to the highest need which he called "self-actualization" i.e., authenticity. [97] Carl Rogers claimed that a "fully functioning person," who showed consistency between self-concept and actions was a person who took responsibility for choices and was true to his or her core values.[98] Common views of authenticity are to be true to yourself, to be who you are, to be genuine, or to think for yourself. This is not everyone's preoccupation, remembering Maslow's well-known pyramid of basic needs. If you're worried about putting food on the table or finding shelter for the night, you're not worried about authenticity.

To mention a more recent theoretical investigation, Kernis and Goldman, have proposed "a multicomponent conceptualization of authenticity." They define authenticity as "the unobstructed operation of one's true or core self in one's daily enterprise." [99] They break authenticity down to four components:

1) awareness: being aware that you possess multifaceted aspects, both good and bad
2) unbiased processing: being honest in your evaluations with regard to yourself
3) behavior: acting in accordance with your values and beliefs, i.e. avoiding hypocrisy 4) relational orientation: being genuine, honest, open, with close others.

They are quick to point out that in certain situations, these components may conflict, in which case one takes priority over another without necessarily rendering one inauthentic, (white-lies etc.). [100]

Being true to our self, or genuine, or to be what-one-is, is complicated, complex, and perhaps even impossible.

(Note that Sartre's "for–itself" or consciousness "is what it is not"). Kernis and Goldman write that concerning "the nature of the "self" that is authentic. [They] believe that it is multifaceted and complex, ever-growing and developing, yet possessing a core that contains one's basic psychological needs (e.g., autonomy, competence, meaning, self-determination), personality characteristics, relational schemas, and values." [101]

I agree to an extent. Our self is a developing process, not a thing. But as far as a core-self is concerned, made up of our psychological needs, as well as our personality characteristics, relational schemas, and values, I believe this to be the product of a multitude of influences, primarily social, coming from others; family, friends, groups, leaders, teachers, etc.

According to Kenneth Gergen's thesis in *The Saturated Self*, "social saturation," has profoundly changed our understanding of the self. The self has become "fragmented," since it corresponds to a "multiplicity of incoherent and disconnected relationships." We are pulled into so many different directions and must play so many different roles, parent, coach, business person, social worker, friend, etc., "that the very concept of an "authentic self" with knowable characteristics recedes from view. The fully saturated self becomes no self at all." [102] Our psychological needs, beliefs; values, and self appraisals depend upon our education and culture which is made up of a multiplicity of influences. Being true to our self somehow implies being true to some particular or generalized other, since values and beliefs only exist in a system of meaning which is dependent upon a social context.

There is another common criticism of the above view of authenticity, one that leads us right back to the importance of recognition. Authenticity -- as being true to one's core values, being in touch with one's true feelings, and as acting with clarity and responsibility -- can lead to instrumentalism, acting in one's own interest, exploiting others or nature, in what is called *ethical subjectivism*. We might say that a sadist, masochist, murderer, terrorist, can be authentic. Many infamous individuals known throughout history could have considered themselves as authentic. They stuck to their core-values right up to the end of their lives. They were probably aware that they had good and bad qualities, acted in accordance with their values and undoubtedly had intimate relationships in their lives.

Some have accused Sartre's philosophy and existential authenticity to be a case of ethical subjectivism, since what is important is acting consistently with one's values, regardless of what those values are. In *Anti-Semite and Jew*, Sartre presents two standard conditions for authenticity, 1) lucid consciousness of one's actions and 2) accepting responsibility for them. The following is a well-known passage. "If it is agreed that man may be defined as a being having freedom within the limits of a situation, then it is easy to see that the exercise of this freedom may be considered as authentic of inauthentic according to the choices made in the situation. Authenticity it is almost needless to say, consists in having a true and lucid consciousness of the situation, in assuming the responsibilities and risks that it involves, in accepting it in pride or humiliation, sometimes in horror and hate." [103]

This is a clear example of ethical subjectivism, as just mentioned. But here again, couldn't a cruel murderer have lucid consciousness of the situation, assume responsibility for his action as well as accept it in pride or humiliation? According to Storm Heter, in his article "*Authenticity and Others: Sartre's Ethics of Recognition*," this would be a gross misinterpretation of Sartre's ethics.

Herter argues that Sartre avoids this subjectivism in several ways. First, being aware of the situation entails being aware of one's role and roles are created in a social context. They are socially constructed identities that involve culturally defined rights and responsibilities. Also, the Anti-Semite, or any oppressor, cannot be authentic because he does not respect others, what Heter calls "a third condition" of authenticity. "An authentic person must recognize the freedom of others. Whereas inauthenticity involves denying one's interdependence upon others, authenticity requires acknowledging the social dimension of self-identity. Self-identities are constructed and validated only though the recognition of other agents. Thus, existential authenticity is not a subjectivist ethical standard." [104]

Sartre is well-known for his claim that man is ultimately free. Of course he was speaking of ontological rather than practical freedom, i.e., freedom to obtain our chosen ends. Man is free in the sense that he can always choose what attitude to adopt within a certain situation. The authentic person must ultimately recognize the ontological freedom of others which is tantamount to recognizing their freedom to think what they please.

If we cannot somehow incorporate the idea of mutual recognition, recognizing as well as being recognized by the other as a free subject, then authenticity as defined above has no ethical value whatsoever. This condition for authenticity will become clear in the following discussion of respect-recognition.

PART IV

MORAL IMPLICATIONS

STEPHEN [rising and looking at him steadily] I know the difference between right and wrong.

UNDERSHAFT [hugely tickled] You don't say so! What! no capacity for business, no knowledge of law, no sympathy with art, no pretension to philosophy; only a simple knowledge of the secret that has puzzled all the philosophers, baffled all the lawyers, muddled all the men of business, and ruined most of the artists: the secret of right and wrong. Why, man, you're a genius, master of masters, a god! At twenty-four," too!

Act 3 Part 1 "Major Barbara"

I appreciate these lines from George Bernard Shaw's play because they perfectly reflect my feelings about morality. I concur with Undershaft's attitude whenever I hear someone claim to know the difference between right and wrong, that they "know in their heart" what is true, that God tells them what they ought to do, or when they speak with unquestionable authority in their moral judgments. Morality and ethics are philosophical subjects I've studied long enough to know how debatable such matters are.

Although I've been emphasizing the importance of recognition for our sense of self, and creating a meaningful existence, I've also been discussing what *is*, rather than what *should be*. I've pointed out the various ways we look for recognition and why we have developed this very vital need. There is a huge presumption in going from a discussion of why or how recognition is important for various individuals, to claiming that we have a duty to recognize one another, turning recognition into a normative concept. However, I do believe that recognition has very significant moral implications inextricably related to other important moral concepts such as equality, justice, fairness, freedom, responsibility and human dignity. It is one of the cornerstones of ethics. Fortunately for me, my position is backed by some of the greatest moral philosophers in European history, most notably Rousseau, Kant, Hegel and Sartre, as well as others.

Chapter IX

Mutual Recognition: Recognition as Respect

As far as moral implications are concerned, I view mutual or reciprocal recognition in much the same way as mutual or reciprocal respect. Throughout my discussion, I've been more or less using recognition in equivocal terms. This is not intentionally ambiguous; it is simply that recognition has many nuances which vary with the context or circumstances in which it's used. Recognition can go from the extremes of simple perception of similarities and differences, to gratitude. As far as recognition in the sense of respect goes, it should be noted that respect is also equivocal.

Stephen Darwall pointed out that two basic notions of respect are either 1) for another person's accomplishments or merit, or 2) for another's status as a person. The former varies from person to person, depending upon the person's character and behavior, and it can vary in degree. Different people are more or less accomplished, and in this sense, some merit more respect and admiration than others. This is what Darwall calls "appraisal respect." The second sense of respect is in recognition of a person's *personhood*; this is what he calls "recognition respect," and this form concerns "not how something is to be evaluated or appraised, but how our relations to it are to be governed. Broadly speaking, we respect something in the recognition sense when we give it standing (authority) in our relations to it." [1] This kind of respect involves the moral standing of individuals as members of a moral community. It is what makes us accountable to others, to respect their freedom as rational human beings and as members of the human race.

This normative sense of recognition, what I'll be calling respect-recognition, seems to have become more important than ever, especially with our current sensitivity to multiculturalism, and basic human rights extending to all individuals of different gender, race, ethnicity, religion, ideology etc. Respect-recognition beckons us to appreciate differences but to respect what we all share in common. Our human community, with the help of modern technology, media and transportation, has gone from our immediate surroundings to the entire world and reciprocal recognition has become increasingly important in order to harmonize world differences while maintaining basic human rights.

Kant, Hegel and Sartre..... to Make my Case

Kant...

Respect-recognition or what was considered mutual recognition was developed in 18th and 19th century moral philosophy, though its roots go back even further. Although Hegel and Sartre speak of recognition as a moral tenet quite explicitly, I'll begin with Kant, whose moral philosophy is implicitly founded on the notion of mutual recognition, in that all people share dignity and merit respect as moral agents with the capacity of reason. "Rational beings are called persons inasmuch as their nature already marks them out as ends in themselves, i.e., as something which is not to be used merely as means and hence there is imposed thereby a limit on all arbitrary use of such beings, which are thus objects of respect." [2]

In order to see how Kant comes to this conclusion, we can begin with his principle that acting morally is acting from a motive of duty rather than love or benevolence. This might seem counterintuitive, but for Kant, if one acts out of altruism, sympathy or love, even if "right and amiable," it is not an action of genuine moral worth, since such actions are a form of self-interest. [3] For example, you might act out of love and sympathy for a friend, and defend her even though she has done wrong or hurt someone else, which would not be acting morally at all according to Kant. On the other hand, he claims that a benevolent or sympathetic action could be moral, but in this case it simply coincides with a universal moral maxim, because the person is fortunate enough to hit upon something right. [4]

For Kant, to be genuinely moral, an agent must act from some principled action based on some universal maxim, which he famously formulated as the Categorical Imperative, "Act only on that maxim through which you can at the same time will that it should become a universal law," or "Act as if the maxim of your action were to become through your will a universal law of nature." [5] Kant's normative theory is often considered the paradigm of deontological, or rule oriented ethics. The Categorical Imperative is founded upon the ideal of agency as well as a rational motivation for creating maxims of conduct rather than considerations of the consequences of behavior. This is the opposite of utilitarianism, which emphasizes maximizing the greatest good for the greatest number.

From here, Kant passes on to the second formulation of the Categorical Imperative, more directly related to the concept of mutual recognition, "act in such a way that you always treat humanity (rational nature,) whether in your own person or in the person of any other, never simply as a means, but always at the same time as an end." [6] For Kant, people are of value, "ends in themselves," because they are first and foremost rational agents with the will and the capacity to act upon reasons, and because they are value-bestowing beings.

As an aside, and in defense of animals and nature, I'd like to add that human beings are perhaps not the only ends-in-themselves. As Joseph Raz pointed out in his book, *Value, Respect and Attachment*, "most likely members of many other animal species who are not moral agents are also ends in themselves, valuable in themselves, and there may be others." [7] I believe animal rights advocates rightly claim that animals are conscious creatures deserving respect. They are *valuers* in that they value things; their food source, their offspring, their habitat, etc., (note, some might say these are not conceptual values but simple needs, but then again, we value what we need). This has been increasingly acknowledged, beginning with the creation of the Society for the Prevention of Cruelty to Animals in the 19th century. It currently extends to the European Union's legal recognition that animals are sentient beings with feelings and consciousness and the establishment of the world-wide organization for protecting animals, PETA. There is even a guarantee for animal rights, in the German constitution.

Kant's moral theory is not without problems and criticism but I'll only mention a couple. Though there is an implicit rule of mutual recognition -- respecting other persons as rational agents -- it must be noted that some people behave more rationally than others. Also, Kant's duty-bound notion of mutual recognition shows little consideration for collective happiness, or the qualities of sympathy, empathy, care and concern in particular situations. Morality however, has *everything* to do with interrelationships and specific individuals in unique situations. It must therefore take more than pure reason into consideration for making moral decisions. I'll discuss the notion of empathy as an important feature of recognition shortly, but first, I'd like to develop Hegel's philosophical reaction to Kant's thesis.

Hegel…

Hegel is one philosopher who explicitly based his moral theory on the concept of recognition. Human consciousness depends upon recognition and maintaining personhood depends upon mutual recognition. But Hegel's sense of recognition extends beyond Kant's emphasis on individuals being rational agents. For him, the interrelation between selves has a more affective foundation of care, esteem, or loving concern as between a mother and child.[8]

Many people are familiar with Hegel's famous master/slave theory, which has been described as an embryonic form of society at large. It expresses the universal dichotomies of freedom and constraint, dominating and dominated, superior and inferior, independent and dependent. I'd like to briefly explain the origin of this theory and discuss Hegel's resolution. He did not pessimistically claim that this is the ultimate human reality, because it is precisely through mutual recognition that we can overcome rivalry and domination and obtain a truly ethical world.

Let's return to the concept of consciousness. Just like contemporary scientists and philosophers, Hegel saw consciousness as having various levels. To review briefly, the first level is "sense certainty." It simply consists of an immediate sensibility to what is present here and now. In order to give unity to this level of simple sensual information processing and in order to act upon it, consciousness must progress to a second level; perception, (classifying objects) and understanding (imposing abstract concepts and laws to help us grasp reality). The third level is self-consciousness, which is primarily expressed in *desire*. We've examined how consciousness of self depends upon other *consciousnesses* in order to exist, from both an anthropological point of view and in terms of psychological development. Hegel's philosophical reasoning confirms this hypothesis.

Hegel's argument is the following. To be conscious of yourself, you need to be conscious of something external to your self, from which to set yourself apart. I define my *self* by distinguishing it from my *not-self*. For Hegel, this is a sort of love-hate relationship between ourselves and objects in the world expressed in desire, "self-consciousness is desire." [9] You desire something and wish to possess it or transform it into being yours, removing its "foreignness." But once possessed, consumed (like food and material goods), it is no longer there and we are again dissatisfied and our desire is renewed. (We are reminded here, of the second Buddhist noble truth: desire leads to dissatisfaction). The self as a reflection of the object, is therefore as transitory as the consumed object and lacks permanence and unity.

Consciousness needs to see itself in something that is enduring and familiar, unlike inanimate things. It needs another consciousness to provide unity, to be more than just fleeting disassociated perceptions. According to Hegel, in order to recognize itself as a self, consciousness must see itself as "Ego that is "we", a plurality of Egos, and "we" that is a single Ego."[10] In other words, my *self*, is constructed by other selves, and these other selves construct my *self.* Individuals can only recognize themselves by recognizing others, which implies mutual recognition. For Hegel, self-consciousness is *selbstbewusstsein,* which in German means being "self-assured," quite unlike the English connotation of self-consciousness as embarrassment. Other consciousnesses "assure" my self-consciousness.

But this state of mutual recognition, between two or more self-consciousnesses, is difficult to achieve and maintain. In the *Phenomenology,* on "recognitive self-consciousness," Hegel describes the process whereby each individual consciousness is an object for the other, and thus inferior, struggling to become a subject for the other, recognized as independent and free,[11] which implies making the other an object.

But why, we might ask, can't each self-conscious individual simply recognize the autonomy of the other and be satisfied without this struggle and combat? The answer, says Hegel, is that each person is imprisoned in his own natural, corporal being, wanting to be seen as an autonomous self, pure and unattached, without need of the other. In this respect, you might assume that the individual wants the death of the other, a complete annihilation in order to declare himself as the victor in the combat. But this is not the case, since by annihilating the other; he would then destroy his only source of recognition. The other person is essential to one's being; "to be" is to be recognized.

So the only possible outcome is an unequal relationship of a victor and loser, master and slave. But this too will prove to be an unsatisfactory situation for the master as well as the slave. For one thing, the master needs recognition from the slave, but a slave cannot give the master true recognition as a free subject because he has been reduced to a mere thing, an object. Secondly, the slave is actively engaged with the world, servicing and producing while the master, who is in control, is nonetheless passive and dependent upon the slave for satisfaction. As for the slave, he or she is also dissatisfied for the obvious reasons of having no freedom, control, nor recognition from the master as an autonomous subject.

This original master/slave situation, as described by Hegel is prior to social formation. It has its roots in the philosophy of Rousseau who blamed civilization for the ills of humanity. Like other living creatures, persons in a state of nature were neither good nor bad, but unlike other animals, humans possessed free will and a potential for perfectibility. While living in small clans, experiencing family love, with an equitable division of labor and sharing of goods; peace and happiness reigned. Rousseau wrote in *The Discourse on the Origins of Inequality,* "Free and independent as men were before, they were now, in consequence of a multiplicity of new wants, brought into subjection, as it were, to all nature, and particularly to one another; and each became in some degree a slave even in becoming the master of other men: if rich, they stood in need of the services of others; if poor, of their assistance…"[12]

With the growing inequalities between men, the results were not only physical and material inequality, but a psychological undermining of everyone's sense of self-worth. In Chapter 1 of *The Social Contract*, Rousseau famously claimed, "Man is born free; but everywhere he is in chains. One thinks himself the master of others, and still remains a greater slave than they."[13] Individuals were driven to seek recognition, but it was in the sense of *amour-propre*, a competitive, comparative need for self-esteem, a transformation from an original *amour de soi*, a positive self-love. Inequality, in Rousseau's line of thinking, is the source of merit-based recognition. Both Kant and Hegel tried to rectify this imbalance by formulating a sense of recognition that supersedes inequality and human differences, showing that the social structure is a way of overcoming the imbalance rather than its cause.

Hegel's theory of mutual recognition was not only expressed implicitly by Kant, but also explicitly by Fichte

(1762-1814). For Fichte, self-consciousness was not possible without recognizing the existence of other free self-consciousnesses. Self-consciousness requires that one identifies oneself as distinct from others, and presupposes that others do the same. However, Fichte did not explain how an explanation of self-consciousness through recognizing the consciousness of others *requires* us to recognize their autonomy and freedom. Hegel attempted to do so, and though I agree with his conclusion, he did no better than Fichte for supplying a logical argument. In the *Phenomenology*, Hegel jumps from his argument explaining the imbalanced master/slave relationship, to his theory that society can offer the ideal of mutual recognition. We arrive at an ideal state in which everyone, master and slave, seem to have come to their senses, with no clear explanation as to how. "Universal self-consciousness is the affirmative awareness of self in an other self: each self as a free individuality has his own 'absolute' independence, yet in virtue of the negation of its immediacy or appetite without distinguishing itself from that other. Each is thus universal self-consciousness and objective; each has 'real' universality in the shape of reciprocity, so far as each knows itself recognized in the other free man, and is aware of this in so far as it recognizes the other and knows him to be free." [14]

Similar to Kant, Hegel affirms that it is *reason* that reveals the universal truth of intersubjective consciousness.[15] But, there must be more to the concept of mutual recognition as a moral foundation than reason alone. A moral theory based on pure practical reasoning, though it can give us a bare universal form of moral law, can't tell us specifically what we ought to do or how to relate to others in practical situations. This is what Hegel set about doing in *The Philosophy of Right*.

In The *Philosophy of Right*, Hegel turned towards ethics and politics. He developed his theory of recognition in the context of practical life, domestic, economic, legal, and political, by using his theory to account for values in the institutions of "The Family," "Civil Society" and "The State." In Part Three, "The Ethical Life," of the *Philosophy of Right*, he described how various levels of recognition, some more abstract and some more concrete were institutionalized in these different structures of society. The increasingly demanding patterns of recognition that are developed by Hegel are not only too complicated to discuss here, but in addition, practical family life, economy and citizenship have changed so much in the last 200 years, that the specifics of his analysis have much less relevance in today's world.

In his article on *Recognition and Moral Obligation*, Axel Honneth refers to Hegel's three-part division in the *Philosophy of Right*, to work out his own positive meaning of recognition for morality, "human subjects can develop an intact self-relation only by virtue of the fact that they see themselves affirmed or recognized according to the value of certain capabilities and rights." [16] He points out that Hegel needed to go beyond the reciprocal recognition of Kant, which was based on universal reason and duty, by adding two other dimensions: 1) love, wherein subjects recognize each other in terms of their needs to attain emotional security, and 2) ethical life on a state level, in which there is a form of recognition allowing for mutual esteem between subjects in forming a social order.

Honneth presents three forms of recognition that reflect Hegel's three part division in the *Philosophy of Right*. The first is a form of recognition that assures our self-confidence; the individual is recognized as one "whose needs and desires are of unique value to another person," wherein we find the moral notions of care or love. The second relation to self is in terms of self-respect, in which "the individual is recognized as a person who is ascribed the same moral accountability as every other human being," which includes the Kantian concept of moral-respect. Thirdly, there is self-worth or self-esteem, in which case "the individual is recognized as a person whose capabilities are of constitutive value to a concrete community." [17]

These different forms of recognition that affirm our self-relations, are more abstract than the institutions that Hegel presented in *The Ethical Life*, but they do reflect what he had in mind. For example, in "'The Family,'" recognition should exist in the relationship of parents to children and between friends in terms of love and care. In "Civil Society," recognition should exist on the level of universal equal treatment with the same moral accountability for all persons, and in "The State," individuals are recognized in terms of their value to the community as far as they participate jointly in a common project. For both Honneth and Hegel, a morality of recognition means recognizing individuals for some aspect of their personal integrity as human beings, which applies to all persons. As Honneth says, a common understanding of the function of morality is "as a collective institution for securing our personal integrity, but the justification of moral rights and duties themselves can be conducted only with regard to the rights of all individuals." [18]

Sartre...

Hegel's influence can be seen quite clearly in the philosophy of Sartre, as Storm Herter pointed out in *"Authenticity and Others: Sartre's Ethics of Recognition."* There are two very clear examples of Hegelian recognition as a moral concept in Sartre's philosophy. Firstly, in Sartre's work, *Anti-Semite and Jew,* he presents a situation much like Hegel's master/slave relationship. Secondly, in *What is Literature?* we have a case for Hegel's ideal of mutual recognition. As we will see, both are based upon the notion of freedom of choice as the essence of being human.

In his work *Anti-Semite and Jew,* which exposes a blatant case of *bad faith*, Sartre exposes an oppressive relationship between the anti-Semite and the Jew that reflects Hegel's master-slave relationship of one-sided recognition. The anti-Semite is like the master, who demands that the slave recognizes him as a free agent, and the Jew is like the slave whose freedom as an agent is refused. But the anti-Semite depends upon the Jew and "finds the existence of the Jew absolutely necessary. Otherwise to whom would he be superior?" [19] This is not just a case of refusing practical freedom because as with Hegel, self-identity requires social validation as a free agent which the Jew is refused. Any recognition from the oppressed, slave or Jew is not genuine because it is not given as a free choice. This was the thesis that Hegel developed in the *Philosophy of Right*. Likewise for Sartre, as Herter writes, "according to Sartre the oppressive relationship is not an absence of recognition per se, but an absence of mutual recognition." [20]

In *What is Literature?* we're presented with a good example of mutual recognition. Rather than an unsymmetrical master/slave relationship, we find that artist and audience, writer and reader are in a pact of mutual respect. As a writer, one has a certain obligation towards one's public, a social role of responsibility towards the reader. Moreover, there is mutual interdependence, since a writer depends upon the reader to the same extent that a reader depends upon the author. As Herter points out, "Sartre might have just as easily used the model of conversation to describe mutual recognition. Speaking requires someone to be spoken to, and listening requires listening to someone." [21]

The point is that between consenting persons, there is not a demand or requirement for recognition, as between a master and a slave, but an appeal or request. There is a solicitation on the part of the author, or speaker, and cooperation from the reader or listener. As Herter says, "the act of requesting preserves the other's independence, since a request builds in the possibility that the other may refuse." [22] The role of writer and reader are roles that accept the other as an intentional free subject. This mutual recognition can be applied to many social roles, family roles, professional roles and even political roles, as between countries. These various forms of mutual recognition are much like what Hegel developed in the *Philosophy of Right* in his description of familial, civil, and state-based roles.

Moreover, what validates our social roles and binds them into a relationship of mutual recognition is a joint project. For example, an author and reader are co-dependently bound in the project of a book, parents and their children are bound in the project of a family, a political leader and his constituents are joined in the project of legislative reform. Interpreting Sartre, I believe there is a relationship between his concept of a joint project and his concept of a "fundamental project," as discussed in *Being and Nothingness*. A fundamental-project is an individual choice of self which is reflected in particular situations. Sartre says that, "in each inclination, in each tendency the person expresses himself completely." [23] We choose and construct our self throughout our lives. We recognize ourselves and are recognized by others in various ways, by what we do and what we have, in our relationships, activities, work, and possessions. As pointed out in the first section, these are all ways and means of recognition that contribute to our self-construction.

I find that Sartre's fundamental-project and a joint project are related since it is through joint projects, or interaction and cooperation with others -- when we recognize other persons as free agents, with various aims, projects and values -- that we are able to realize our individual fundamental projects. In the terms of Kant, it would be a manifestation of each person's "end-setting capacity."

In a similar vein, in "*Respect, Recognition and Public Reason*," James Boettcher says that "from the more philosophically modest standpoint of political liberalism, we should simply say that others are committed to various aims, projects, and values, whatever their ultimate source, and that such aims, projects, and values are central to each person's identity and self-understanding." However, he adds that in considering the source of these aims, projects and values "there is an individual choice of self but within a necessary cultural and social dimension, deriving from common practices, traditional values, beliefs, and doctrines bound up with our roles and institutions within a social group." [24]

There is a notable problem with the moral arguments of Johann Fichte, Hegel, and Sartre for universal mutual recognition. None of them supplied a *logical* reason for recognizing the other's freedom. But again, it seems to me that supplying a logical reason is analogous to looking for a logical reason for any other human relationship; love, concern, understanding, as well as hate, contempt, or indifference. Human emotions and relationships are not necessarily logical. Mutually recognizing each other as free human subjects is good for people and good for the human species in an emotional and practical sense, regardless of logic. Mutual recognition feels good. If our sense of well-being, identity, the validity of our aims and projects, and our human dignity are dependent upon the affirmative recognition of others, do we need a logical argument to prove that it is immoral when such recognition is withheld?

Chapter X

Non-Recognition II, Denying the Other as Other

In Avishai Margalit's distinguished book, *The Decent Society,* he implicitly discusses the importance of recognition in negative terms by identifying ways in which individuals are injured or humiliated. By exploring the contradicttory aspects of human dignity, he arrives at a positive concept of recognition. Margalit describes Hegel's master/slave relationship in terms of humiliation and respect. "Humiliation is intended both to prove absolute superiority and to win recognition, which is a conceptual impossibility. Absolute superiority can be achieved only with regard to what is not human; recognition can be attained only from other humans."[25]

Slavery, exploitation, torture, and genocide are but a few examples of our human history of non-recognition. The tragic treatment of our fellow human beings, treating others as subhuman, is more than likely a product of cultural education says Margalit. "Just as there are partially color-blind people, there are also people who are blind to the human aspect in others." [26] This can be relatively mild stigmatization, as when we mock the strange or deformed, or it can be devastating, as in extreme racial or religious prejudice. The deplorable aspect of such non-recognition is, as Sartre said, that one must "treat man as a dog, by first recognizing him as a man."[27] As both Hegel and Sartre pointed out, and as history has proven, non-recognition or rejection requires recognizing people as human first. Humiliation and injury is the result of refusing recognition to those who are conscious of being treated inhumanely. Slaves in the South are a telling example. The following is a quote from a book of actual testimonies from slaves before the Civil War.

> *"To be a slave. To know, despite the suffering and deprivation, that you were human, more human than he who said you were not human. To know joy, laughter, sorrow, and tears and yet be considered only the equal of a table. To be a slave was to be a human being under conditions in which that humanity was denied. They were no slaves. They were people. Their condition was slavery. They who were held as slaves looked upon themselves and the servitude in which they found themselves with the eyes and minds of human beings, conscious of everything that happened to them, conscious of all that went on around them. Yet slaves are often pictured as little more than dumb, brute animals, whole sole attributes were found in working, singing, and dancing."* [28]

Even though the slaves were treated as subhuman they were none-the-less baptized in church. There was therefore at least a spark of recognition for their potential humanity in order to treat them inhumanely. For Margalit, his "central claim is that humiliation typically presupposed the humanity of the humiliated. Humiliating behavior rejects the other as nonhuman, but the act of rejection presupposes that it is a person that is being rejected." [29] A decent society for Margalit is one in which every subject has a sense of being recognized as a member of the human community. This is where there is a moral difference between mistreating people and mistreating animals. With all due respect to animals, they cannot be insulted or humiliated as people can. Victimized animals, unlike humans, do not have "accusing eyes." [30]

There are other forms of non-recognition, less heinous than slavery or the countless cases of oppression, torture, or genocide. Simple lack of respect for a person as a person, overlooking significant features of his life and details that he feels pertinent to his identity can cause both anxiety and a loss of self. I agree with Harry Frankfurt who said that when a person is treated as insignificant it is "an assault upon his reality." …. "It is as though, in denying him suitable respect, his very existence is reduced." [31] This was the point made in the song "Mr. Cellophane," from the musical *Chicago*, when the melancholic Amos sang, "Mr. Cellophane should have been my name, Mr. Cellophane, 'cause you can look right through me, walk right by me, and never know I'm there." Not being noticed, not being taken into consideration, treated with indifference or totally ignored, leads to despondence, depression and a destabilized sense of self.

Another good illustration of this form of non-recognition is in my favorite modern play, *Waiting for Godot* by Samuel Beckett. One of the most overlooked but very important roles in this play is that of the "Boy." Throughout the play, the two bums, Vladimir and Estragon are waiting in a sort of limbo-nowhere-land waiting for Godot. To their great chagrin and existential pain, they are visited from time to time by a young boy who fails to recognize them each time he returns. I was not surprised to read in *The Philosophy of Beckett,* that recognition is an important and recurrent theme for Beckett. John Calder writes, "Everyone has to know that in some way he or she matters, that the life lived has some point. The need to be recognized and remembered becomes the motivation behind the creation of new concepts about human life and destiny, surfacing many times in Beckett's work." [32]

The point that has been made by both 19th century and contemporary moral philosophers is that mutual recognition is important for man's essence as a conscious agent with beliefs, values and aims. This is a recognition that should be accorded unconditionally to all human beings. According to this Kantian premise, even wrongdoers and villains must be accorded a minimum of recognition. Our justice system is based on the principle that captured criminals, no matter how evil, must be treated as "ends in themselves" -- they are due a fair trial. This is the founding principal for any declaration of human rights. It must guarantee certain basic rights due to all persons, regardless of age, gender, ethnicity, beliefs, etc., simply in virtue of being human. This is an egalitarian and universal requirement.

This concept of equal justice is the basis of all our modern ethical systems. There is perhaps nothing so infuriating and psychologically unbearable as injustice.

Even very young children know quickly, almost instinctively, when something is "not fair." Blatant injustice is something that doesn't need to be taught. In fact, the Categorical Imperative could be considered as having its roots in animal nature. Our distant ancestors the primates possess what is called "inequity aversion." Frans de Waal, who has done extensive study of primate behavior, has shown that there is solid evidence of "strong reciprocity." [33] There is a universal belief that there should be equal treatment between members of the group, and experiments have shown that most primates and even dogs are sensitive to injustice. A minimum of egalitarianism undoubtedly evolved because it encouraged cooperation. It was in the best interest of everyone to discourage exploitation and free-riding.

We all want fairness and justice. Equal respect and recognition are vital human needs. However, equality is not a value in itself and recognition-respect without appraisal-respect might hinder rather than promote the welfare of the human condition. Harry Frankfurt in his article *Equality and Respect*, says that "the widespread conviction that equality itself and as such has some basic value as an independently important moral ideal is not only mistaken. It is an impediment to the identification of what truly is of fundamental moral and social worth." [34] Equality is a necessary value but it must be accompanied by other values that take into accordance our differences in order for there to be true justice.

When someone demands equal treatment, it is in terms of what he shares with all other persons, not what is specific to him personally, his own needs and interests or his own particular situation. Frankfurt claims that a concern for being equal even "tends to alienate people from themselves," and inhibits authenticity by ignoring their own personal nature, ambitions and character. "Someone who insists that he be treated equally is calculating his demands on the basis of what other people have rather than on the basis of what will accord with the realities of his own condition and most suitably provide for his own interests and needs." [35]

On one hand, insisting on being treated equally seems justified, especially when "what other people have" are the basic necessities for survival. The drama of unequal or underdeveloped societies, in which people are dying of hunger or are oppressed, is that people are not treated equally for even the simplest of needs; such as food, and shelter. As we said earlier, authenticity is not a preoccupation when you are starving. Such societies are not "decent" in Margalit's terms. However, when the general condition of the society becomes more comfortable, more decent and civil, we "up the ante," to go beyond free education, police protection, health care, retirement funds, etc., and expect a two-car garage, a flat screen television, and various other commodities. In this case, Frankfurt might argue that our individual interests and needs are no longer equal. Our capacities, efforts, goals and aims quite naturally differ and equal treatment in all domains is not only unrealistic, but in some cases, quite unjust.

Our individual differences inspired Nietzsche to challenge Kant's deontological ethics of universal equality. His radical view was that it was a moral error to think that every individual was a free and autonomous agent, responsible for his actions. There is a natural hierarchy among people, some are superior to others, some more capable of achievement than others. Nietzsche claimed that morality was born of resentment on the part of the inferior and less incapable, who were envious of the superior and accomplished. He bemoaned the fact that religion and moral philosophy turned what he called the "natural hierarchy" on its head, valuing the weak and devaluing the strong. Morality, for Nietzsche, should be based on merit, not on basic equality. Obviously for Nietzsche, appraisal-respect is more important than recognition-respect, since he found the notion of good as coming from those "belonging to the highest rank, in contradistinction to all that was base, low-minded and plebeian." [36] He took Rousseau's *amour propre*, which led to competition, self-comparison, and an urge for power, and turned it into a virtue.

But before condemning Nietzsche as some kind of insensitive moral fascist, it must be noted that for him, the noble character traits that we should admire and promote are not necessarily egotistical and self-serving. They are on the contrary, positive in a humanitarian sense, and belong to people with a sort of Kantian "good will." They are people who are realistic, honest with themselves, express warmth and care towards their fellow humans. Nietzsche's unpopular assertion was that "the noble lives before his own conscience with confidence and frankness," and "it is the "superior" man who "has veneration for his enemy" and "such veneration is already a bridge to love." [37]

Nietzsche was not the first philosopher to challenge the notion of a universal moral law which required reciprocity and the mutual respect. His emphasis on prioritizing a noble character has its roots in ancient Greek philosophy. Aristotle who had no deontological, rule-bound doctrine of universal morality said that ethical knowledge was based upon wisdom and judgment and could not be systemized. In ancient Greek philosophy, the emphasis was on the cultivation of a strong and noble character rather than criterions of right and wrong, or the inculcation of moral rules. In fact, Aristotle emphasized the importance of an integrated social life, friendship and personal relationships as essential to virtue and a satisfying life.

This brings us back to the importance of esteem or what we've been calling appraisal-recognition. When we seek the esteem-recognition of others, it's not just any others we encounter, but those whom we esteem ourselves. Esteem from people we value renders us conscious of our personal merit and intrinsic worth. For example, a writer who is held in esteem by other writers, a farmer by other farmers, a scientist by other scientists, an adolescent by other adolescents, feels that the esteem is merited to a far greater extent than if judged by someone who is not part of his group or has no familiarity with the extent of his achievements.

Chapter XI

A Psychological Approach
to Moral Recognition

The two ethical systems I've been discussing, one based on a universal moral law, the other based on individual character and particular situations, can also be found in psychological theories concerning moral development. I'll just briefly consider two lines of thought and their bearing on mutual recognition.

In the late 1950's, Lawrence Kohlberg developed a three-level, six-stage theory of moral development, inspired by the famous Swiss child psychologist Jean Piaget who argued that moral thinking was related to cognitive development. Kohlberg proposed that "universal and regular age trends of development may be found in moral judgment, and these have a formal cognitive base." [38] Kohlberg's first level is "pre-conventional" (stage 1); when children associate what is right and wrong based on reward and punishment. Stage 2 is based on some basic notions of reciprocity, and fairness, "I'll scratch your back if you scratch mine." Level two is "conventional" (stage 3); what constitutes right or good is what others approve of or what conforms to other's expectations. Stage 4 means accepting social rules according to some authority and doing one's duty. Level three is "post-conventional" (stage 5); when there is some sensitivity to different beliefs and values, although morality is still based on socially agreed rules and laws. In the final and highest level of moral reasoning, (stage 6), what is right is based on universal moral principles and abstract reasoning.

These stages of moral development reflect cognitive development as a product of socialization, and are quite similar from one society or culture to another. The latter stages of moral development are in no way inevitable, since individual and social circumstances differ. Moral development may be retarded or arrested at any point. But as we can see, the final stages of moral development coincide with Kantian ethics of moral reasoning and universal moral principles. Level 6, the final stage, implies an ethics of universal justice.

In reaction to Kohlberg's theory, one of his protégés, Carol Gilligan, in her book, *In a Different Voice*, observed that Kohlberg's theory did not take into account a difference of gender since his studies of moral development were based upon boys. She conducted her own studies of both girls and boys and found that girls and women tended to cluster more in Kolberg's Stage 3 of development, which emphasizes pleasing others. Her studies led her to conclude that there were decidedly two different themes or "voices" when thinking about ethics. She called those whose moral judgment corresponded with Kohlberg's categories an "ethics of rights" as opposed to a more supple approach, an "ethics of care." These ethical voices are not *necessarily* male or female but there is a tendency according to empirical observation, for boys to express the former and girls the latter. Obviously, Gilligan was aware that men *feel* and women *think*, so there is no gender exclusivity concerning these two moral attitudes, one more emotionally based and the other more rationally based.

I believe that these two psychological theories correspond to the positions in moral philosophy I've been discussing. The "ethics of right" is universalistic, in that it is more concerned with "the elaboration of rules and the development of fair procedures for adjudicating conflicts." [39] I would add that the ethics-of-right corresponds closely with Kantian ethics, or what we've been calling respect-recognition. On the other hand, Gilligan's "ethics of care," brings in a very important emotive element, which is somewhat associable with appraisal-recognition, since it emphasizes particularities rather than universalities or how a person judges a particular person in a situation. Gilligan pointed out that we have responsibilities towards others in terms of care that cannot be simplified to principles of universal justice. Whereas male morality has a "justice orientation," female morality has a "responsibility orientation," and whereas males are more concerned with establishing a hierarchy, women are concerned with connecting with one another. "The morality of rights is predicated on equality and centered on the understanding of fairness, while the ethic of responsibility relies on the concept of equity, the recognition of differences in need."[40]

How we evaluate a situation and how we decide to act ethically, is often based on an emotive rather than cognitive judgment. Instead of resorting to a categorical principle, we might say "I don't know, it depends upon the situation." But rather than arriving at a moral relativism, a problem we noted earlier, (good & right = my belief & opinion) Gilligan says that woman's reluctance to judge categorically is a recognition of the complexities of real-world situations and how each individual's experience is unique. "An ethics of care is a psychological logic of relationships, which contrasts with the formal logic of fairness that informs the justice approach" [41] In the end, even if we respond emotively and thus subjectively, there can still be an implicit general principle behind our decision. "Care becomes the self-chosen principle of a judgment that remains psychological in its concern with relationships and response but becomes universal in its condemnation of exploitation and hurt." [42] For example, if we spontaneously act to help a lost child, we are helping a particular child in a particular circumstance, but we would probably help any child in a similar circumstance.

In her book *Feminist Morality, Transforming culture, society, and politics*, Virginia Held discusses a feminist transformation of moral concepts. She exposes three aspects that reflect the dominance of a male point of view in traditional ethics:

1) the split between reason and emotion
2) the public and private distinction
3) our concept of the self. [43]

Concerning (1), the split between reason and emotion, Held elaborates upon Gilligan's former argument in which males tend to aggregate towards a more rational view of ethics and females a more emotional view. As for aspect (2), the distinction between the public and private; the familiar view is one in which man transcends his human nature by occupying the public realm, while women occupy the private realm, i.e., the household, fulfilling the natural function of reproducing and mothering. In other words, the male public world transcends animal nature whereas women are seen as being closer to nature and relatively excluded from the domain of public life. However, this doesn't exclude women from the public realm since as Held argues, "human mothering shapes language and culture, it forms human social personhood, it develops mortality." [44] As for aspect (3), a concept of self, Held believes that the paradigm of the mother-child relationship, which is mutually empathetic, may be extended to a "larger relational unit." This relationship does not imply a loss of self and autonomy, but is a "relationship of mutuality in which self and other both express an understanding of each other's subjectivity." [45] The self comes to be defined in relation to others. Held's feminist view of moral concepts is reminiscent of what was discussed earlier, both in the Shinto-Buddhist ontology of the concept of self as collectivist, co-extensive and interdependent, and in Hegel's inclusion of the family, in which love and care is an important element in an ethical life that can be extended into civil society and the state.

Empathetic Recognition, Feeling vs. Rationale

Empathy has been a popular subject lately and a number of distinguished thinkers have pointed out its importance. I'm including it in a discussion of moral implications because empathy is a form of recognition that we consider virtuous or of moral worth. As was pointed out earlier, the word empathy has to do with our ability to understand how another person thinks and feels. Empathy is an ability to imagine oneself in the condition or predicament of another person, to vicariously feel what he or she feels. It is clearly a form of recognition i.e., empathetic-recognition. As the psychology professor Martin Hoffman said, empathy is "the involvement of psychological processes that make a person have feelings that are more congruent with another's situation than with his own situation." [46]

It's important to note that empathy has both a cognitive and an emotional component. When I spoke about the development of a theory of mind, I emphasized the cognitive aspect, when children learn that others have a different point of view or perspective from their own. We usually consider this a learned capacity. However, empathy seems to be basic to our nature as the experiments of the Swedish psychologist Ulf Dimberg showed; we don't decide to be empathetic, we just are. For example, we spontaneously smile when others smile and frown when they frown, which is exactly what Dimberg's experiments proved. People mimicked photos of smiling or frowning faces with a smile or frown, even when the photos were flashed too fast for conscious perception.[47] Similarly, the psychologist Lipps, who popularized the term empathy, pointed out that it is like an "instinct," and as Jeremy Rifken says, there is mounting evidence that humans are "wired for empathy." [48] In fact, recent cognitive research has explored the hypothesis of cerebral wiring. The neuroscientist Marco Iacoboni has proposed that a "core imitation circuitry" in our brains, simulates the emotional expressions of others, which activates our limbic system, causing an observer to feel what another is feeling.[49]

Looking at human evolution, it is evident that human empathy has its roots in animal behavior and was important for our survival. In all mammalian species, mothers are immediately reactive to their babies, whether they're cubs, calves or kittens. The babies of unresponsive mothers were less likely to survive so genes of unresponsiveness were not passed on. Furthermore, as Frans de Waals points out, "having descended from a long line of mothers who nursed, fed, cleaned, carried, comforted and defended their young, we should not be surprised by gender differences in human empathy." [50] This fits in perfectly with the feminist morality of Virginia Held, who emphasized the importance of a relational-self, "maternal thinking," and "natural sentiments," [51] as well as Gilligan's observation that woman have a "responsibility orientation." This emotive responsiveness is not exclusively feminine, and it will probably continue to become more balanced between men and women in the future as we progressively share social roles more equally.

In any case, the origin of empathy logically seems to come from parental care. It is our limbic system, the emotional part of our brain that allowed us to have feelings of pleasure and affection that as it evolved, prepared us for family life, friendship and caring relationships. We are social animals for whom bonding is essential. I appreciate the de Waals comment that, "We have a tendency to describe the human condition in lofty terms, such as a quest for freedom or striving for a virtuous life, but the life sciences hold a more mundane view: It's all about security, social companionships, and a full belly." [52] (I find it interesting to reflect on how Aristotle might have modified his vision of human virtue in light of Darwinian evolutionary theory).

De Waals' extensive research incontestably shows that animals, from mice to elephants to chimpanzees, all demonstrate empathy. It is not unique to humans. "Empathy engages brain areas that are more than a hundred million years old. The capacity arose long ago with motor mimicry and emotional contagion, after which evolution added layer after layer, until our ancestors not only felt what others felt, but understood what others might want or need," writes de Waals. [53] Empathy, along with compassion, gratitude, sympathy, altruism, fairness, trust, cooperation is every bit as old and as important for our survival as a species as self-interest, strength and competition.

On the other hand, just as we noticed with self-esteem, there is also ironically and sadly, a "dark side" to empathy. If we think about sadists; those who humiliate, maim, or torture, we must admit that they are empathetic to the other's suffering. That is exactly the point. They are able to take satisfaction or even pleasure in another's suffering because empathy has both a cognitive and an emotional component. We can know intellectually how the other feels and remain emotionally detached, without *actually* feeling their pain, and thus show no compassion or pity. The newspaper and television brings us stories of war, famine, oppression, and national disaster every day, but we have become more or less emotionally inured to other's suffering. We may find it horrible or even tragic, but we seldom break down in tears. Like doctors or social workers who see so much suffering every day, we remain cognitively aware but emotionally detached.

However, the closer the problem, the more we feel for those involved. When something happens to loved ones or close friends, seeing them suffer or hearing their story, we actually feel their pain. In fact, part of the talent of a good writer or film director is to put us into the skin of another. We can easily be moved to tears reading a good book or seeing a great film (in my case, even Disney's Bambi or Pinocchio I'm ashamed to admit), because we really do identify emotionally. In her book *Poetic Justice*, the philosopher Martha Nussbaum made the point that reading good novels actually helped to make us better citizens as they made us more sensitive to social issues. So, as a result of cognitive and emotional empathetic recognition, there are occasions when we are actually moved to act upon our feelings of empathy. Millions of people were moved to help in response to recent natural disasters, tsunamis, hurricanes, earthquakes, especially since we were exposed to on-the-spot films and first-hand stories of victims. But in the case of actually helping others, it is probably much more frequent when our own family, close friends or other members of our group are involved.

The advantage of modern technology, the wide accessibility of the Internet for example, is that it can bring us closer together. Distant problems become near and actual, here and now. In spite of that, the danger with technology is that it can also estrange us. In modern societies, we see more and more people interacting with their mobile devices than with other people. In the U.S., tests for empathy have fallen sharply since 2000, very likely from a lack of face-to-face time. Today's narcissist younger generation not only lack the empathy that allows them to feel concerned for others, but even to intellectually understand the other's points of view.[54]

These observations concerning empathy have been developed by the psychologist Paul Ekman, who divided empathy up into several types; the first is "cognitive empathy," the second is "emotional empathy," and the third, when we are moved to action, "compassionate empathy." [55] I would add that the degree to which we empathize cognitively, emotionally or compassionately, is relative to the degree to which we recognize the other, not as a virtual image but as a flesh and blood human being. As mentioned above with non-recognition, when we refuse to recognize others we turn off our empathetic mode. When another person is only virtual or considered sub-human, as slaves or enemies of war, we are capable of acting atrociously, not so much from cruelty as from indifference.

Chapter XII

The Ambiguity of Mutual Recognition: The Never Ending Dilemma

We have been considering recognition as a moral concept enlightened by various philosophical and psychological theories. They confirm our common sense intuition that justice, fairness, and human dignity are founded upon mutual recognition. Nonetheless, we have seen a repeated dichotomy, two opposing but complementary levels upon which mutual recognition functions. The first takes into consideration how we are alike as human beings in our nature and in our needs, irrespective of individual differences. The second is based on how we are not alike, recognizing persons as separate and unique individuals who merit respect for their differences. All individuals are due equal recognition with respect to their personhood, as free, intentional agents. However, each particular individual merits recognition for his or her personal and distinct capacities, efforts and accomplishments. For example, it's commonly believed that those who put in more time and effort deserve greater reward. A child who works harder at school expects better grades than a child who is lazy and skips classes. A worker who produces ten times more than a co-worker who makes no effort expects better pay. If effort and accomplishment are not rewarded, we claim that it's "not fair," to the same extent that inequality is not fair.

Complete egalitarianism is impossible since humans are not all equal in physical or mental capability. There will always be some outperforming others, stronger, smarter, or richer. Some hierarchy naturally exists, from insects to animal packs, to primate communes, and isolated hunter-gathering societies. However, such differences tend to be mild.[56] They are tolerated as natural differences and the group continues to function harmoniously.

Perhaps what has gone terribly amuck in certain modern societies is that there are countless examples of a small privileged wealthy elite supported by a majority who work hard and gain little relative to their labor. We feel infuriated with the inordinate wealth that is gained by CEO's, bankers, financial managers, traders, etc. Do they deserve millions of times more than the rest of us? As Natalie Angier, has pointed out, Homo sapiens naturally have an innate distaste for extremes in hierarchy, as it violates our sense of fairness, that "is both cerebral and visceral, cortical and limbic," that is to say both an affront to our sense of logic and a negative stimulus on our emotions.[57] Extreme unfairness ticks off the amygdala, the ancient seat of outrage and aggression in the brain. Unfortunately today, according to recent and frequently published data, there is the widest rich-poor income gap on record in the United States. The land of opportunity and equality now has the largest disparity of any Western nation, and this trend is not only firmly entrenched but on the rise. Unfortunately, there is no easy solution for this economic disparity that is increasing around the world, as inequality begets more inequality.

Justice is an unending ethical dilemma, which is reflected in my opening statement from Shaw's play. As far as recognition as a moral concept is concerned, we need both respect- recognition and appraisal-recognition; recognition for what we share in common, our basic human rights, and recognition for our capacities and accomplishments and what makes us unique individuals.

Conclusion

It was difficult for me to find a sub-title for this book. Recognition is such a vast subject; it ranges from perceiving similarities and differences to mutual respect. Any aspect of it could constitute a book in itself.

I have claimed that recognition is the key to identity. There is of course no single feature of human life that creates our identity. But I hope to have successfully argued that recognition plays a major role in constructing what we call our *self*. It is not an exhaustive discussion of the subject, but ideally, a substantive introduction to the many ways in which we seek recognition and why it is important to creating self-consciousness.

In my introduction, I said that I waver between a Darwinian determinism and Sartrean existentialism. This may or may not have been evident throughout this work. However, you might have noticed that when I mentioned the word *choice,* I put the word in italics or pointed out its equivocal nature. I believe that our choices in life are always more-or-less free choices. We are made just as much as we make ourselves. The first three parts of this book should clarify this affirmation.

There were several times I mentioned the influence of both nature (what we inherit genetically) and nurture (our early education and life experiences). These are two elements that determine our identity; and two factors in our lives that we did not willfully choose. They influence the way in which we are recognized and contribute to our identity.

On the other hand, I do not completely defend determinism. Opposing determinism, existentialists declare the fact of "existence before essence." Existentialism purports that human beings have no ready-made essence; they progressively define themselves as they exist. This is why I continually emphasize the importance of consciousness in a discussion of recognition. Through consciousness, we create value and bestow meaning in our lives.

The first part of this book is an attempt to explain how everything that contributes to a person's identity comes through recognition from others in a social milieu. What makes me who I am, my physical body, the objects I own, the work I do, and the people I know, are givens that take on value and meaning within a particular context. There are many aspects of that context that I didn't choose; for example, being born in California or raised speaking English. However, I had the possibility to change my environment, learn a new language, and meet new people. What is recognized and hence valued in our lives, changes from one relationship to another, one group to another, one society and culture to another. Recognition and identity evolve simultaneously.

Human consciousness developed through a series of evolutionary changes and our individual consciousness developed as a result of initial caretaking and education. Every human being is born into an arbitrary situation. An individual develops in a particular environment and social construct, with a language and meanings that he or she didn't create. What becomes a person's reality is a *shared* reality that depends upon others, mediated by their recognition.

Although we don't construct the social reality that surrounds us, we do create an identity through our personal story, through creating an image, and through our behavior and interaction with others. How we interact, out of self-interest or altruistically, looking for self-validation or excessive approval constitutes our evaluative self. However, the search for recognition shouldn't be reduced to a search for self-esteem. My argument is much more existential. We don't only need recognition to feel good about ourselves. We need recognition to *know* ourselves and to actually *be* who we are.

My favorite existentialist philosopher Sartre, in his play *Huis Clos*, is often quoted but misinterpreted, for the expression "*l'enfer c'est les autres*" ("hell is other people"). This reflects my argument concerning recognition. Through the "look" of the other, we are an object for another person. In other words, we are dependent upon recognition from others for being the person we are. But, as we saw with Hegel, and his master/slave theory, the opposite is also true. The other person is an object for me. The only way out of this subject/object dyad, is through mutual recognition. This is where volition and moral responsibility become more apparent.

As mentioned above, reality is a communal enterprise; meaning and value depend upon other people and in an ideal world everybody respectfully recognizes everybody else. I have decidedly taken an existential approach to recognition. Despite its simple basis, the perception of similarities and differences, recognition evolves into a prescriptive/normative principle of mutual recognition, i.e., an appreciation and respect for similarities and differences.

This book defends the importance of recognition. As an essential function of consciousness, it is indispensable for constructing our notion of *self.* It is fundamental for creating and sustaining inter-relationships by establishing strong human bonds and enhancing understanding and trust. Recognition is absolutely necessary for a harmonious society, and therefore contributes to creating a meaningful existence. Recognition is something we naturally want, something we existentially need, and, in the form of mutual recognition, it is something that we ethically ought to seek. To quote Hegel, "being-recognized (*Anerkanntseyn*) is immediate actuality." [58] It is the very foundation of our human and *humane* existence.

ENDNOTES

INTRODUCTION

[1] William James, *The Principles of Psychology.* Vol. 1, (New York: Cosimo Classics, 2007), 293. (Originally published, 1890).

[2] Ibid. 292.

PART I

[1] Matilda White Riley, Beth B. Hess, Kathleen Bond, ed., *Aging in Society: Selected Reviews of Recent Research* (Hillsdale, NJ: Lawrence Erlbaum Associates, 1983), 253.

[2] Erik H. Erickson, "Reflections on Dr. Borg's Life Cycle," *Aging, Death, and the Completion of Being.* ed. David D. Van Tassel (Philadelphia: University of Pennsylvania Press, 1979).

[3] John Tagliabue, "Tears and dolls for everyone," *International Herald Tribune,* November 15, 2012.

[4] Gary D. Fireman, Ted E. McVay Jr., Owen J. Flanagan, "Sexual Identities and Narratives of Self," *Narrative and Consciousness, Literature, Psychology and the Brain* (New York: Oxford University Press, 2003), 218.

[5] Alan N. Shore, *Affect Regulation and the Origin of the Self: The Neurobiology of Emotional Development* (Hillsdale NJ: Lawrence Erlbaum Associates, 1994), 267.

274 Catherine Monnet, Ph.D.

[6] Gillian Einstein & Owen J. Flannagan, "Sexual Identities and Narratives of Self," 218.

[7] Alan N., Schore, *Affect Regulation and the Origin of the Self,* 264.

[8] G. Einstein & O. Flanagan, "Sexual Identities and Narratives of Self," 220.

[9] Kenneth J. Gergen, *The Saturated Self: Dilemmas of Identity in Contemporary Life* (New York: Basic Book, 2000), 155.

[10] Anthony P. Cohen, *Self Consciousness: An Alternative Anthropology of Identity* (New York: Routledge, 1994), 147.

[11] Ibid. 177.

[12] Jean Paul Sartre, *Being and Nothingness,* trans. Hazel Barnes (London: Methuen and Co. Ltd. 1958), 591.

[13] Currie Lee, CNN news broadcast, October 2010.

[14] T. Veblen, *The Theory of the Leisure Class* (NJ: Transaction Publishers, 1992), 61. (Original work published 1899).

[15] William B. Swann Jr., *Resilient Identities: Self-Relationships and the Construction of Social Reality* (New York: Basic Books, 1999), 125.

[16] S. Coontz, *The Way We Never Were: American Families and the Nostalgia Trap* (New York: Basic Books, 1992), 170.

[17] John Locke, *Second Treatise on Government,* §27.

[18] G.W.F. Hegel, *Philosophy of Spirit,* Jena Lectures (1805-1806), Part II Actual Spirit Recognition, A. i. Immediate Recognition.

[19] J.P. Sartre, *Being and Nothingness,* 576.

[20] Ibid. 577.

[21] Ibid. 589.

[22] Ibid. 590.

23   M. Weber, "Status groups and classes" G. Roth & C. Wittich eds., *Max Weber: Economy and society* (Berkeley: University of California Press, 1913), Vol. 1, 302-311.

24   Robert M. Galatzer-Levy & Bertram J. Cohler, *The Essential Other: A Developmental Psychology of the Self* (New York: Basic Books, 1993), 232.

25   Roger B Hill. Ph.D., University of Georgia, Copyright©1999.

26   Robert M. Galatzer-Levy et al., *The Essential Other,* 248.

27   G. W. F. Hegel, "*Jenaer Systementwürfe III*", Rolf-Peter Horstmann, ed., *Gesammelte Werke* Band 8, Rheinisch-Westfälische Akademie der Wissenschaften (Hamburg: Felix Meiner Verlag, 1976), 22.

28   Karl Marx, *Early Writings,* trans. T. B. Bottomores, (New York: McGraw Hill, 1964), 124-125.

29   A. Maslow, "A theory of human motivation," *Psychological Review,* 50, (1943): 370-396.

30   William B. Swann Jr., *Resilient Identities,* 128.

31   Roger B. Hill. Ph.D., University of Georgia, Copyrigh©1999.

32   William B. Swann Jr., *Resilient Identities: Self-Relationships and the Construction of Social Reality,* 130. (See Harry Helson, *Adaptation Level Theory.* New York: Harper & Row, 1964).

33   William B. Swann Jr., *Resilient Identities,*132.

34   Ibid. 95.

35   E. H. Erickson, *Childhood and Society,* 2nd ed. (New York: Norton 1963). A. Maslow, *Motivation and Personality* (New York: Harper & Row 1954). Carl Rogers, *On Becoming a Person,* (Boston: Houghton Mifflin 1961).

36   For a review see Lynn Hoffman, *Foundations of Family Therapy,* (New York: Basic Books, 1981).

37   William James, *The Principles of Psychology,* Vol. 1, 294.

38 Helen Fisher, *Why We Love: The Nature and Chemistry of Romantic Love* (USA: Henry Holt, 2004).

39 B. L. Murstein, *Love, Sex, and Marriage through the Ages,* (New York: Springer Publishing, 1974), 98.

40 S. Freud, (1910c), A special type of choice of object made by men (contributions to the psychology of love). trans. & ed. J. Strachey, *The standard edition of the complete psychological works of Sigmund Freud,* (London: Hogarth Press 1957), Vol. 11, 165-175.

41 Robert M. Galatzer-Levy & Bertram J. Cohler, *The Essential Other: A Developmental Psychology of the Self*, 253.

42 Helen Fisher, *The Anatomy of Love.* (New York: W.W. Norton, 1992).

43 Helen Fisher, *Why Him? Why Her? Finding Real Love By Understanding Your Personality Type* (USA-Canada: Henry Holt, 2009).

44 J.P. Sartre, *Being and Nothingness,* 367.

45 Ibid. 367.

46 Ibid. 367.

47 Ibid. 375.

48 William Swann, Alan Stein-Seroussi, Brian Geisler, "Why People Self-Verify," *Journal of Personality and Social Psychology*, (1992) 62:392-401.

49 Sheldon Stryker, Timothy Owens, Robert White, eds., *Self Identity and Social Movements*, (Minneapolis: University of Minnesota Press, 2000), 134.

50 Carlye E. Rusbult, Madoka Kumashiro, Shevaun L. Stocker, Scott T. Wolf "The Michelangelo Phenomenon" in *On Building, Defending, and Regulating the Self: A Psychological Perspective*, Abraham Tesser et al. (New York: Psychology Press, 2005), 2.

[51] Ibid. 3.

[52] Ibid. 17.

[53] Ibid. 21.

[54] Ibid. 23.

[55] Z. Rubin, *Liking and Loving*, (New York: Holt, Rinehart &Winston, 1973).

[56] Claud Levi-Strauss, *Les Structures élémentaires de la parenté* (rev. ed.), (Paris: Universitaires de France, 1967).

[57] A. Preston, "The ideals of the bride-to-be," *Ladies Home Journal* (June, 1905):26.

[58] Time/Pew Research Center Poll, *Time Magazine,* Nov. 29, 2010.

[59] Andrew Cherlin, John Hopkins University *Time Magazine*, Nov. 29, 2010, 44.

[60] D. McAdams & G. Vaillant, "Intimacy motivation and psychosocial adjustment: A longitudinal study," *Journal of Personality Assessment*, 46(6), (1982): 586-593. P. Berger & H. Kellner, "Marriage and the construction of reality," *Diogenes*, 46, (1964):1-24. R. Sternberg & S. Grajek, "The nature of love," *Journal of Personality and Social Psychology*, 47, (1984): 312-329.

[61] E. Waring, M. Tilman, L. Frelick, L. Russell, G. Weisz, "Concepts of intimacy in the general population," *Journal of Nervous and mental Disorder*, 168, (1980): 471-474.

[62] J.R. Wilson, R.E. Kuehn, E.A. Beach, *The Evolution of Human Sexuality* (Oxford: Oxford University Press, 1963).

[63] R.D. Laing, *Self and Others*, (London: Routledge, 1999) 67-69, quote, 68.

[64] William B. Swann Jr., *Resilient Identities,* 95.

[65] E. H. Erickson, *Childhood and Society.* 2nd ed. (New York: Norton, 1963). A. Maslow, *Motivation and Personality*, (New

York: Harper & Row, 1954). Carl Rogers, *On Becoming a Person*, (Boston: Houghton Mifflin, 1961).

[66]   William James, *The Principles of Psychology,* 294.

[67]   R. D. Laing, *Self and Others*, 70.

[68]   James M. Olson & Mark P. Zanna, eds., *Self-Inference Processes* (Hillsdale, NJ: Lawrence Erlbaum Associates, 1990), 265.

[69]   William James*, The Principles of Psychology,* 295.

[70]   John Locke, *Locke's Essay.* Book II, Ch. 28 § 12.

[71]   Patricia S Churchland, *Braintrust: What Neuroscience Tells Us about Morality*, (NJ: Princeton University Press, 2011), 114.

[72]   Richard Jenkins, *Social Identity* (London: Routledge, 2004), 85.

[73]   Olson, James M, Zanna, Mark P., editors, *Self-Inference Processes,* 116.

[74]   Robert M. Galatzer-Levy, *The Essential Other,* 159.

[75]   Ibid. 159.

[76]   Jerry, Suls, ed., *Psychological Perspectives on the Self. Volume: 4* (Hillsdale, NJ: Lawrence Erlbaum Associates, 1993), 196.

[77]   William B. Swann Jr., *Resilient Identities: Self-Relationships and the Construction of Social Reality.* ibid., 83. (For a discussion of opportunity structures, see McCall and Simmons (1966). For a discussion of lifestyle enclaves, see R. N. Bellah, R. Madsen, W. M. Sullivan, A. Swidler, & S. M. Tipton *Habits of the Heart: Individualism and Commitment in American Life.* New York: Harper & Row, 1985).

[78]   E. Pinel, & W.B. Swann, "Finding the Self Through Others; Self-Verification and Social Movement Participation," ed., Sheldon Stryker et al., *Self, Identity and Social Movements.* (Minneapolis: University of Minnesota Press, 2000), 148.

[79]   Robert Galatzer-Levy, *The Essential Other*, 153.

[80]   Ibid. 160.

[81] For example, see Soraya Mehdizadeh, *Cyberpsychology, Behavior and Social Networking.*

[82] Joel Stein, "The New Greatest Generation," *Time Magazine*, May 20, 2013, 31.

[83] Jeremy Rifkin, *The Empathic Civilization* (New York: Jeremy P. Tarcher/Penguin, 2009), 580.

[84] Ibid. 582.

[85] For example, see Frans de Waal, *Good Natured, The Origins of Right and Wrong in Humans and Other Animals* (MA: Harvard University Press, 1996).

[86] Frans de Waal, *The Age of Empathy* (New York: Three Rivers Press, 2009), 11.

[87] Avishai Margalit, *The Decent Society* (MA: Harvard University Press, 1998), 61-62.

[88] Thomas Moore, *Care of the Soul* (New York: Harper Collins, 1992), 5.

[89] William James, *Principles of Psychology*, 296.

[90] Ibid. 298.

[91] Ibid. 301- 302.

[92] See, a list of past and present definitions in, R. Paloutzian, & C. Park ed., *Handbook of the Psychology of Spirituality and Religion* (New York: Guilford Press, 2005), 23.

[93] Acccording to the NISET scale by J. Van der Ven.

[94] R. Paloutzian, *Handbook of the Psychology of Spirituality and Religion*, 24.

[95] William James, *Principles of Psychology*, 316.

[96] R. D. Laing, *Self and Others,* 117-118.

[97] G. H. Mead, *Mind, Self and Society from the Standpoint of a Social Behaviorist*, C.W. Morris ed. (Chicago, IL: University of Chicago Press. 1934), 155-156.

[98] Donald J. Moore, *Martin Buber, Prophet of Religious Secularism* (New York: Fordham University Press, 1996), 132.

[99] Martin Buber, *I and Thou*. A new translation with Prologue by Walter Kaufmann, (New York: Charles Scribner's Sons, 1970), 80, 112.

[100] William James, *Principles of Psychology*, 316.

[101] Friedrich Heiler, *Prayer: A Study in the History and Psychology of Religion*, Samuel McComb & John Edgar Park, ed., (Oxford University Press, London, 1932), 356.

[102] Ibid. 357.

[103] Ibid. 358.

[104] William James, *Principles and Psychology*, 316.

[105] It is: 1. Practical and Ritual, 2. Experiential and Emotional, 3. Narrative and Mythic, 4. Doctrinal and Philosophical, 5. Ethical and Legal, 6. Social and Institutional, 7. Material. Damien Keown, *Buddhism: A Very Short Introduction*, (Oxford: Oxford University Press, 1996), 5.

[106] See, Allen B Wallace. "Intersubjectivity in Indo-Tibetan Buddhism," *Journal of Consciousness Studies*, 8, No. 5-7, (2001), 209-30.

[107] Ibid. 213.

[108] Damien Keown, *Buddhism: A Very Short Introduction* (Oxford: Oxford University Press, 1996), 92.

[109] Allen B. Wallace, "Intersubjectivity," 214.

[110] Ibid. 217.

[111] See, Edward Felton, *Scientific American*, September 2010, 76.

PART II

[1] William James, *Principles of Psychology*, 225.

[2] Ibid. 146.

3   D.J. Chalmers, "The puzzle of conscious experience," *Scientific American*, Dec. 1995, 63.

4   Karl Popper, *The Open Universe: An Argument for Indeterminism* (London: Hutchinson: 1982), 150.

5   John C. Eccles, *Evolution of the Brain: Creation of the Self* (London: Routledge, 1989), 176.

6   Francis Crick, *The Astonishing Hypothesis. The Scientific Search for the Soul* (New York: Touchstone, 1994).

7   Such as Hans Moravec, *Mind Children* 1988, and Colin Blakemore, *The Mind Machine*, 1988.

8   John Searle, "The Problem of Consciousness," *Consciousness in Philosophy and Cognitive Neuroscience,* Revonsuo Anitti, & Kamppinen, Matti, eds., (Hillsdale, NJ: Lawrence Erlbaum Associates, 1994), 103.

9   John Searle, *The Rediscovery of Mind,* (Cambridge MA: MIT Press, 1992).

10 David Chalmers, *The Conscious Mind: In Search of a Fundamental Theory* (New York: Oxford University Press, 1996), 297.

11 G.M. Edelman, *Bright Air, Brilliant Fire: On The Matter of the Mind* (New York: Harper Collins, 1992), 7.

12 Antonio Damasio, *The Feeling of What Happens: Body and Emotion in the Making of Consciousness* (New York: Harcourt Brace & Company, 1999), 314-315.

13 Rodolfo R. Llinás, *I of the Vortex* (Cambridge MA: MIT Press, 2001), 168.

14 D. Dennett, *Consciousness Explained* (London: Penguin, 1991).

15 See for example: Colin McGinn, *The Problem of Consciousness.* (Oxford: Blackwell 1992). Patricia Churchland, "Can neurobiology teach us anything about consciousness?" *Proceedings and Addresses of the American Philosophical Association,*

(1994), 67(4): 23-40. John Eccles, *How the Self Controls Its Brain* (London: Springer-Verlag 1994). And Jerry Fodor, "Can there be a science of mind?" *TLS*, 3 July:1992, 5-7.

[16]   As Rudolpho Llinàs explains, the thalamus is at the center of connectivity to the cortex and consciousness is generated by recursive looping between the thalamus and cortex. (R.R. Llinàs, *I of the Vortex: From Neurons to Self*).

[17]   Karl Popper & Eccles, John, *The Self and its Brain*. (New York: Routledge, 1983), 141.

[18]   John Eccles, *Evolution of the Brain, Creation of the Self*, 174.

[19]   Merlin Donald, *A Mind So Rare*. (New York/London: W.W. Norton & Co., 2001), 179.

[20]   Ibid. 195.

[21]   Ibid. 197.

[22]   "Chimpanzees: Self recognition," *Science*, 167 (1970), 86-87. "Self awareness and the emergence of mind in primates," *American Journal of Primatology*, 2, (1982), 237-248.

[23]   Denise R. Beike, James M. Lampinen, Douglas A. Behrend, eds., *The Self and Memory*, New York: Psychology Press, 2004), 13.

[24]   Merlin Donald, *Origins of the Modern Mind* (Cambridge/London: Harvard University Press, 1991), 168.

[25]   Frans de Waal, *Age of Empathy*, Ch. 3.

[26]   Rizzolatti, Giacomo & Laila Craihero, "The mirror-Neuron System," *Annual Review of Neuroscience* 27, no. 1, (2004), 169-92.

[27]   Frans de Waal, *Age of Empathy*, 60.

[28]   Merlin Donald, *Origins of the Modern Mind*,186.

[29]   Patricia Churchland, *Braintrust: What Neuroscience Tells Us about Morality* (Princeton, NJ: University Press, 2011), 145.

30   See, Susan Blackmore, "State of the Art-The Psychology of Consciousness," *The Psychologist*, vol. 14, (2001), 522-525.

31   Patricia Churchland, *Braintrust,* 159.

32   Donald, Merlin, *Origins of the Modern Mind,* 116-117.

33   Ibid.214

34   Ibid. 133

35   Julian Jaynes, *The Origin of Consciousness in the Breakdown of the Bicameral Mind* (Boston/New York: Houghton Mifflin Co., 1976), 128.

36   Preben Bertelsen, *Free Will, Consciousness, and Self: Anthropological Perspectives on Psychology* (New York: Berghahn Books, 2005), 75.

37   Ibid. 79.

38   Julian Jaynes, *The Origin of Consciousness,* 140.

39   Ibid. 141.

40   Ibid. 217.

41   Robert Dunbar, *Gossip, Grooming and the Evolution of Language.* (MA: Harvard University Press, 1998).

42   John Eccles, *Evolution of the Brain*, 80.

43   Ibid. 216.

44   Ibid. 95.

45   Merlin Donald, *A Mind So Rare,* 326.

46   Margaret S. Mahler, Annie Bergman, Fred Pine, *The Psychological Birth of the Human Infant: Symbiosis and Individuation* (New York: Basic Books, 2000), 46.

47   H. Kohut, *The Analysis of the Self* (1971) & *The Restoration of Self* (New York: International Universities Press, 1977).

48   Allan N. Shore, *Affect Regulation and the Origin of the Self: The Neurobiology of Emotional Development.* (Hillsdale, NJ: Lawrence Erlbaum Associates, 1994), 66.

[49]   Ibid. 12.

[50]   G.E. McClearn & J.H.C. DeFries, *Introduction to behavioral genetics.* (San Francisco: W.H. Freeman, 1973).

[51]   Mahler, et al. *The Psychological Birth of the Human Infant,* 8.

[52]   Malcom Pines, "Mirroring and Child Development: Psychodynamic and psychological interpretations," Terry Honess & Krysia Yardley, eds., *Self and Identity: Perspectives across the Lifespan* (London: Routledge & Kegan Paul, 1987), 19.

[53]   Ibid. 20.

[54]   Ibid. 21.

[55]   Patricia Churchland, *Braintrust,* 158-159.

[56]   D.W. Winnicot, "Mirroring and Child Development," *Self and Identity,* 25, 26.

[57]   Ibid. 23.

[58]   K. Nelson, "Narrative and the emergence of a conscious self," Gary D. Fireman, Ted E. McVay Jr., Owen J. Flanagan, eds., *Narrative and Consciousness: Literature, Psychology, and the Brain* (New York: Oxford University Press, 2003), 27.

[59]   M. Malcom, "Mirroring and Child Development," *Self and Identity,* 27.

[60]   Herbert Terrace, Janet Metcalf, eds., *The Missing Link in Cognition: Origins of Self-reflective Consciousness.* (New York: Oxford University Press, 2005), 104 ★{According to Frans de Waal, we shouldn't restrict our notion of pointing to an outstretched arm and a pointed finger. He gives several examples of chimpanzees and great apes who attract a person's or another primate's attention to notice an unseen object, food for example, thus demonstrating that they are capable of taking the perspective of the other's ignorance of the object.} Frans de Waals, *Age of Empathy,* 151-157.

[61]   Higgens & Vookles, "Patterns of Self-Belief," James Olson, Mark P. Zanna, eds., *Self-Inference Processes* (Hillsdale, NJ: Lawrence Erlbaum Associates, 1990), 155.

[62]   Ibid.156.

[63]   U. Neisser, "Five kinds of self-knowledge," *Philosophical Psychology*, 1, (1988), 35-59.

[64]   U. Neisser, "The Development of Consciousness and the Acquisition of Skill," Frank S. Kessel, Pamela M. Cole, Dale L. Johnson, eds., *Self and Consciousness: Multiple Perspectives* (Hillsdale, NJ: Lawrence Erlbaum Associates,1992), 7.

[65]   Ibid. 9.

[66]   Ibid. 11.

[67]   Ibid. 11.

[68]   Ibid. 12.

[69]   M. Merleu-Ponty, *Les relations à autrui chez l'enfant.* ed. Les cours de la Sorbonne, 55-57.

[70]   G. C. Gallup & M. K. McClure, "Preference for mirror-image stimulation in differentially reared rhesus; monkeys," *Journal of Comparative and Physiological Psychology*, 75, (1971) 403-407.

[71]   Mahler, et al. *The Psychological Birth of the Human Infant,* 90.

[72]   Ibid. 90.

[73]   Ibid. 90.

[74]   Frank S. Kessel, et al. eds., *Self and Identity,* 33.

[75]   C. Buhler, *From Birth to Maturity* (London: Kegan, Paul, Trench, Trubner, 1935).

[76]   Allan N. Shore, *Affect Regulation and the Origin of the Self,* 201.

[77]   Ibid. 202.

[78]   Heinz Kohut, "Thoughts on narcissism and narcissistic rage" In P. Ornstein ed. *The Search for the Self* (New York: International Universities Press, 1978), 655.

[79]   Allan N. Shore, *Affect Regulation and the Origin of the Self,* 208. & (K. Wright, *Vision and separation: Between mother and baby* (Northvale NJ: Jason Aronson, 1991, 30).

[80]   K. Wright, *Vision and separation: Between mother and baby* (Northvale NJ: Jason Aronson, 1991), 30.

[81]   Gershen Kaufman, *The Psychology of Shame* (New York: Springer, 1989), 36.

[82]   Allan N. Shore, *Affect Regulation and the Origin of the Self,* 208.

[83]   Ibid. 207, 424.

[84]   Sartre, *Being and Nothingness*, 261.

[85]   Freud S., *"On narcissism: An introduction"* 1914, & Sartre, *Being and Nothingness* 256.

[86]   Sartre, *Being and Nothingness,* 289.

[87]   Rebecca Saxe, et al., "Theory of Mind Performance in Children Correlates With Functional Specialization of a Brain Region for Thinking about Thoughts," Saxelab Website.

[88]   Herbert Terrace, *The Missing Link in Cognition,* 133.

[89]   K. Nelson, "Narrative and the Emergence of a Consciousness of Self," Gary Fireman et al, *Narrative and Consciousness,* Chapter 2.

[90]   Herbert, Mead, *Mind, Self and Society,* (Chicago: University of Chicago Press, 1934), part III Ch. 3.

[91]   Robyn Fivush, & Catherine A. Haden, eds., *Autobiographical Memory and the Construction of a Narrative Self: Developmental and Cultural Perspectives.* (Mahwah, NJ: Lawrence Erlbaum Associates, 2003), Chapter IV.

[92]   Robert M. Galater-Levy &, Bertram J. Cohler, *The Essential Other: A Developmental Psychology of the Self* (New York: Basic Books, 1993), 74.

[93]   Ibid. 138.

[94]   Baldwin, J. M., "Handbook of psychology: Feeling & will," (New York: Holt, 1894), 338.

PART III

[1]   William James, *Psychology: The Briefer Course* (New York: Collier Books, 1962).

[2]   Charles Cooley, *Human nature and the Social Order* (New York: Scribners,1902), 90.

[3]   Charles Cooley, *Human Nature and the Social Order* (New York: Schocken, 1964, 184. (First published 1902).

[4]   Charles Cooley, *Social Organization: A Study of the Larger Mind.* (New York: Schocken, 1962) 4. (First published 1909).

[5]   G. H. Mead & C. W. Morris eds., *Mind, Self and Society from the Standpoint of a Social Behaviorist* (Chicago: University of Chicago Press, 1934), 1.

[6]   Ibid. 7- 8.

[7]   Ibid. 140.

[8]   J. H. Griffen, *Black Like Me* (Boston: Houghton Mifflin, 2nd ed., 1977), 12.

[9]   G. H. Mead, *Mind, Self and Society,* 133.

[10]   U. Neisser, & R. Fivush, *The remembering self: Construction and accuracy in the self-narrative* (Cambridge University Press, Cambridge, 1994), p vii.

[11]   Gary D. Fireman, Ted E. McVay Jr., Owen J. Flanagan, eds., *Narrative and Consciousness: Literature, Psychology, and the Brain* (New York: Oxford University Press, 2003), 5.

[12]   K. Nelson, & J. Gruendel, "Generalized event representations: Basic building blocks of cognitive development," In M. Lamb & A. Brown eds., *Advances in developmental psychology* (Hillsdale, NJ: Lawrence Erlbaum Associates, 1981), vol. 1, 131- 158.

[13]   K. Nelson, "Narrative and the Emergence of a Consciousness of Self," in Gary D. Fireman, et al eds., *Narrative and Consciousness,* 28.

[14]   D. Dennett, *The intentional stance.* (Cambridge, MA: MIT Press, 1987).

[15]   Paul Ricoeur, *Temps et Récit III: Le temps raconté,* (Paris: Editions du Seuil, 1985), 443.

[16]   D. Dennett, *Consciousness Explained* (Boston: Little, Brown and Company,1991), 418.

[17]   Paul Ricoeur, *Temps et Récit III,* 446.

[18]   Jerome Bruner, *Making Stories: Law Literature, Life* (Cambridge, MA: Harvard University Press, 2002), 14.

[19]   Dan Zahavi, "Self and Other: The Limits of Narrative Understanding," in D.D. Hutto, ed., *Narrative and Understanding Persons*, Royal Institute of Philosophy Supplement 60, (Cambridge: Cambridge University Press2007), 179-201.

[20]   B. Baars, *In the Theater of Consciousness* (New York: Oxford University Press, 1997).

[21]   T. Smith, "Introduction: Autobiography in fresh contexts" *a/b: Auto/Biographical Studies. 13(1),* (1998), 2.

[22]   J. Kotre, *White gloves: How we create ourselves through memory.* (New York: Norton, 1996), 111.

[23]   Ibid. 118.

[24]   M. S. Gazzaniga, *The Mind's Past* (Berkley: University of California Press, 1998), 2.

[25]   Ibid. 174.

[26]   Ibid. 26.

[27]   D. L. Hull, "In defense of presentism," *History and Theory, 18,* (1979), 1-5.

[28]   Denise R. Beike, James M. Lampinen, Douglas A. Behrend, eds., *The Self and Memory.* (New York: Psychology Press, 2004), 208.

[29]   M. A. Conway, & C.W. Pleydell-Pearce, "The construction of autobiographical memories in the self-memory system," *Psychological Review, 107,* (2000), 261–288.

[30]   Dan McAdams, "Identity of the Life Story," Robyn Fivush, Catherine A. Haden, eds., *Autobiographical Memory and the Construction of a Narrative Self: Developmental and Cultural Perspectives* (Mahway, NJ: Lawrence Erlbaum Associates, 2003), 195.

[31]   Marc Freeman, "Rethinking the Fictive, Reclaiming the Real," Gary D. Fireman, et al eds., *Narrative and Consciousness,*123.

[32]   Sartre, *Being and Nothingness,* 496-504.

[33]   Dan McAdams, "Identity of the Life Story," Robyn Fivush, eds., *Autobiographical Memory and the Construction of a Narrative Self,* 189.

[34]   Denise R. Beike, et al eds., *The Self and Memory,* 210.

[35]   William B. Swann, *Resilient Identities: Self-Relationships and the Construction of Social Reality* (New York: Basic Books, 1999), 47.

[36]   Karl R. Popper, *Conjectures and Refutations* (London: Routledge 1963), 47-48. For a discussion, see V.F. Guidano, and G. Liotti, *Cognitive Processes and Emotional Disorders.* (New York: Guilford, 1983).

[37]   Swann, William B. Swann, *Resilient Identities,* 48.

38   Rollo May, *The Meaning of Anxiety* (New York: Washington Square Press, 1979), 192-193.

39   Denise R. Beike, et al eds., *The Self and Memory,* Ch. 1.

40   G. Strawson, Ch. 4, "Against narrativity," *The Self* (Oxford: Blackwell Publishing, 2005).

41   Roy Baumeister, "Anxiety and Deconstruction, Escaping the Self," James M. Olson & Mark P. Zanna, eds., *Self-Inference Processes* (Hillsdale NJ: Lawrence Erlbaum Associates,1990), 276.

42   Ibid. 276, 277.

43   Ibid. 278.

44   Ibid. 278-282.

45   Jerry Suls, *Psychological Perspectives on the Self Volume: 4* (Hillsdale, NJ: Lawrence Erlbaum Associates, 1993), 133.

46   Mark Snyder, "Self-monitoring Processes," Leonard Berkowitz, ed., *Advances in Experimental Social Psychology, vol. 12* (New York; Academic Press, 1979).

47   B. R. Schlenker, *Impression management: The self-concept, social identity, and interpersonal relations* (Monterey, CA: Brooks/Cole, 1980).

48   Erving Goffman, *The Presentation of Self in Everyday Life* (Garden City, NY: Doubleday, 1959), *Strategic Interaction* (Philadelphia: University of Pennsylvania Press,1969), *Stigma,* (Englewood Cliffs, NJ: Prentice-Hall, 1963).

49   Sartre, *Being and Nothingness*, 59.

50   Ibid. 555.

51   Kenneth J. Gergen, *The Saturated Self: Dilemmas of Identity in Contemporary Life* (New York: Basic Books, 2000), 147.

52   Ibid. 150.

53   Louis A. Zurcher Jr., *The Mutable Self* (Beverly Hills, Sage, 1977).

54   William B. Swann, *Resilient Identities,* 29.

55   Dan McAdams, "Identity of the Life Story," Fivush, Robyn Fivush et al eds., *Autobiographical Memory and the Construction of a Narrative Self,* 200.

56   Fivush, Robyn Fivush, et al eds., *Autobiographical Memory and the Construction of a Narrative Self,* 82.

57   Ibid. 78.

58   Clare Ulrich, "My Memory, Myself: The Role of Culture in Memory and Self-Identity," *Human Ecology.* Volume: 32. Issue: 1 (2004), Page Number: 2+, COPYRIGHT 2004 Cornell University, Human Ecology.

59   Robyn Fivush et al eds., *Autobiographical Memory and the Construction of a Narrative Self,* 82.

60   Clare Ulrich, "My Memory, Myself."

61   Jerry Suls, *Psychological Perspectives on the Self,* 207– 208.

62   T. S. Lebra, *Culture, Self, and Communication.* Paper presented at the University of Michigan, Ann Arbor, MI, June, 1992.

63   R.B. Cattel, *The scientific analysis of personality* (Baltimore: Penguin, 1965). (Originally in 1943).

64   Christopher J. Murk, *Towards a Positive Psychology of Self-Esteem* (New York: Springer Publishing Company, 2006).

65   Ibid. 22.

66   Ibid. 28.

67   William James, *The Principles of Psychology, Volume 1*, 310– 311.

68   Ibid. 310.

69   Jerry Suls, *Psychological Perspectives on the Self. Volume: 4,* 30.

70   William James, *The Principles of Psychology, Volume 1*, 306.

71   Jerry Suls, *Psychological Perspectives on the Self. Volume: 4*, 3.

72   L.A. Sroufe, "Relationships, self, and individual adaptation" In A. J. Sameroff and R. N. Emde, eds., *Relationships, Self, and Individual Adaptation in Early Childhood: A Developmental Approach* (New York: Basic Books, 1989).

73   J. Bowlby, *Attachment and Loss. Vol. II, Separation* (New York: Basic Books, 1973), 204-205.

74   R.G. Wahler, & J. E. Dumas, "'A chip off the old block'": Some interpersonal characteristics of coercive children across generations". In P. Strain, ed. *Children's Social Behavior. Development, Assessment, and Modification* (New York: Academic, 1986).

75   D. Stern, *The First Relationship* (Cambridge, MA: Harvard University Press, 1977), 142.

76   E.S. Wolf, *Treating the Self: Elements of Clinical Self Psychology* (New York: Guildford, 1988), 39.

77   Nathaniel Branden, *Honoring the Self* (New York: Bantam Books, 1983), 33.

78   Branden, Nathaniel, *Six Pillars of Self-Esteem* (New York: Bantam, 1994), 95. See pp. xv and 21.

79   Po Bronson & Ashly Merryman, *Nurture Shock,* (New York: Twelve, 2009).

80   William B. Swann, *Resilient Identities,* 79.

81   P. Wachtel, "Vicious circles: The self and the rhetoric of emerging and unfolding," *Contemporary Psychoanalysis* (1982), 18:259-273.

82   R. L. Bray, "Self-esteem: Hoax or reality," *New York Times*, Educ-33, December 19, 1990.

83   J. Adler, "Hey I'm terrific!" *Newsweek* (February 17, 1992): 46-51.

84   F. Nietzsche, *Beyond good and evil*, H. Zimmerman, trans., (New York: MacMillan, 1911).

85   Denise R. Beike, et al eds., *The Self and Memory,*174.

86   G.W. Allport, *Personality: A Psychological Interpretation*, (New York: Holt, 1939), 422.

87   Frans de Waal, *The Age of Empathy*, 75.

88   John Eccles, *The Evolution of the Brain, The Creation of Self* (New York: Routledge, 1989), 114.

89   Frans de Waal, *The Age of Empathy*, 75.

90   Jeremy Rifkin, *The Empathetic Civilization*, 131.

91   Jean M. Twenge, Keith W. Campbell, *The Narcissism Epidemic, Living in the Age of Entitlement* (New York: Atria Paperback, 2009), 2.

92   Ibid. 4.

93   M. Heidegger, *Sein und Zeit* (Tübingen: Max Niemeyer Verlag, 1957), 186.

94   Thomas Nagel, *The View from Nowhere* (USA: Oxford University Press, 1989), 3.

95   Ibid. 64.

96   Preben Bertelsen, *Free Will, Consciousness, and Self, Anthropological Perspectives on Psychology* (Oxford: Berghahn Books, 2003), 93.

97   A.H. Maslow, *Toward a Psychology of Being* (Princeton, NJ: Van Nostrand, 1968).

98   C.R. Rodgers, *On Becoming a Person: A Therapist's View of Psychotherapy* (Boston: Houghton Mifflin, 1961).

99   M. Kernis & B. Goldman, "From Thought and Experience to Behavior and Personal Relationships," in Abraham Tesser, Joanne V. Wood, Diederick A. Stapel, eds., *On Building,*

Defending, and Regulating the Self: A Psychological Perspective (New York: Psychology Press, 2005), 32.

[100] Ibid. Ch. 2.

[101] Ibid. 41.

[102] Kenneth J. Gergen, *The Saturated Self,* 7.

[103] Sartre, *Anti-Semite and Jew,* trans. George Becker, (New York: Grove Press, 1968), 90. (Reflexions sur la question juive, 1943).

[104] Storm T. Heter,"Authenticity and Others: Sartre's Ethics of Recognition" *Sartre Studies International.* Volume: 12. Issue: 2, (2006): Section 5.

PART IV

[1] Stephen Darwall, *The Second-Person Standpoint* (Cambridge, MA: Harvard University Press, 2006),123.

[2] Immanual Kant, *Groundwork for the Metaphysics of Morals.* trans./ed., Allen Wood, (CT: Yale University Press, 2002), 46 ((Die Metaphysik der Sitten 4:428).

[3] Ibid. 13. (Die Metaphysik der Sitten 4:398)

[4] Ibid. 13. (Die Metaphysik der Sitten 4:398)

[5] Ibid. 38. (Die Metaphysik der Sitten 4:421)

[6] Ibid. 46-47. (Die Metaphysik der Sitten 4:429)

[7] Joseph Raz, *Value, Respect and Attachment* (MA: Cambridge University Press, 2001), 152.

[8] Leo Rauch, *Hegel and the Human Spirit.* (Detroit, MI: Wayne State University Press, 1983), 120. This is a translation, with commentary, of the *Jena Lectures on the Philosophy of Spirit* (1805-6).

[9] W.F.H. Hegel, *The Phenomenology of Mind/Spirit* (1807) trans. J.B. Baillie, (London: Harper & Row, 1931), 'B' Self-Consciousness, IV: 1, §174.

[10]   Ibid. §177

[11]   W.F.H. Hegel, *The Philosophy of Spirit*. (1830) trans. William Wallace, (Oxford: Oxford Clerendon Press, 1971), Part III, Section 1, B. Phenomenology of Mind and Consciousness, §§ 430-435.

[12]   Jean Jacques Rousseau, *The Discourse on the Origins of Inequality*. *(Discours sur l'origine et les fondaments de l'inégalité parmi les hommes)*, (Paris : Les integrals de philo/Nathan, 1981), 2ⁿᵈ Partie, 82.

[13]   Jean Jaques, Rousseau *The Social Contract (Du Contrat social*, 1761), (Paris : GF Flammaron, 1966), Ch. 1, 41.

[14]   W.F.H. Hegel, *The Philosophy of Spirit*. § 436.

[15]   Ibid. § 437.

[16]   Axel Honneth, "Recognition and Moral Obligation," trans., John Farrell, *Social Research*, Volume: 64. Issue: 1, (1997): 29.

[17]   Ibid. 25-26.

[18]   Ibid. 28.

[19]   Sartre, *Anti-Semite and Jew*, (Reflexions sur la question juive, 1943) (New York : Schoecken Books, 1948), 28.

[20]   Storm, T. Heter, "Authenticity and Others: Sartre's Ethics of Recognition" *Sartre Studies International*, Volume: 12. Issue: 2, (2006): Section 5.

[21]   Ibid. Section 6.

[22]   Ibid. Section 6.

[23]   Sartre, *Being and Nothingness*, 563.

[24]   James Boettcher, "Respect, Recognition and Public Reason," *Social Theory and Practice*. Volume: 33. Issue: 2, 2007. Page Number: 223+. COPYRIGHT 2007 Social Theory and Practice-Florida State University; COPYRIGHT 2007

25   Avishai Margalit, *The Decent Society*, trans. Naomi Goldblum, (Cambridge, MA: Harvard University Press, 1998), 110.

26   Ibid. 101.

27   Sartre, *Critique of Dialectical Reason*, (London: Verson, 1976), Vol. 1, 110.

28   Julius Lester, *To be a Slave*, (New York: Scholastic Inc., 1968), 28.

29   Avishai Margalit, *The Decent Society,* 109.

30   Ibid. 112.

31   Harry Frankfurt, "Equality and Respect," *Social Research*, Volume: 64. Issue: 1, (1997): 13. Also, in *Necessity, Volition and Love* (New York: Cambridge University Press 1999), 153.

32   John Calder, *The Philosophy of Beckett* (London: Calder publications, 2001), 33.

33   Frans de Waal, *The Age of Empathy*, 181-182.

34   Harry Frankfurt, "Equality and Respect," 13.

35   Ibid.

36   F. Nietzsche, *Genealogy of Morality* (1870-71), trans. F. Golffing, (New York: Doubleday Anchor Books, 1956), I. 2.

37   Ibid. I. 10.

38   Lawrence Kohlberg, "Handbook of Socialization Theory of Research" (Chicago: Rand McNally, 1969), 375.

39   Carol Gilligan, *In a Different Voice* (Cambridge MA: Harvard University Press, 1982), 9-10.

40   Ibid. 164-165.

41   Ibid. 73.

42   Ibid. 74.

43   Virginia Held, *Feminist Morality: Transforming culture, society, and politics* (Chicago-London: University of Chicago Press, 1993), 49-63.

[44]   Ibid. 55.

[45]   Ibid. 60.

[46]   Martin Hoffman, *Empathy and Moral Development: Implications for Caring and Justice* (Cambridge, UK: University Press, 2000), 30.

[47]   Frans de Waal, *The Age of Empathy*, 66.

[48]   Jeremy Rifkin, *The Empathetic Civilization*, 131.

[49]   Marco Iacoboni, "Neurology of Imitation," *Current Opinion in Neurobiology,* 19, no. 6 (2009): 663.

[50]   Frans de Waal, *The Age of Empathy*, 67.

[51]   Virginia Held, *Feminist Morality: Transforming culture, society, and politics,* 67.

[52]   Frans de Waal, *The Age of Empathy*, 68.

[53]   Ibid. 208.

[54]   Joel Stein, "The New Greatest Generation," *Time Magazine*, May 20, 2013, 31.

[55]   Dacher Keltner, Jason Marsh, Jeremy Adam Smith, *The Compassionate Instinct: The Science of Human Goodness* (New York: W.W. Norton and Co., 2010), 171-174.

[56]   Natalie Angier, "Where what's fair-and –square meets hierarchy," *International Herald Tribune,* July 6, 2011.

[57]   Ibid.

[58]   W.F.H. Hegel, *Philosophy of Spirit,* Jena Lectures (1805-1806), Part II Actual Spirit Recognition, A. i. Immediate Recognition.

SELECTED BIBLIOGRAPHY

Baars, Bernard. *In the Theater of Consciousness.* New York: Oxford University Press, 1997.

Beike, Denise R., James M. Lampinen, Douglas A. Behrend, Editors. *The Self and Memory,* New York: Psychology Press, 2004.

Bertelsen, Preben. *Free Will, Consciousness, and Self: Anthropological Perspectives on Psychology.* New York: Berghahn Books, 2005.

Boettcher, James. "Respect, Recognition and Public Reason," *Social Theory and Practice.* Volume: 33. Issue: 2, (2007).

Bowlby, John. *Attachment and Loss - Vol. II,* New York: Basic Books, 1973.

Branden, Nathaniel. *Honoring the Self.* New York: Bantam Books, 1983.

Branden, Nathaniel. *Six Pillars of Self-Esteem.* New York: Bantam, 1994.

Buber, Martin, *I and Thou*. Translation with Prologue by Walter Kaufmann. New York: Charles Scribner's Sons, 1970.

Calder, John, *The Philosophy of Beckett*. London: Calder publications, 2001.

Chalmers, David. *The Conscious Mind: In Search of a Fundamental Theory*. New York: Oxford University Press, 1996.

Churchland, Patricia S. *Braintrust: What Neuroscience Tells Us about Morality*. NJ: Princeton University Press, 2011.

Cohen, Anthony P. *Self Consciousness: An Alternative Anthropology of Identity*. New York: Routledge, 1994.

Cooley, Charles. *Human nature and the Social Order*. New York: Scribners, 1902

Crick, Francis. *The Astonishing Hypothesis. The Scientific Search for the Soul*. NewYork: Simon & Schuster, 1994

Damasio, Antonio, *The Feeling of What Happens: Body and Emotion in the Making of Consciousness*. New York: Harcourt Brace & Company, 1999.

Darwall, Stephen, *The Second-Person Standpoint*. MA: Harvard University Press, 2006.

Dennett, D., *Consciousness Explained*. Harmondsworth: Penguin, 1991

Donald, Merlin. *A Mind So Rare*. NewYork/London: W.W. Norton & Co., 2001.

Donald, Merlin. *Origins of the Modern Mind*. MA/London: Harvard University Press, 1991.

Dunbar, Robert. *Gossip, Grooming and the Evolution of Language*. MA: Harvard University Press, 1998.

Eccles, John C., *Evolution of the Brain: Creation of the Self*. London: Routledge, 1989.

Edelman, G.M. *Bright Air, Brilliant Fire: On The Matter of the Mind*. New York: Harper Collins, 1992.

Erikson, Erik. *Childhood and Society*. 2nd edition. New York: Norton, 1963.

Fireman, Gary D., Ted E. McVay Jr, and Owen J. Flanagan. *Narrative and Consciousness, Literature, Psychology and the Brain*. New York : Oxford University Press, 2003.

Fivush, Robyn and Catherine A. Haden, Editors. *Autobiographical Memory and the Construction of a Narrative Self: Developmental and Cultural Perspectives*. NJ: Lawrence Erlbaum Associates, 2003.

Frankfurt, Harry. "Equality and Respect," *Social Research*. Volume: 64. Issue: 1, 1997. also, in *Necessity, Volition and Love*. New York: Cambridge University Press 1999.

Freud, S. *"On narcissism: An introduction"* 1914. London: Yale University Press, 1991.

Galatzer-Levy, Robert M. and Bertram J. Cohler. *The Essential Other: A Developmental Psychology of the Self*. New York: Basic Books, 1993.

Gazzaniga, M. S. *The Mind's Past.* Berkley: University of California Press, 1998.

Gergen, Kenneth J. *The Saturated Self: Dilemmas of Identity in Contemporary Life.* New York: Basic Books, 2000.

Gilligan, Carol, *In a Different Voice.* MA: Harvard University Press, 1982.

Goffman, Erving. *The Presentation of Self in Everyday Life,* Garden City NY: Doubleday, 1959.

Griffin, John H. *Black Like Me.* Boston: Houghton Mifflin, 1977.

Hegel, G.W.F. *The Philosophy of Spirit.* (Jena Lectures 1805-6).

Hegel, Georg W. F. *The Phenomenology of Mind/Spirit.* (1807) Translated by J.B. Baillie. London: Harper and Row, 1967.

Hegel, Georg W.F. *The Philosophy of Spirit.* (1830) Translated by William Walace, MA: Oxford Clarendon Press, 1971.

Heidegger, Martin. *Sein und Zeit.* Tübingen: Max Niemeyer Verlag, 1957.

Heiler, Friedrich. Samuel McComb, John, E. Park, Editors. *Prayer: A Study in the History and Psychology of Religion.* London: Oxford University Press, 1932.

Held, Virginia, *Feminist Morality: Transforming culture, society, and politics*. Chicago/London: University of Chicago Press, 1993.

Heter, Storm, T. "Authenticity and Others: Sartre's Ethics of Recognition." *Sartre Studies International*. Volume: 12. Issue: 2 (2006)

Hoffman, Martin. *Empathy and Moral Development: Implications for Caring and Justice*. Cambridge: Cambridge University Press, 2000.

Honess, Terri and Krysia Yardly, Editors. *Self and Identity: Perspectives across the Lifespan*. London: Routledge & Kegan Paul, 1987.

James, William. *The Principles of Psychology* Vol. 1 New York : Cosimo Classics, 2007 (originally published, 1890).

James, William. *Psychology: The Briefer Course*. New York: Harper, 1961

Jaynes, Julian, *The Origin of Consciousness in the Breakdown of the Bicameral Mind*. Boston/New York: Houghton Mifflin Co., 1976.

Jenkins, Richard, *Social Identity*, London: Routledge 2004.

Kant, Immanuel, *Groundwork for the Metaphysics of Morals*. Translated/Edited by Allen Wood. CT: Yale University Press, 2002.

Kaufman, Gershen, *The psychology of shame*. New York: Springer, 1989

Keown, Damien. *Buddhism: A Very Short Introduction.* Oxford: Oxford University Press, 1996.

Keltner, David, Jeremy Smith, and Jason Marsh. *The Compassionate Instinct: The Science of Human Goodness.* New York: W.W. Norton and Co., 2010.

Kessel, Frank S., Pamela M. Cole, Dale L. Johnson, Editors, *Self and Consciousness: Multiple Perspectives.* NJ: Lawrence Erlbaum Associates, 1992.

Kohlberg, Lawrence. *Handbook of Socialization Theory of Research.* Chicago: Rand McNally, 1969.

Kohut, Heinz. *The Analysis of the Self.* New York: International Universities Press, 1971.

Kohut, Heinz. *The Restoration of Self.* New York: International Universities Press, 1977.

Kotre, John. *White gloves: How we create ourselves through memory.* New York: Norton, 1996,

Laing, R. D. *Self and Others.* Routledge, London: Routledge, 1999.

Lester, Julius. *To be a Slave.* New York: Scholastic Inc., 1968.

Levi-Strauss, Claude. *Les Structures élémentaires de la parenté.* (rev. ed.) Paris: Universitaires de France, 1967.

Llinás, Rodolfo R., *I of the Vortex.* MA: MIT Press, 2001.

Locke, John, *AN Essay Concerning Human Understanding* Book II. 1690.

Mahler, Margaret, Annie Bergman, and Fred Pine. *The Psychological Birth of the Human Infant: Symbiosis and Individuation*. New York: Basic Books, 2000.

Margalit, Avishai, *The Decent Society*. Translated by Naomi Goldblum. MA: Harvard University Press, 1998.

Marx, Karl, *Early Writings*. Translated and edited by T.B. Bottomore. New York: McGraw Hill, 1964.

Maslow, Abraham. *Motivation and Personality*. New York: Harper & Row, 1954.

Maslow, Abraham. *Toward a Psychology of Being*. (2nd Ed.) Princeton, NJ: Van Nostrand, 1968.

May, Rollo. *The Meaning of Anxiety*. New York: Washington Square Press, 1979.

Mead, G. H. Edited by C. W. Morris. *Mind, Self and Society from the Standpoint of a Social Behaviorist*. IL: University of Chicago Press, 1934.

Murk, Christopher J. *Towards a Positive Psychology of Self-Esteem*, New York: Springer Publishing Company, 2006.

Nagel, Thomas. *The View from Nowhere*. MA: Oxford University Press, 1989.

Neisser, Ulric. "Five kinds of self-knowledge". *Philosophical Psychology* 1 (1988) 35-59

Nietzsche, Friedrich. *Beyond good and evil.* Translated by H. Zimmerman. New York: MacMillan, 1911.

Nietzsche, Friedrich. *Genealogy of Morality.* (1870-71). Translated by F. Golffing. New York: Doubleday Anchor Books, 1956.

Olson, James M. and Mark P. Zanna, Editors. *Self-Inference Processes.* Hillsdale, NJ: Lawrence Erlbaum Associates, 1990.

Popper, Karl. *The Open Universe: An Argument for Indeterminism.* London: Hutchinson, 1982.

Popper, Karl, John Eccles. *The Self and its Brain.* Routledge, New York, 1983.

Rauch, Leo. *Hegel and the Human Spirit.* MI: Wayne State University Press, 1983.

Raz, Joseph. *Value, Respect and Attachment,* MA: Cambridge University Press. 2001.

Ricoeur, Paul. *Temps et Récit III: Le temps raconté,* Paris: Editions du Seuil, 1985.

Rifkin, Jeremy. *The Empathic Civilization.* New York: Jeremy P. Tarcher/Penguin, 2009.

Rodgers, Carl. *On Becoming a Person: A Therapist's View of Psychotherapy.* Boston: Houghton Mifflin, 1961.

Rousseau, Jean Jaques. *Discours sur l'origine et les fondaments de l'inégalité parmi les hommes (The Discourse on the Origins of Inequality).* Paris : Les integrals de philo/Nathan. 1981.

Rousseau, Jean Jaques. *Du Contrat social (The Social Contract)* (1761). Paris : GF Flammaron, 1966.

Sartre, Jean Paul. *Anti-Semite and Jew.* Translated by George Becker. New York: Grove Press, 1968.

Sartre, Jean Paul. *Being and Nothingness.* Translated by Hazel Barnes. London: Methuen and Co. Ltd., 1958.

Sartre, Jean Paul. *Critique of Dialectical Reason.* Vol. 1 London: Verson, 1976.

Schlenker Barry R. *Impression management: The self-concept, social identity, and interpersonal relations.* Monterey CA: Brooks/Cole, 1980.

Schore, Allan N. *Affect Regulation and the Origin of the Self: The Neurobiology of Emotional Development.* NJ: Lawrence Erlbaum Associates, 1994.

Searle, John. *The Rediscovery of Mind.* MA: MIT Press, 1992.

Stryker, Sheldon, Timothy J. Owens, Robert White, Editors. *Self Identity and Social Movements.* Minneapolis: University of Minnesota Press, 2000.

Suls, Jerry, *Psychological Perspectives on the Self. Volume: 4.* NJ: Lawrence Erlbaum Associates, 1993.

Swann Jr., William B. *Resilient Identities: Self-Relationships and the Construction of Social Reality.* New York: Basic Books, 1999.

Terrace, Herbert and Janet Metcalf, Editors. *The Missing Link in Cognition: Origins of Self-reflective Consciousness.* New York: Oxford University Press, 2005.

Tesser, Abraham, Joanne V. Wood, and Diederick A. Stapel, Editors. *On Building, Defending, and Regulating the Self: A Psychological Perspective.* New York: Psychology Press, 2005.

Twenge, Jean M. and Keith W. Campbell. *The Narcissism Epidemic, Living in the Age of Entitlement.* New York: Atria Paperback, 2009.

de Waal, Frans *Good Natured, The Origins of Right and Wrong in Humans and Other Animals.* MA: Harvard University Press, 1996.

de Waal, Frans *The Age of Empathy.* New York: Three Rivers Press, 2009.

Zahavi, Dan, "Self and Other: The Limits of Narrative Understanding" In Hutto, D.D.,(eds): *Narrative and Understanding Persons.* Royal Institute of Philosophy Supplement 60, Cambridge University Press, Cambridge, 2007, pp 179-201

Zurcher Jr., Louis A., *The Mutable Self.* Sage, Beverly Hills, 1977

INDEX

A

Adam and Eve, 63, 151
"adaptation theory," 45
admiration, xiii, 26, 104, 217
advertising, 28
aging,10-13
Allport, G., 89, 133
alienation, 40, 41
altruism, 216, 217, 235, 264
America, 27, 56, 155, 205,
        220, 221
amour-propre, 255
anatta, 95
angoisse, 222
Angier, N., 268
angst, 222, 223, 231
anonymity, 24, 104
anticipation, 144
appearance, physical, 4,
        6-10, 53
appraisal- recognition, 256,
        259, 269,
appraisal-respect, 234,
        253, 255

approval, xi, 76, 104, 149, 214,
        220, 271
anxiety, 191, 210, 222, 251,
        (disintegration), 184,
        185, 187
aristocracy, 8, 44
Aristotle, 164, 256, 264
artist, 34-36, 103, 105,
        231, 246
Asia, 155, 196
attachment, 4, 59, 60, 70,
        96, 236
attention, (joint), 143, 176
Auster, P., 105
authenticity, 221-229, 254
autonomy, xiv, 42, 155, 199,
        222, 226, 240, 242, 261
Australopithecus, 125
awareness, 98, 117, 118,
        121-124

B

Baars, B., 177
Baumeister, R., 185, 186
Beckett, S., 251, 252
behaviorism, 142, 169
beliefs, (religious), 21, 95,
        130, 165, 186
Bertelsen, P., 133, 224
Bhavanga, 99
binding, 119, 121
bonding, 58, 125, 127,
        129, 264
Bowlby, J., 208
Boettcher, J., 248
Branden, N., 209, 210
Buber, M., 91, 92
Buddhism, 95-101
Buhler, C., 148
Bush, G. W., 27

C

California Task Force, 210
*Cambridge Declaration of
        Consciousness*, 80
caregiver, 16, 48, 59, 67,
        139-143, 149-151, 154,
        209, 220
caretaker, 145, 150, 155, 158,
        190, 209
Categorical Imperative, 235,
        236, 253
Chalmers, D., 116,118
Chomsky, N., 136
childhood, 11, 60, 156, 219
China, xvii, 74, 81, 196, 199

Chinese Room
        Argument, 117
choice, (free), 49, 52, 195,
        223, 224, 245, 246, 270
Christians, 26, 38, 164, 185
clothing, 21-24, 102, 130, 192
Cohen, A., 22
Cohler, B., 72
compassion, 99-101, 203,
        264-266
Comte, A., 216
confirmation, (behavioral), 53
conformity, 23, 66, 69, 127,
        155, 157, 196
Conscience collective, 90
"conspicuous
        consumption," 27
consumerism, consumer
        society, 27, 28
Cooley, C. H., 168-170, 188
"cost signaling," 64
Crick, F., 117, 121

D

"dark side," 204, 218, 264
Damasio, A., 118
Darwall, S., 233, 234
das Man, 223
deconstruction, (cognitive),
        185, 187
Delphic oracle, 163, 213
Dennett, D., 116, 119,
        173, 174
depression, (cosmic), 224

Descartes, R., 4, 76, 116, 123, 164, 166, 173, 174

determinism, xiv, 51, 201, 269, 270

dignity, (human), 221, 232, 235, 248, 249, 267

Dimberg, U., 262

disunity, (diachronic), 184, 187

DNA, 4, 120, 121

Donald, M., 121, 122, 125, 126, 130-132, 137, 143, 153

DSM 5, 75

dualism, 85, 119, 164; 165, 174

Durkheim, E., 88, 90, 93

E

Eccles, J., 117, 120, 136, 216

"ecological-self," 140, 145, 146

Edelman, G., 118

ego, 2, 78, 83, 98, 160, 164, 167, 187, 212, 218, 239

egoism, egotism, xvi, 96, 204, 205, 214, 217

Einstein, G., 15, 17

Ekman, P., 266

empathy, 262-266

"empirical self," 1, 25, 97, 166, 168, 182

Entrustet, 105

equality, xvii, 15, 221, 232, 253-255, 269

Erickson, E., 12, 46, 60, 182

Eternal thou, 91, 95

"ethics, of care", "ethics of rights," 258-260

"evaluative-self," 153, 202, 221, 271

existentialism, xiv, 269, 270

F

Facebook, 74, 218

faith, (bad), 179, 191, 212, 245

fame, 6, 36, 76,- 78

FAP, 119

Festinger, L., 213

Fichte, J., 242, 248

fictive-self, 179, 190

Flanagan, O., 15, 17

Frankfurt, H., 251-254

Freud, S., 46, 49, 88, 140, 151, 166, 167, 208, 218

Freeman, M., 180

"fundamental project," 186, 247

G

Gallup, 124, 146

Galatzer-Levy, R., 72

Gazzaniga, M., 178, 179

genotype, 116

Gergen, K., 21, 22, 193, 226

"ghost in the machine," 119, 221

Gilligan, C., 258-263

God, 63, 73, 87-96, 98, 102, 106, 134, 151, 156, 164, 207, 221, 232

Goffman, I., 190
Goldman, B., 225,226
Griffen, J., 170
Gurung, R., 23

H

Hamilton's rule, 67
harmony, (group), 155, 196
Hegel,G.W., 29, 30, 40, 41,
    166, 176, 232, 235,
    237-250, 261, 272
Heiler, F., 93, 94
Held, V., 260, 261, 263
Helson, H., 45
Heraclitus, 174, 182
Heter, S., 228
Hill, R., 42
Hobbes, T., 205
Homo erectus, 126, 129
Homo habilis, 125, 126
Homo sapiens, 17, 123, 125,
    129, 130, 142, 145,
    173, 268
Honneth, A., 243-245
Hume, D., 165, 166, 183, 193
humiliation, 63, 207, 227,
    249-251

I

Iacoboni, M., 263
ideal-self, 53, 54, 150
identity crisis, 11, 33, 184,
    "negotiation," 134

image, 20, 23, 28, 34, 55, 110,
    121, 153, 187-194, 217-
    220, 266, 271,
image (body), 5,6, "specular,"
    146, 147
immortality, 36, 78, 106,
    107, 149
"impression management,"/
    "impression
    monitoring,"
    188,189, 193
independence, xiv, 12, 155,
    199, 242, 246
individuality, 155, 196,
    206, 242
inequality, 38, 241, 268, 269
infancy, xvi, 13, 15, 16, 113,
    138, 140, 141, 171, 214
infant, 58-60, 126, 127, 138-
    151, 160, 171, 172
injustice, 78, 252, 253
intelligence, 127, 135, 218
intentional stance, 173
Internet, 6, 23, 36, 73-79,
    106, 135, 206, 218 –
    220, 266
Interpreter, 178, 179
intersubjectivity, xii, 3, 62,
    98, 100, 142, 152, 168
I-Thou, 91

J

James, W., xiv, xv, 1, 2, 47, 61,
    63, 85, 86, 88, 90, 93,
    94, 116, 120, 134, 138,

167-169, 182, 188, 193,
206-208
Jaynes, J., 131-134
Jena Lectures, 29, 40
Jesus, 26, 103, 107
Jones, J., 71,
Jung, C., 88
justice, xvii, 221, 232, 252,
253, 258-260, 265,
267, 269

K

Kant, I., 236, 237, 241-244,
247, 252, 254, 255,
258, 259
karma, 97,98
Kaufman, G., 150
Kernberg, O., 219, 220
Kernis, M., 225, 226
knowledge, *a priori*, 183
Koch, C., 121
Kohut, H., 140, 142, 184, 219
Kohlberg, L., 257, 258
Kotre, J., 178

L

Lacan, J., 141, 146
LAD, 136
Laing, R.D., 58, 61, 90
language, (symbolic), 80, 123,
127, 131, 132,
Lebra, T., 200
Legacy Locker, 105
Levi-Strauss, C., 55
limbic system, 263

"lifestyle enclave," 70,
(Western), 196, 199
Lipps, T., 128, 262
Llinàs, R., 119
Locke, J., 29, 64, 138,
165, 169
"looking-glass self," 91, 168,
170, 188
Luther, M., 38

M

Mahler, M., 139, 141, 147-
149, 155
manipulation, 153, 180, 181,
194, "strategic," 192
Margalit, A., 82, 249-251, 254
marriage, 56-58, 102
Marx, K., 40, 41
Maslow, A., 41, 46, 60, 224
(Maslow's pyramid),
25, 225
master/slave, 166, 238, 241,
242, 245, 246, 249, 272
material self, 2, 3, 24, 31, 32,
92, 167
Mauss, M., 93, 94
mauvaise foi, 179, 191, 212, 223
May, R., 184
McAdams, D., 180, 182, 195
Mead; G. H., 91, 154, 168-172
meditation, 88, 96-99,
110, 187
"me generation," 76, 218, 219
memory, (autobiographic),
197, (episodic), 80, 125,

(external), 105, (loss), 107, 108, (narrative), 179, (pre-organic), 120, (selective), 180-182

Michelangelo (phenomenon), 53

Middle Ages, 38, 164

"middle way," 97

mimesis, 126-128, 143

"mirror neurons," 127

Moore, T., 85

morality, (feminist), 259, 260, 263

Murk, C., 206

N

Nagel, T., 123, 223

narcissism, (infantile) 149, (epidemic), 220, 221

narrative-self, 175

Neisser, U., 140, 145, 153, 172

Nelson, K.,143, 153, 173

nurture & nature, 14, 15, 67, 68, 201, 270

neuroscience, xv, 152, 179

Nietzsche, F., 212, 254, 255

Nirvana, 97, 98

norms, (cultural), 8, 11

Nussbaum, M., 265

O

ontology, 200, 261

other, (generalized), 91, 170, 226

ought self, 53

P

peer group, 66, 157, 190

People's Temple Agricultural Project, 71

personality, "big 5 model," 202, (disorder), 75, 110, 218, 220, "pastiche," 21, 192

personhood, 7, 30, 139, 186, 234, 237, 261, 267

PETA, 237

physical-self, xv, 6-8, 124, 125, 140, 156, 164, 224

Pinel, E., 71

Pines, M., 141

Plato, 85, 163

politicians, 4, 18, 43, 109, 191

Ponty, M., 147

Popper, K., 117, 183

prayer, 93; 94; 131

presentism, 180, 182

primates, 104, 122, 124-127, 131, 135, 253

public eye, 6, 36, 109

Princess Diana, 103

Protestant (work ethic), 26, 27, 37-40

pseudaltruism, 216

psychology, (child), 139, (developmental), xvi, 138, 161, (religious), 90, social, 46, 169, 190

Pygmalion, 20, "phenomenon," 55

Q

Qi Wang, 197

R

Raz, J., 236
reality, (shared) /(social), 271
regard (*le*), 151
relativism, (cultural), 199,
    (moral), 271
religion, 93, 95, 96, 98, 165,
    234, 255
Religious Orientation
    Scale, 89
respect-recognition, 221,
    229, 234
revolution, (industrial), 41,
    (Agrarian), 133
Ricoeur, P., 174
Rifkin, J., 76
rights, (animal), 1, 123, 236,
    237, (human), 17, 234,
    252, 269
Rizzolatti, G., 127
Rogers, C., 46, 60, 224
roles, (playing), 190, 192, 193,
    (social), 7, 133, 228,
    246, 247, 263, (work),
    37, 38
Rosenberg Scale, 206
Rousseau, J. J., 232, 241, 255
Ryle, G., 119, 221

S

Sartre, J.P., 24, 30, 51, 52,
    150, 151, 166, 167,
    179-181, 191, 193, 222,
    225-228, 232, 234,
    235, 245-248, 250,
    269, 271
Saxe, R., 152
schizophrenia, 59, 106, 187
sculpting, 53, 54
separation-individuation, 147,
    155, 157
shame, 83, 145, 148-151,
Shaw, G. B., 20, 55, 231, 269
slavery, 249-251
slaves, 38, 250, 266
soul, 84-86, 93, 95-98, 163-
    165, 174
state-sharing, 142, 143
stream of consciousness, 167,
    168, 182, 193
suicide, 71, 78, 106, 210
Sroufe, A., 208
Stern, D., 209
Swann, W., 27, 46, 60, 71,
    183, 194
symbiotic stage, 139, 140,
    141, 147
synchronicity, 128

T

tabula rasa, 138, 159, 165, 169
technology, (modern), 73, 76,
    234, 266

theory of mind, xii, 151, 152,
        173, 189, 262
true-self, 55, 90, 92, 93, 163,
        192, 204, 221
two-factor theory, 205, 206

U

utilitarianism, 236

V

validation, 70, 71, 104, 194,
        245 (self) 70, 194, 204
Veblen, T., 26, 37
Virtual Eternity, 106
vorhanden, 223

W

de Waal, F., 127, 128, 216,
        253, 263, 264
Wallace, A., 99
Watchtel, P., 211
Weber, M., 33, 37, 39
we-community, 176
will, (free), xiv, 117, 195, 222,
        241 (good), 255
wisdom, 12, 97, 100, 256
World Wide Cemetery, 105

Printed in the United States
By Bookmasters